*Higher Education
and the Practice
of Democratic Politics*

Higher Education and the Practice of Democratic Politics:

A Political Education Reader

**Edited and with an Introduction
by Bernard Murchland**

*published by
the Kettering Foundation*

ISBN 0-923993-01-0

This book is printed on recycled paper.

Inquiries, book orders and catalogue
requests should be addressed to
Kettering Foundation,
200 Commons Road,
Dayton, OH 45459

Contents

Foreword

Before you plunge into this collection of articles, a word on how this volume came about might be useful. Over five years ago, a small, informal group of faculty, administrators, and students from a wide range of institutions began meeting to discuss a common concern with the way academia is educating young people for political responsibility, civic competence, and public leadership. The group met on a number of campuses and, occasionally, at the Kettering Foundation. They began to share articles that brought the problems of political education into sharper focus or offered richer insights into their nature. The members of the group came from different institutions and drew on a wide variety of experiences and intellectual traditions. Their difficulty, however, was finding a vehicle for sharing an inquiry that combined so many disciplines and professions. That difficulty led to this book, which brings perspectives from many different fields to bear on one subject. Still, the group managed to create a common dialogue. In this volume the group is sharing their conversations with a wider audience, welcoming to this exchange anyone who is concerned with preparing the next generation for public life.

The articles in this volume were selected from the larger collection of materials that were exchanged in the group. They were the basis for discussions on what some called "civic" and others called "political" education. While the titles suggest an emphasis on education, the articles actually find the problem of political education to be more philosophic than pedagogical. Together, these essays make the claim that the current academic definition of politics is too narrowly modern—too preoccupied with governments, elections, and interest groups—to comprehend all that is in the political realm. The big losers in the narrow definition are citizens and the public. Citizens are reduced to political consumers or special interest advocates. The public disappears into political mythology.

These articles treat the age-old political questions of how to make the many into one (without losing individual freedoms) and how to deal with values (without teaching values). They make a case for citizen participation. However, they also take us beyond these customary ways of framing the challenges of democratic politics. They invite us to reconsider the meaning of basic political terms. Is "participation" simply to be understood as the right to vote, or is it more? Should "the political" be considered a realm of politicians and governments, separate from our everyday lives, or is politics a dimension of nearly everything we do? Should we think of the "public" as the antithesis of the "private" and be ever alert to protect the one from the other? Or are the public and private realms interdependent corollaries? Is politics exclusively competitive or does it have an equally important unifying function?

The authors' perspectives on politics cause them to raise questions both about the role of the university and the nature of political education. Their questions go so far as to challenge the very definition of knowledge itself.

David Mathews
President, Kettering Foundation

Acknowledgments

The idea for this book was born out of those far-ranging, fertile seminar-discussions for which the Kettering Foundation has become justly famous. As is often the case, Foundation President David Mathews had a major role in framing the concept. I also want to acknowledge the contributions of Suzanne Morse, director of programs at the Kettering Foundation, as well as the talents of the publications staff, particularly Robert E. Daley, Betty Frecker, George Cavanaugh, Val Breidenbach, Judy McGeorge, and Christopher Baron. Maria Farland and Manfred Stanley made helpful suggestions. The research efforts of Cheryl Carr and Deborah Witte were indispensable. Michael Briand, research director at the Foundation, guided each step of the production process with persistence, skill, and unfailing good humor. Thanks is also owed to Cynthia Horton and Karen Reppen of A-R Editions. Above all, I want to thank the contributors. It is quite literally their book.

Bernard Murchland

Introduction

by Bernard Murchland

Mortimer Adler has said that in a democracy we have two important things in common: we are all citizens, and we are all philosophers. By this he means that we all have to *think* about what it means to *be* a citizen. Judged by that standard, democracy in the United States today is not in very good shape. Our involvement in civic life is shallow, the public will is enfeebled, and once-honored ideas such as the common good are largely vestigial. In short, we have a weak sense of citizenship.

As I read history, we last had a strong sense of citizenship in the forties. We were at war then; we believed it was a just war; we were clear about our goals and values; and we were drawn together in a common effort to put our convictions into action. By the fifties, that sense of common purpose had evaporated, principally because our peacetime priority was economic prosperity. The metaphor of the marketplace powerfully shaped our self-understanding as a nation. We began to think of democracy as akin to market transactions, and to see ourselves more as producers and consumers than as citizens. Higher education adapted accordingly: education for career skills displaced other purposes of education, including education for citizenship.

In the postwar period, the ruling philosophy of our political leaders became what the social analyst Daniel Yankelovich has called "the money and missiles sense of reality." This philosophy, Yankelovich explains,

> assumes that what really counts in this world are military power and economic realities, and all the rest is sentimental stuff. It has overly constricted the domain of what is real and transformed the large political and moral dilemmas of our time into narrow technical questions that fit the experts' own specialized expertise. This process of technicalizing political issues renders them inaccessible to public understanding and judgment because the public exists in the very domain that is excluded. To narrow issues artificially is to exclude the bulk of the citizenry from the policy-shaping process.

This is a book about educating for democratic citizenship—about *political* education. The authors, each in his or her own way, argue for a revitalized conception of democracy and in the process attempt to *reinvigorate* the vocabulary of citizenship, civic virtue, and the common good. Against a background of compelling evidence that Americans generally, and young people in particular, are increasingly alienated from the political system, the authors explore anew the questions: What understanding of democracy informs our public discourse? What must we do to educate citizens for a democratic society? Are educators correct in maintaining that they are already providing such an education?

In regard to this last question, it is instructive to read college catalogues. Some time ago, I examined a number of these catalogues to see what they had to say about educating for citizenship. The gap between their rhetoric and the reality of higher education is great. Every one I read promised to educate students for public service, social responsibility, and leadership. They listed objectives such as these: to provide students with a deep understanding of American democracy and the citizen's role in maintaining its strength and vitality; to prepare graduates for participation as citizens in a free and open society; to educate for lives of responsible citizenship; to prepare students to accept the demands of a responsible citizenship; to develop in students a willingness to meet the responsibilities of citizenship in a free society. And so forth and so on.

One wonders how educational institutions justify the rhetoric of their catalogues. Do they see the gap between what they claim and what they actually produce? Do students see it? In the recent past I have conducted informal polls among students I have encountered on my own campus and elsewhere. Specifically, I have asked them three questions: What are the responsibilities of citizenship in a free society? What is your college doing to fulfill the aims of citizenship education stated in its catalogue? Do you think your college constitutes a civic community? The impressions I formed may not be scientifically rigorous. But they do support the conclusions reached by numerous reports on the state of civic education today.

The Responsibilities of Citizenship

The answers to my question about the responsibilities of citizenship fell into five categories. Predictably, some reflected the academic community's emphasis on "knowledge": "A citizen must be well educated." "Only with a sound education can we make the right choices." "We must have knowledge to be productive members of society." "We must have knowledge of current events, a basic knowledge of how government works, be knowledgeable about issues, etc." These students regard "being knowledgeable" as an important aspect of citizenship.

A second category of answers reflects the prominence in our society of the therapeutic approach to social problems. Thus, some students spoke of the need to help the poor, the homeless, the disadvantaged. They see community service as the principal method by which this goal can be achieved. For such students, citizenship is a form of altruism.

Other answers, by contrast, reflected the emphasis on individualism in our society: "Citizenship is the responsibility of the individual student." "Citizenship means pursuing your own happiness without infringing on the rights of others." "The responsibility of the citizen is to do as little harm as possible."

I heard muffled echos of some civics course long ago that a student might have taken. But I heard no statement to the effect that "a citizen is someone who has an active voice in the government of his country or in shaping the values of his society." Although there were frequent references to voting, joining a political party, and the connection between rights and citizenship ("A citizen is someone who has the right to. . . .") the word "responsibility" was less in evidence.

Saddest of all were the voices of cynicism. To the question, "What does citizenship mean to you?" a group of college students in Wisconsin offered replies such as, "A bad word"; "Not the kind of word that has ever entered my vocabulary"; "It is a question I cannot answer"; "I can't imagine where the word would ever come into my thinking"; "The word 'citizen' turns me off"; "It has about as much meaning as a 'thousand points of light.' "

What Colleges and Universities Are Doing to Educate for Citizenship

We can distinguish between what happens in the classroom and what occurs outside it. Rarely do students associate the curriculum with citizenship education. The vast majority of those I queried reported as follows: "Few classes raise the question"; "I don't think I ever heard the matter discussed"; "My classes are largely devoid of any talk about citizenship"; "Not very many classes talk about it."

Occasionally, a student might refer to a course in government or public policy. But most of them detected political education—if they detected it at all—in activities outside the classroom. In this context, many of their answers were quite positive. They mentioned organizations on campus such as fraternities, political clubs, and, above all, student government, which a number of them described as "like real government on a smaller scale." In such organizations they had "many options" to learn about what they take to be the art of democratic politics. Community service again ranked high, as did internships and participation in advocacy groups. The students I spoke with thought that in their extra- and para-curricular activities they had some opportunity to exercise the office of citizenship. To me, this indicates that students are not as apathetic as they are sometimes portrayed. But they do tend to feel powerless, and this breeds a high degree of cynicism.

Furthermore, their citizenship activities are quite divorced from their academic pursuits.

Colleges as Civic Communities

Asking students whether their campuses are civic communities proved to be my toughest question. Many said they simply didn't understand it. They said, "That question is new to me," or "I don't know what a civic community is." Others gave confused answers: "My college is a civic community because it functions at various levels and each level is independent of the other." "Mine provides a gathering of diverse individuals. This alone constitutes a community." The only categorical responses I obtained were negative: "My college is not a civic community. Period. That is all I will say on that subject." Not once did I receive a positive response to this question. The closest I came was a reference to a campus organization where the individual could associate with people having a shared interest.

I can think of two reasons why the students I queried had trouble with this question. The first has to do with the language I used. "Civic" and "community" are not exactly coin of the realm in student vocabularies. Such terminology appears to be a lost language for a whole generation. Second, there is little in the campus experience to which students might relate a question about political community. Their answers to my questions reflected their political alienation.

What the Profs Say

One clear inference from my samplings would be that students aren't receiving much in the way of an education for democratic citizenship. Political education in any robust sense appears to be minimal. To get a better sense of what is—and isn't—being taught I pursued my inquiry among the professoriate with some variation of the question: "What are you doing to ensure the political education of the next generation?"

One of the liveliest debates in American history about the nature of education and the role of educational institutions in society is now under way. As with all important debates, it is both philosophical and political in nature—philosophical because it is about the nature of knowledge and our conceptions of the good; political because it involves fundamental choices about how we wish to live together in society. To prescribe a curriculum is a public act; it makes a political statement. Looked at this way, the curriculum is shorthand for what we take to be the range and depth of the political choices open to us as individuals and as a society. It might be helpful at this juncture to call attention to the ideological climate of the American college and university. We are presently witnessing one of the liveliest debates in American history about the nature of education and the role of educational institutions in society.

To grasp the contours of this debate, imagine a pentagon. On one corner are the traditionalists who want to base the curriculum on the great ideas of Western civilization as they are found in the "great books." We can usually count on someone from the University of Chicago to defend this view, Robert Hutchins in an earlier day and more recently Allan Bloom. On an opposite corner is an articulate band of postmodernists who might include on any given day some deconstructionists, Marxists, ethnicists, African-Americans, Native Americans, feminists, and latter-day pragmatists. These are sometimes called multiculturalists. They take up cudgels against the traditionalists to argue for the radical contingency and pluralism of practices, values, and principles. In their view, all ideas are constructs; traditional "foundations" for knowledge claims—reason, nature, divine authority—are so many masked attempts to protect the vested interests of the powerful. Richard Rorty, a proponent of this view, is given to such expressions as "the best hope for philosophy is not to practice philosophy" and "the mind is not equipped with any truth tracking mechanism." Rorty recommends an education "without dogma" and urges us all to be nice to one another.

On a third corner of the pentagon are the progressive (sometimes called radical) educators, whose membership overlaps to some extent with the postmodernists. They argue for citizenship education in the tradition of civic humanism and classical republicanism. Often they take their inspiration from John Dewey and invoke authors who talk about strong citizenship, strong democracy, and strong republicanism.

A fourth and large group comprises those who think the primary purpose of education is to provide students with skills useful in a high-tech, postindustrial economy. This is education for economic efficiency, vocational education. On this view, the successor generation is a human resource that must be marshaled for a competitive work force against such economies as Japan and Germany. This view is one typically put forth in political speeches, commission reports, and books by corporate CEOs. University administrators are inclined to talk this way, and they give students the clear impression that their education will make them better off economically. Large numbers of students return the compliment and come to college with precisely that end in mind.

By far the largest group represented on the pentagon is composed of those who might be called the silent majority of academia, the (more or less) unreflective defenders of the status quo. And what is the status quo? It is revealed in the metaphor of the university as a marketplace of ideas. Adam Smith introduced the invisible hand into economics in 1776; James Madison introduced it into politics in 1787; and Charles William Elliot, president of Harvard University, introduced it into the curriculum in the late 1890s when he devised the elective system. Each of these men proceeded from the ideological position that the greatest freedom is the pursuit of self-interest and that the "public good" is a mere aggregate of individual goods.

With the introduction of the elective system the "liberal" in liberal education underwent a sea change of meaning. From the traditional sense of the freeing arts, those disciplines that made us autonomous subjects, it came to take on the quasi-market meaning of the pursuit of interest. Thus professors should be free to teach what they want to teach without administrative (or governmental) interference (this is a large part of what is meant by academic freedom) and students should be free to choose what they want to learn from the cafeteria of knowledge—a little of this, a little of that randomly strung along a line of distribution requirements and arbitrarily terminated with the conferring of a degree. This strikes many as a highly antiseptic concept of what education should be but it is far and away the prominent one in America today.

Obviously, different answers to my question about political education were given by professors in the different corners of the pentagon. But in practice, nine out of ten of those I encountered were defenders of the status quo. The national debate leaves relatively untouched whole faculties and even whole institutions.

This group gave one of two answers to my question. Either they adopted a value-neutral position and said that political education was not part of their responsibility. Their job is to retail the hardware of their disciplines and pursue their research interests, taking some time out to logroll for academic scarcities in committee work. Citizenship strikes them as a soft, unwieldy slightly antiquarian notion.

Or they answered that in modern-day society there is a division of labor such that professors have the assigned task of teaching critical thinking. They view that as their contribution to citizenship education. As one of them told me: "We can't do everything and we don't want to do more." When I pointed out that college graduates aren't conspicuous in their ability to think, critically or otherwise, they were inclined to change the subject.

The specialization of faculty is perhaps the major impediment to effective political education. What Thomas Bender calls the "culture of professionalism" has eclipsed public culture. Says Bender: "Intellectual specialization took on a new character in the process of becoming a system of disciplines . . . each new disciplinary profession developed its own conceptual basis. Each became a distinct epistemic community. Disciplinary peers, not a diverse urban public, became the only legitimate evaluators of intellectual work."

But the matter is more complex. Whether they realize it or not, faculty inevitably engage in political education. What they say or don't say, what they do or don't do through the curricula they approve, sends a powerful political message to their students. Academicians implicitly accept the liberal conception of society as a collection of competing interest groups (just as academia is divided into competing departments), and see politics as voting and support of the activities of interest groups, which exercise the power they accumulate to secure a competitive advantage. Government's role (like that of the administration on campus) is to referee the competition to ensure a modicum of fairness. This is the message beamed to students. And it is a good message for students to get. It describes quite accurately what we have permitted the practice of democratic politics to become. But it falls short of exhausting further and richer meanings of both "democracy" and "politics."

The Dialogic Tradition

In my own struggle with the problem of how to educate young people for practicing the art of democratic politics, I have been driven back to a reexamination of dialectical thinking as first illustrated by Socrates in his attempt to devise a language with which to talk about justice and other political concepts. Such language begins in confusion and puzzlement rather than clarity, relies primarily upon dialogue rather than logical demonstration, and yields a moral or political outcome. Socrates went about asking his fellow citizens questions. He wanted to know how the world looked to them and what they thought about things. Political meaning is disclosed—and here I follow Hannah Arendt—when the citizen enters into dialogue with other citizens, not primarily to persuade them of anything but to find out what is on their minds, what their concerns and interests are. And Socrates found out that the world appears different to each individual. This sets both the philosophical and political problem: How can we find the common in the diverse? The answer is "more of the same"—more dialogue, hammering out in the public forum not only what we think, but also what we think *together*. In this way a common world, a public world, is created.

The means by which Socrates elicited this world was called "midwifery," which is to say the political art of determining the public through conversation. The effort often remains inconclusive, to be sure. But without it, no beginning is possible. Arendt puts it clearly: through conversation "we become equal partners in a common world and together constitute a community." We can converse precisely because we see things differently; we can find common ground when we are able to talk to one another. This is the political meaning of deliberation. Our reigning conception of politics—call it interest group politics for short—makes deliberative conversation difficult. Americans do not lack free speech, but the constraints on free speech are considerable. A young executive in a Fortune 500 company had better not claim too much of it. An untenured professor in a major university would be considered wise to adhere rather closely to the canons of judgment shared by those who will have a say in her future. We do not lack plurality; what we do lack is an effective means of finding the *unum* in the *plurum*, of making our pluralism cohere. Americans are good at talking past one another, much better at focusing on what divides us than on what unites us.

Democracy, then, requires a deliberating citizenry. And it requires forums where such deliberation is encouraged. Americans have traditionally prized such forums and they can be traced to colonial times. Tocqueville lauded them. And John Dewey caught their spirit when he wrote: "I am inclined to believe that the heart and final guarantee of democracy is in free gatherings of neighbors on the street corner and in living rooms to discuss what is read in the uncensored news of the day."

What has become of these forums? They have not exactly disappeared. But they have suffered a curious paralysis. Two logical sites for forums of civic dialogue today are our educational institutions and the media. But each in its own way has become the enemy of civic discourse. The media—parading a seemingly endless waggle of talking heads—inundates us with trivia and "expertise," the latter probably as much an enemy of public dialogue as the former. Educational institutions have failed even more grievously to provide the kind of civic forums we need. In fact, one could easily conclude that the principal purposes of our schools is to deprive successor generations of their civic voice, to turn them into mute and uncomprehending spectators in the drama of political life.

In my opinion, the best thing that colleges could do to make good on their promises of political education is to educate students in the dialectical tradition. It was no accident that Socrates invented the dialogic method in philosophy at precisely the time when the Greeks were experiencing the first flush of democracy. It is the democratic way of arriving at public truth. The public is created, and Socrates teaches us this, through dialogue or what in a more modern idiom Jürgen Habermas calls the praxis of communicative action—that is, through language that leads to public-building action. "Public" in the strong sense means knowing and doing in common what we never can do alone.

This volume of essays constitutes an argument for a strong public. The writers, from a variety of viewpoints and backgrounds, succeed in respiriting the core concepts of citizenship, democracy, and liberal education. Moreover, they succeed in establishing crucial linkages between these concepts.

The debate about the purposes of education is in important respects a debate about the nature of democracy, which in turn raises unavoidable questions about how we understand citizenship. It may be the case, as some have suggested, that citizenship will anchor our political deliberations in the years ahead.

Let us hope so.

Bernard Murchland is professor of Philosophy at Ohio Wesleyan University and editor of the Civic Arts Review.

Part 1

Restoring the Lost Dimension

The cluster of essays in this section call attention to the "lost dimension" of political education—what is missing in our efforts to educate for democratic citizenship. They indicate some of the reasons for this and show in a general way how we might begin restoring what has been lost.

J. Peter Euben raises the critical questions: What does it mean to be a citizen in a democratic polity? What if the primary question asked of any policy was whether and how it helped us think of ourselves in a democratic polity? What if the central aim of education were to increase students' knowledge of past democratic experiences and expand the democratic culture they experience as a preparation for living a public life? We are quite far from giving satisfactory answers to such questions. Drawing upon the example of

Vaclav Havel and recent experiences in Eastern Europe, Euben fears our own politics by contrast is becoming more and more "the preserve of kings and priests, of professionals and professors, and less and less the subject of widespread debate."

Robert B. Woyach notes five changes in attitude we will have to achieve if we are to overcome "the root causes of political alienation" and strengthen citizenship: (1) we must stop thinking of politics as what politicians and bureaucrats do and think of it as a process by which the community defines the public good; (2) we must extend our horizons beyond government to include civic and neighborhood forums, which are the proper sites for the exercise of citizenship; (3) widespread participation must be centered in small-scale, local settings rather than in remote institutions such as Congress or the Department of Education; (4) citizens should be leaders and not followers, taking the initiative in organizing and setting the public agenda; (5) citizens must have a greater role in seeking and defining the public good.

Sara M. Evans and **Harry C. Boyte** show how the concept of democracy, proceeding from its origins in classical Greece, came to emphasize the values of citizenship: a concern for the common good; the welfare of the community as a whole; willingness to honor the same rights for others that oneself possesses; tolerance of diverse religious, political, and social beliefs; acceptance of the primacy of the community's decisions over one's own private inclinations; and a recognition of one's obligations to defend and serve the public. In America, this understanding of citizenship was severely compromised, in part, by the views of Founders such as Alexander Hamilton who had little faith in the common person's capacity for self-government; and, in part, by the development of large-scale social entities such as industry, cities, and the federal government itself. After the Civil War, elite views of democracy came to predominate, and continue to do so through the prevalence of the marketplace conception of democracy. As the authors point out, however, participatory democracy is not a mere "nostalgic echo from the past," but a living value revived time and again by citizens who organize to pursue their common interests and reassert control over their lives. The practice of democracy has always been the best school for citizenship, educating people in the "varied skills and values which are essential to sustaining effective participation."

Parker Palmer addresses the idea of the public. Citizenship, democracy, and civic virtue are impossible without a vital and vibrant sense of what the public is and how it works. The idea has an honorable lineage, and efforts to rehabilitate it today are in our own best interests. Palmer discusses three factors pertinent to our current impoverished sense of public life: (1) the availability of public spaces such as parks, cafes, galleries, forums, neighborhoods, and voluntary associations; (2) the psychology of public space—the way we relate to others in such spaces, particularly to strangers; and (3) a structure of myth and symbol. Public life cannot thrive without public space. "Relations in public," says Palmer, "are the relations of strangers who do not, and need not, know each other in depth. And such relations have real virtue." Finally, we require myths and symbols to define us as a community. These provide narrative space within which meanings are generated. They come from the *Bible*, literature, and from our political traditions. A central image is that of "covenant," which reminds us that the foundation of our common life has a personal as well as a public dimension.

The selections by **David Mathews** and **Hannah Arendt** bring us closer to the theoretical underpinnings of democratic political education. Mathews identifies four ways we usually attempt to educate for civic responsibility: by teaching civic literacy, by teaching values, by teaching civic skills, and by teaching civics by indirection; e.g., through mastery of a discipline. (If students pursue a sound curriculum, this last argument goes, civic education will be a by-product.) Each of these approaches has merit, according to Mathews, but each falls short of what is required. To teach civic intelligence properly, we must develop the *public* capacities of judgment and dialogue. Civic competence, he says, "is not a matter of aggregate individual intelligence, but of *civic* intelligence."

Arendt offers a philosophical justification and argument for the necessity of a strong sense of the public. Arendt is preeminent among political theorists in this century who have called for a restoration of the lost dimension of civic learning, what she calls "the public realm." The public realm is (1) the sphere of activity in which our private experiences are transformed into a larger, "public" reality that can be shared by others, and (2) the world that is common (*koinon*) to all of us. This common world "gathers us together and yet prevents our falling over each other." The public realm is what preserves the *pluribus* in the *unum*. Or, as Mathews would put it, the public realm is the space in which civic intelligence is nourished.

"Clearly we need to think anew and more deeply about the education of democratic citizens."

Democracy in America: Bringing It All Back Home

by J. Peter Euben

Last March, the *New York Times* ran a series of articles entitled "The Trouble with Politics." The series and the issues it raised have since been eclipsed by the Iraq crisis but, whenever and however that crisis is "resolved," the trouble with politics will remain.

The *Times* articles suggested that our public life is being inundated with banality. As America's "democratic visions and values seem to triumph around the world, an unhappy consensus has emerged at home that domestic politics has become so shallow, mean, and even meaningless, that it is failing to produce the ideas and leadership needed to guide the United States in a rapidly changing world." Too much of our political discourse is "trivial," "obscurantist," and defined by the search for the image, code, or picture that will grab the attention of an information-saturated, entertainment-hardened, easily bored public. We have too many "wet-fingered politicians" who rely on political professionals to track the public mood which, since Watergate and Vietnam, has been "profoundly disenchanted." As a result, no vigorous, substantive debate is possible on the major issues that confront the nation: the prospect of an economically integrated Europe and the challenge of Japanese economic power, the rootlessness and homelessness of our people, and the second-rate educational performance of our young. The lament is summed up in Representative David Obey's (D-WI) question: "Is American politics so brain-dead that we are reduced to having political shysters manipulate symbols?"

The occasion for the articles—and Obey's lament—was the upheaval in Eastern Europe, symbolized by Czechoslovakian President Vaclav Havel's address before a joint session of Congress. Havel's presence and presidency vividly reminded Americans that the Cold War had ended, and that our pallid but useful self-congratulatory claim to be the leader of the free world was now obsolete. Some celebrated "our victory" over communism as a sign of our chosenness: we were, unknowingly, the *apotheosis* of civilization, the ideal become real, and the *telos* of history. But the *Times* articles presented a different mood, one of anxiety about who "we" are, an unease over whether the emperor is, if not entirely naked, then too shabbily dressed to keep up appearances. It is an anxiety likely to return as patriotic fervor for Middle Eastern intervention wanes.

As the *Times* articles made clear, whatever it is about us that inspires Polish workers, Czech intellectuals, and Chinese students no longer inspires us. Though we are part (and only a part) of the democratic vision and vistas that animate them, we ourselves have grown oblivious to both. We have no Pericles or Lincoln, no Whitman or Martin Luther King, Jr., no Adam Michnik or Havel, which is exactly what the latter's speech "brought home." (Asked how a man of Havel's thoughtfulness and sophistication would fare if he ran for office here, Representative Bill Thomas replied: "How much money does he have? Which consultant does he have? And is he willing to shave his moustache?") Opinion polls that report satisfaction with the Bush administration need to be understood in a broader context: of other polls indicating that, for the first time in our history, we expect the lives of our children to be harder than our own; of rising apathy as evidenced by a continuing decline in voter turnout; of two national studies which claim that "the typical young person" is indifferent, lethargic, alienated, ignorant, and uninterested in anything except parochial and trivial matters.

Havel's speech was particularly noteworthy, given his immediate audience. In front of those with power he mocked his own power. Facing those often complacent about the power of human beings to control nature and destiny, he warned against the "vain belief" that "man is the pinnacle of creation" rather than part of it, and the corresponding delusion that "therefore, everything is permitted." Speaking before those who have inordinate faith in economics and science, and who offer moral platitudes while keeping their ethics committees busy, Havel insists on the primacy of moral principles that eschew self-righteousness and Manichaeanism. A student of American democracy, he also appears as a teacher schooled by a totalitarianism that has, unintentionally, provided him and his compatriots with "a special capacity to look, from time to time, somewhat further than someone who had not undergone this bitter experience."

What, then, is it that Havel's speech, his presence, and his character can teach us? First of all, that there are no lessons, if by lessons we mean terse hypotheses about politics or morality. Havel is too shrewd and too much the ironist for that, having learned through experience to appreciate Aristotle's injunction that an educated person should bring no more precision to a subject matter (politics and morality) than that subject warrants. Having lived under a regime in which everyday mendacity was obscured by grandiose ideological defenses, he knows that life is always richer than our categories, and that action, choice, and character confound the self-serving polarity between "we" who act righteously and justly because of what we know and "they" who are unjust, evil, and ignorant. He is too much the student of absurdist theater not to recognize how often compromise and baseness lurk within nobility and how often redemptive moments shine forth from what is ordinary and unexpected. In his New Year's speech to his people, Havel speaks of how their "education" under the communist regime has developed in them "a profound distrust of all generalizations, ideological platitudes, clichés, slogans, intellectual stereotypes, and insidious appeals to various levels of our emotions, from the base to the loftier."

Havel (like Michnik) chooses his own words carefully and there is a lesson in that, too. Many of those words—democracy, freedom, power, citizenship, and justice—are familiar enough, in fact, so familiar that many of us regard them as pieties ritually invoked to sustain a lapsed (and, therefore, manipulative) cultural myth. Yet Havel's voice lends these words urgency and depth. For example, consider the dignity he accords "citizen" in his speech before Congress. Paying homage to the Declaration of Independence, the Constitution, and the Bill of Rights, he sums up their significance by saying they "inspire us all to be citizens."

But that is not how they inspire Americans, at least not if we take citizenship as a serious public responsibility. Indeed, much of our political discourse exemplifies what Havel distrusts: platitudes, clichés, slogans, stereotypes, and manipulative emotional appeals. That is, surely, another lesson Havel (inadvertently) taught his listeners. While many Americans wince at the banal invocations of our democratic past by our own political leaders, that same past moves Walesa, Havel, and Mandela, and moves us anew when such figures lay claim to its legacy. Given who they are, what they have done and must yet accomplish, they have earned the right to invoke Jefferson and Lincoln in a way our leaders have not. While they are founding or renewing democracies, our domestic politics consists in trying to extricate ourselves from a savings and loan scandal that touches the President's son and the second highest-ranking Democrat in the Senate.

The end of the Cold War has only widened the gap between our past and present, between our political life and public discourse and those taking shape in Eastern Europe. That is because our political identity can no longer be defined in terms of antagonisms and alliances and by what we are not: totalitarian. As even this thin cultural narrative loses its hold, formerly inconceivable, marginal, or very old questions become central, compelling, and new. What does it mean to be a citizen of a democratic polity? Why do so many value public life so highly? Why do demands for freedom appear as demands for political participation?

The Cold War's demise not only raises these general questions about our political identity, but also problematizes specific policies justified in its name. Consider for a moment, how it framed the educational reform movement. There was the Gardner Commission's call in 1983 for "educational excellence" defined in terms of national security imperatives. And William Bennett insisted in 1988 that "the survival of Western civilization and the protection of our children" mandated a strong "arsenal of democracy," stocked with military hardware and fueled by the Manichaean contrast between the evil Communist East and the good free West. What is curious about this language and these sentiments is that they share more with the Communist regimes Havel and Michnik helped to overthrow than with the movements they helped to lead. The language of the Cold War educational reform is now curiously old-fashioned. Clearly, we need to think anew and more deeply about the education of democratic citizens.

Havel's speech and the events in Eastern Europe can teach us to honor both what we have and what we lack. What we have is a democracy based on an independent judiciary, individual rights, and free elections; what we don't have is democracy in the sense of sustained and direct citizen participation. For Havel, "democracy in the full sense of the word" is an ideal one may approach as one would a horizon. We steadily move toward it while recognizing that there is no finality to the goal that nonetheless guides us, that the distance between it and ourselves mandates that we treat every means as an end and every end as a means.

Since the upheavals in Eastern Europe, fewer and fewer observers casually dismiss what we have as "bourgeois rights and liberties" though critics remain who rightly condemn our inconsistent fidelity to those rights. Many more dismiss what we do not have as unworthy of honor.

Redressing this imbalance requires, at a minimum, that we add depth to central terms of our political discourse: democracy, power, freedom, and politics. We could begin by taking seriously Lincoln's belief that government is rightly of, by, and for the people. This means viewing with suspicion the arguments by "responsible elites" that, because government for the people cannot be government by or of them, the few must rule in order to save democracy from itself. Havel agrees that there is no democratic heaven on earth, but disagrees with many conventional "realists" that our fallen political state entitles some intellectual or political elite to claims of special power or privilege. Dissident leaders have no monopoly on truth and goodness, and their opponents are not permanently immune to appeals based on justice and freedom. For all of his insistence that "intellectuals cannot go on forever avoiding their share of responsibility for the world and hiding their distaste for politics under an alleged need to be independent," he is himself modest about his own views, self-mocking about his present position, and as we have seen, suspicious of politics. Havel understands democracy as the participatory process by which free citizens take their places in the deliberative forums which shape their individual and collective lives. He is suspicious of political experts and expertise, and this suspicion raises the question of whether "democracies" must rely on institutional leadership to the degree they do or whether ordinary citizens can handle complex political matters without specialized knowledge.

In Eastern Europe, popular citizen committees took the political initiative away from governments and, in the case of the German Democratic Republic's Round Table, from *all* parties. This opening up of public life contrasts with the attempts of the Reagan and Bush administrations to close it down. Consider how these administrations have dismantled our already compromised democratic life piece by piece: limiting the Freedom of Information Act, systematically deceiving the press, arrogantly lying in the Iran-Contra affair, and unilaterally invading Grenada and Panama. Compare this sorry record with the opening up of public discourse and life in Eastern Europe, where the redefinition of public space was accompanied by what might be called a redefinition of mental space; the change in who could talk and where such talk could happen was matched by an expansion of what could be talked about. As this widening of public discourse has occurred, the people as a whole have progressively appropriated the conduct, knowledge, and procedures that originally were the exclusive domain of the party and government elites. As knowledge, values, and techniques became elements of a common culture, they were submitted to criticism and controversy: in other words they became "politicized."

In many respects our politics is becoming more and more the preserve of kings and priests, of professionals and professors, and less and less the subject of widespread public debate. Fewer things are brought before the commons, and more are claimed as the eminent domain of experts who reappropriate knowledge while forming a caste of initiates.

To be skeptical of the idea of self-appointed responsible elites, political experts, and the narrow public life in which they thrive is not to ignore the fact that citizens possess different degrees of courage, eloquence, wealth, and political acumen, or to deny that special competence can serve democratic ends. Some citizens more fully embody a nation's ideal of character than others (even when that ideal is democratic pluralism) and so contribute more to public life. Perhaps they deserve special public recognition for so doing. Indeed, a *political* community presupposes difference in experience, function, interests, identities, and points of view among citizens. Public life exists precisely to recognize and sustain those differences and provide a forum in which they can be expressed. "We" are, for all that separates us, one people who share, however imperfectly and contentiously, a common past, present, and future. Political participation brings such differences before others, translates opinions and interests from the "private" idiom of personal interest ("I want") into the more impersonal public idiom ("what should we do?"). For this to occur, the superiority of the one or the few cannot entail inferiority or passivity of the many.

Here is where so many of the various national reports on education have failed. They vacillate between platitudinous references to democratic citizenship and quantitative hysteria over declining test scores—which are taken to demonstrate both the steady slide away from earlier pedagogic standards and the pressing need to regain our scientific, military, or commercial hegemony. But what if the primary questions asked of any policy—and especially of any educational policy—were whether and how it helped students think of themselves as potential citizens of a democratic polity? What if a central aim of education were to increase students' knowledge of past democratic experiences (both exemplary and cautionary) and expand the democratic culture they experience as preparation for living a public life? I do not think there are single or simple answers to these questions, or any one place or way wisdom or judgment can be learned. If Sheldon Wolin is right that "American politics in all its ramifications requires a multiple self, one who is required to act the citizen in diverse settings" such as "nation, state, city or town, neighborhood and voluntary association," then many sites present themselves as places where a deliberative self can be formed and political judgment cultivated. That is surely one of the lessons the Solidarity movement can teach us.

Redressing the imbalance would also require rethinking the nature of power. During the Cold War, power was largely defined (as it is now in the Middle East) in military terms, which was doubly useful for the United States since power could be quantified and we could be seen to have more of it than anyone else. But as the significance of military power as an aspect of national power recedes (even in spite of its dismaying resurgence in the Middle East), what it means to be "powerful" is unclear. Once again Havel, Adam Michnik, and the events in Eastern Europe can help us. Havel has argued that anyone with the courage to insist on the truth at the risk of his or her life has more power than thousands of anonymous voters. The refusal of such exemplary individuals to live lies (refusing, for example, to put up signs with

Marxist slogans in their shops) can move others to speak the truth and even to risk justice and freedom. The seemingly unpolitical jailing of a rock group, Havel argues in *Disturbing the Peace,* revealed power's hidden intention to make "life entirely the same, to surgically remove from it everything that was even slightly different, everything that was highly individual, everything that stood out, that was independent and unclassifiable." The events argue that, while absolute power corrupts absolutely, the absence of power corrupts just as absolutely. Both facts speak to the need to share power and responsibility. Finally, Michnik argues (or rather anticipates) that mass movements for democracy must create power within civil society rather than attempt simply to wrest power from the state. In practicing the politics of everyday life, Solidarity was reacting to a totalitarian regime that had itself politicized social life. But it was more than a reaction, it was also a recognition that power is created whenever people work together for a common aim, no matter how local or particular that aim might be. The point of such action was not only to deal with a particular need—obtaining food, getting a friend out of jail, or protecting jobs—but to enlarge both the capacity to act collectively and the commitment to such action. The new power could not be narrowly partisan or conspiratorial since that would imitate the kind of state politics one was opposing. "Every conspiracy," Michnik writes, "demoralizes. In its depths flourishes the spirit of a sect that uses a language all its own, that is based on rites of initiation, on tactics to which everything is subordinated, on an instrumental attitude toward truth, and on disregard for any values that are not political."

Johnathan Schell summarizes Michnik's views (and elaborates some of Havel's) in the following words: "Do you believe in freedom of speech? Then speak freely. Do you love truth? Then tell it. Do you believe in an open society? Then act in the open." If you wish to act locally, "then what could be more local than yourself?" And if you wish to produce results today, "then what area of life [is] more ready to hand, more thoroughly within your grasp, than your own actions?" And if, accordingly, you make yourself and your own actions the starting point for the reform of society, then how can you "permit those actions to be degraded by brutality, deception, or any other disfigurement?"

Events in Eastern Europe have given new dignity to politics, and new meaning to the phrase "political freedom." Some understand political freedom as a contradiction in terms; one might become political to protect one's freedom but hardly to *be* free. Yet the demands for freedom by Civic Forum, the East German Round Table, and Solidarity were not simply (or even primarily) demands for individual liberties, but for direct participation in the collective decisions that shape individual lives. To be political is to be free and vice versa, because it is in the realm of politics that people unite to constitute a human world, to empower each other in order to jointly take control and responsibility for forces that might otherwise control them. Here is

Havel: "Only by looking outward, only by caring for things that in terms of pure survival he needn't bother with at all, by constantly asking himself all sorts of questions, and by throwing himself over and over again into the tumult of the world, with the intention of making his voice count, only thus does one really become a person." The challenge to selfhood Havel locates in "the tumult of the world" is akin to what Sethe, a newly escaped slave woman now living in a freed community, faces in Toni Morrison's *Beloved:*

> She had twenty-eight days . . . of unslaved life. . . . Days of healing, ease and real-talk. Days of company: knowing the names of forty, fifty other Negroes, their views, habits; where they had been and what done; of feeling their fun and sorrow along with her own, which made it better. One taught her the alphabet; another a stitch. All taught her how it felt to wake up at dawn and *decide* what to do with the day. . . . Bit by bit . . . along with others, she had claimed herself. Freeing yourself is one thing; claiming land ownership of that freed self was another.

The realms of the political are not simply places for private interests to be expressed or protected, but have their own intrinsic value. Or so Aristotle thought. People who participate in politics, he believed, become morally and politically educated because of their participation. They learn to think in public and as public beings, to make public claims and give reasons that appeal to shared predicament and tradition. In acting politically they confront those beyond the immediate sphere of family or neighborhood; they encounter difference through deliberation and thereby develop the judgment and practical wisdom unattainable except by living a public life. If Aristotle is right then "representative democracy," not "political freedom," is a contradiction in terms. For if politics is a "partnership in virtue" (in Aristotle's phrase), how can I delegate someone to be virtuous for me? (It would be as absurd as going to a gym and having someone else do workouts for me.) No one can act for me or in my name, not because he or she will misrepresent my interests, but because such delegation is a renunciation of what is distinctively human about me. That, I think, is one of the lessons, perhaps even the foremost lesson, to be learned from Havel, Michnik, and the events in Eastern Europe.

I do not want to romanticize politics or slight Havel's suspicion of it. To say politics is the only thing that matters is fanaticism. Nor do I want to romanticize events in Eastern Europe or Havel himself, who warns us against doing either. Still less do I want to exaggerate the significance, let alone the content, of the *Times* articles. They are too often superficial, the complaints by political leaders too often self-serving. Politicians are too quick to blame public opinion rather than themselves. More often, they portray themselves as victims of media control, pointedly overlooking their frequent collusion with the media to create an exclusive political discourse of experts and insiders.

I do want to suggest that the *Times* is right about our cynicism and the corruption of our political discourse. Even something as momentous as the Kuwait crisis will not long obscure the truths brought home to us by events in Eastern Europe and Havel's presence here: the American policy elite, once so anxious to claim credit for democracy's advance in Eastern Europe, is clearly becoming uncomfortable. If the first step in ending political cynicism and corruption is for those responsible to *recognize* they are responsible, then the *Times* articles are a healthy sign.

It may even be that some members of Congress in attendance responded to Havel as they did because they saw their best selves in him, and that, too, would be a healthy sign. Perhaps he reminded them of what leadership could be and why public life mattered beyond the demands of political survival, moral posturing, and the sovereignty of oil. Here was a man of principle for whom tolerance represented not the passive acceptance of differences or grudging pluralism but an active generosity of spirit and a recognition of his own partiality, in the double sense of incompleteness and one-sidedness. Here was a cautionary visionary who saw politics as a calling and a responsibility of the highest order, without idealizing it or denying that he cared for other things more.

The overwhelming response Havel (and Mandela) elicit when they invoke our founding myths and otherwise moribund political language may also be a healthy sign. It may be that the democratic experiments in Eastern Europe (as well as the anti-apartheid struggle in South Africa and the failed revolution in China) can reconnect us with neglected legacies of our own democratic past (with Daniel Shays, the Anti-Federalists, and the Populists for example) and alert us to the continuing democratic experiments in our midst (neighborhood associations, women's health collectives, public interest research groups, and the sanctuary movement) which exist outside established centers of power.

In a press conference Havel said, "For 21 years we have lived outside of time. The students gave our history back to us." If we are good enough students it may be that Havel (and the Czech students), Michnik (and the workers of Solidarity), Mandela (and the black people of South Africa), and the single figure in Tiananmen Square halting a column of tanks will give us back some of ours.

J. Peter Euben is a professor of Politics and the History of Consciousness at the University of California–Santa Cruz. He is the author of The Tragedy of Political Theory *(Princeton, NJ: Princeton University Press, 1990).*

Originally published in Tikkun, *Vol. 5, no. 6, pp. 13–16. Reprinted with permission of the author.*

"One of the chief failings of the American political system over the past half century has been the inability to encourage average citizens to participate in the search for the public good."

Strengthening Citizenship

by Robert B. Woyach

During the last two decades, many political analysts have concluded that political alienation represents a growing problem in the United States. They have not agreed, however, on either the root causes of alienation or on the best responses to it. Indeed, elitists and populists alike have become increasingly skeptical that citizenship can be strengthened.

For their part, elitists face an inherent contradiction between their image of a workable political system and the goal of reducing alienation. Since political alienation reflects a sense of powerlessness, it can probably only be reduced through fundamental reforms of the political system. Those reforms probably must in some way enhance citizen efficacy. However, such reforms violate basic elitist beliefs about how democracy in the modern world must be structured to work effectively.

Populists also have little reason to be confident. Experience with institutions that do empower people have not been without their frustrations. Citizen participation requires an appropriate attitudinal foundation. Not all people are interested in political participation, nor are they willing to participate in democratic dialogue and learning. Many of those who do participate are unwilling to seek the public good along with their private interests. In short, people socialized within an elitist political system do not necessarily develop the attitudes required for a healthy citizenship.

What kinds of attitudes are necessary? In this article I outline five distinct changes in the way we approach politics, government, citizenship, and the civic community which are essential for building the foundations for a healthier citizenship. These are not recommendations for institutional change; nor are they suggestions for how to accomplish the needed attitudinal changes. Rather, they point out key attitudes, some of which have been neglected even by populists, that currently inhibit citizen participation. I then suggest alternative attitudes necessary to encourage or liberate participation.

Attitudes toward Politics

In the United States the term "politics" has come to be equated with special interests, unethical deal making, and the compromise of basic values. The routine denigration of politics may well make political alienation inevitable.

People in groups require politics. It is through politics that groups or communities determine the criteria for distributing values among members. Politics allows free people living in groups to create shared goals, to come to common understandings of needs, and to pool their resources to accomplish shared images of the future. Politics is not a process reserved to government; it is a part of everyday life. Without politics a group cannot make decisions. Unless it accepts authoritarian rule, it cannot act as a group. Groups and communities that cannot decide or act ultimately die.

The denigration of politics cannot lead to an apolitical society. It does, however, deprive a group or community of a *legitimate* process for defining the public good. As people withdraw from the disdainful world of politics, public policy formation becomes a technical activity, controlled by a narrow, tainted group of people. These bureaucrats, autocrats, or politicians are left to "do politics" while the rest go about the allegedly more legitimate and more honest work of achieving personal goals.

If citizenship is to be strengthened, we must recognize that citizenship implies participation in politics! We must reassert that politics is a healthy and intrinsic part of social life. This is not the same as pretending that there are no mean-spirited, self-interested, or evil people in the world. However, only if we see politics as an essential and healthy process can we see unethical politics as an aberration that can and should be resisted through healthy citizenship.

Attitudes toward Government as the Focus of the Civic Community

Since the 1930s, American political culture has increasingly seen government as the institution within which the public agenda is set and responses to public needs and opportunities implemented. The tendency to see government as the center of civic life is natural. In a representative democracy it is the only institution whose key figures are chosen by a broad electorate expressly for the purpose of making public policy. However, the more we have made government the surrogate for the civic community, the more politically alienated the society has become. In this sense, conservatives who criticize the tendency to look to government to solve all problems and rectify all injustices may be correct.

Reforming elitist institutions in order to encourage greater participation can only succeed up to a point. Representative government is not designed to engage large portions of the citizenry in the process of setting public agendas, making decisions, or implementing public policies. Merely opening up elitist institutions to broader participation may only encourage special interest politics. Organized interest groups are better positioned to capture institutions like political parties and to use new opportunities to lobby legislatures than the disorganized body of citizens.

If we are to respond to the problem of political alienation effectively, we must broaden our image of the civic community and citizenship in ways which legitimatize and empower organizations and institutions other than government. While important, government is not the *only* focus for civic community. Civic and neighborhood groups (e.g., neighborhood watches, world affairs councils, Chambers of Commerce, Rotary and Zonta International are examples) and groups organized around common needs and interests (such as welfare rights and environmental groups) are quasi-public institutions. Their goals are related to public life. As long as government remains the focus of civic community, such groups operate within the public sector primarily as lobbyists for special interests. However, if such groups were challenged to work toward the public interest and if their members were challenged to work openly to identify and work toward legitimate public interest goals within their areas of interest, it might be possible to transform these and similar groups into arenas for the healthy exercise of citizenship.

Attitudes toward the Efficacy of Local Communities

One of the most fundamental causes of political alienation in the modern world can be summed up in a simple dichotomy: widespread participation must be centered in small-scale, local settings; but the power to mobilize the resources needed to address public needs and opportunities effectively is often centered in large-scale, remote institutions like national governments. The globalization of everyday life only reinforces the basic dilemma that power resides in one place and participation in another. In short, the trend toward increasing scale in modern life seems destined to increase political alienation.

As we have learned about the complexity of social, political, economic, and ecological systems, we have become painfully aware that local communities cannot solve many problems on their own. But has our emphasis on the power of national governments and international cooperation been myopic as well? Have we lost sight of critical ways in which local communities can and must contribute to recognizing and addressing public needs? Some problems may best be addressed within local communities. Many problems which require national or international policies may be solvable only if small-scale institutions effectively mobilize individual concern and cooperation. Much of the current research on management and corporate effectiveness supports this idea. As organizations grow larger, they must work harder at listening to workers at all levels and at involving even the smallest work group in decentralized management.

The only solution to the alienating effects of giantism may well be a vibrant localism. Thus, if we are to strengthen citizenship in the United States, we must develop a more realistic image of the power of local communities, not only in matters of purely local concern but also in matters of national and international concern. It is impossible, for example, for any one local community to alter those trends that are leading to a warming of the global climate. But it may also be impossible to alter those trends if local communities are *not* involved in discussing the problem and implementing strategies to address it. Not everyone will participate in the process, but citizenship can only be strengthened if we create institutions and develop images of local communities that make it possible and reasonable for citizens interested in issues to participate efficaciously.

Attitudes toward Citizens as Leaders

For most political scientists, citizenship within the political arena implies "active" participation in politics. It may be more accurate, however, to say that citizenship involves "reactive" participation. Citizenship has, by and large, come to be treated as the equivalent of "followership." Leadership, the more proactive role in political life, is primarily associated with positions of authority. Leaders are people who sit atop the management hierarchy of organizations. Sometimes charismatic leaders emerge from the masses. By virtue of their ability to inspire and mobilize people, they ultimately take their place atop some organizational hierarchy. Citizens, presumably, follow these hierarchical or charismatic leaders.

The equation of citizenship with followership has the happy consequence of making the role of citizen accessible to everyone. If citizenship requires little skill—other than being able to make personal judgments and decisions in a voting booth—then virtually anyone can be a good citizen. Unfortunately, equating citizenship with followership also has insidious side effects.

For one thing, it absolves the average citizen from the need to exercise leadership, whatever the crisis or need. When problems arise, we look to those in authority to respond and bemoan the lack of leadership if they cannot. No one looks to the average citizen to exercise creativity or leadership in the public realm, least of all the average citizen. What has been widely regarded as a leadership crisis in America today stems largely from the unwillingness of average citizens to exercise leadership in the public arena.

By equating citizenship with followership, we also deflate the role of citizens. Citizens become part of a lesser class that observes political life, judges it, but can do little more. We define citizens as inefficacious when we see them merely as observers. We also deprive citizenship of any allure. In their private lives people can be proactive. They can participate in setting agendas. They can create the basis for their own futures. Business entrepreneurs, union officials, even girl scout leaders *lead*. In civic life, by contrast, these same people—as citizens—merely follow.

The effort to revitalize citizenship in America probably requires a reconceptualization of the role of citizenship to stress such modes of participation as community organizing. We must, in short, reassert the leadership dimension of citizenship. Given the commonly accepted assumptions about the complexity of issues and the pull of private life, it may seem counterproductive to stress the more intensive modes of citizen participation in this way. Indeed, it would be inappropriate to denigrate the less intensive modes of participation. However, the *overall* role of citizen must be elevated to something more than just observing and judging if we want it to be exciting and desirable. Only if citizens perceive that they have opportunities to take the initiative in setting public agendas and mobilizing groups to address public needs—independent of any formal position of authority—can we expect to capture the kind of entrepreneurship which most "leaders" now reserve for their private lives.

Attitudes toward the Public Good

Greater participation in civic life may lead to a healthier citizenship. It may also make alienated participation more widespread. The fundamental difference between healthy citizenship and alienated participation lies in the search for the public good. Political participation only reflects a healthy citizenship if it balances the pursuit of private interests with a genuine concern for achieving what is best for the civic community as a whole.

One of the chief failings of the American political system over the past half century has been its inability to encourage average citizens to participate in the search for the public good. While Americans may feel patriotic toward their community, their state and their nation, they feel little or no responsibility to help define the public good, especially with respect to issues that involve their private interests. Within representative systems, citizens are sometimes encouraged to advocate their particular viewpoints and interests to elected officials. But it is the elected elite, not citizens, who aggregate those interests into some vision of the public good. Those who care too much for the public good may find themselves at a disadvantage vis-à-vis those who seek only their private interest. It is hardly surprising, therefore, that most citizens feel little personal responsibility for the public good and lack the skills necessary to participate in defining it.

If we wish to strengthen citizenship, we must reassert the role of average citizens in seeking and defining the public good. We must also build more realistic images of the public good and the process through which it is defined. People's interest in the public good and commitment to searching for it must be constantly reinforced and nurtured if they are to take time from private pursuits and participate in public life. At the same time, we must not encourage images of the public good or the civic community that are totalist or unrealistic. Conflict over private interests is endemic in any human group—from the family to the globe. But genuine conflicts over what constitutes the public good are just as endemic. Conflict cannot be assumed to come solely from the pursuit of private interests. The public good and the best way to achieve it are almost never clearly defined. The most realistic images of the public good only emerge from discussions in which many points of view are recognized as legitimate and listened to carefully. Even then, the image of the public good remains tentative—an imperfect reflection based on limited human understanding.

Unless we expect and legitimize conflict within human communities, we encourage disillusionment. Unless we encourage the average citizen to participate in the search for the public good, we can never encourage a healthy citizenship.

Robert B. Woyach is professor of Political Science at The Ohio State University. This article is excerpted from a longer article entitled "The Political Perspective: Civic Participation and the Public Good."

Originally published in Gross, Richard E. and Thomas L. Dynneson. Social Science Perspectives on Citizenship Education *(New York: Teachers College Press, 1989), pp. 57–63, © 1991 by Teachers College, Columbia University. All rights reserved.*

"Americans have again and again articulated a broad
and inclusive vision of direct participation and civic
virtue that renews and enriches earlier conceptions
of democracy."

The People
Shall Rule

by Sara M. Evans and Harry C. Boyte

In 1975, a writer for *Business Week* magazine sounded a theme heard often
in the business press during the decade. What previously people had
accepted with gratitude, the man complained, now were assumed to be
rights. The sixties' social unrest had made the American public all too
demanding and self-assertive about concerns that ranged from taxes to the
environment. But the problem was not new. Current unruliness brought to
the surface "a conflict as old as the American republic: the conflict between
a political democracy and a capitalist economy."

To say a fundamental conflict exists between capitalism and democracy
sounds odd. The two are entwined in most people's minds, supposedly inseparable. But in fact up until the late nineteenth century "democracy" was seen
as a disturbing, even as a subversive, idea in polite society. The source of
unease was obvious enough. From antiquity, democracy—simply, the notion
that "the people shall rule"—had been associated with a constellation of
ideas that accompanied wide-ranging efforts at social change.

Indeed, both subject and verb of the formulation that "the people shall
rule" held unsettling implications. In the first instance, the meaning of "the

people" denoted the idea of *popular power* locating control over the institutions of society and government in the majority of the population, the common people. As Aristotle defined it, "a democracy is a state where the freemen and the poor, being in the majority, are invested with the power of the state." According to Plato, Socrates predicted that violence would inevitably accompany the transition to such government: "Democracy comes into being after the poor have conquered their opponents, slaughtering some and banishing others, while to the remainder they give an equal share of freedom and power."

The insurgent content of the term, with its implications of a "world turned upside down," asserted itself repeatedly in democratic popular uprisings. One can imagine the terror which John Ball, leader of a fourteenth-century English peasant revolt, struck in the hearts of the powerful when he orated: "Things cannot go well in England, nor ever will, until all goods are held in common and until there will be neither serfs nor gentlemen, and we shall be equal." For subsequent democratic rebels in English history, the vision of a far-reaching "commonwealth" proved a recurring pattern. Thus Gerrard Winstanley, theoretician of a radical faction of the seventeenth-century English Civil War, which had in fact established what was called "The Commonwealth," took the term with a shocking literalness: "The whole earth shall be a common treasury," Winstanley wrote. "For the earth is the Lord's. . . . There shall be no lords over others, but everyone shall be a lord of himself, subject to the law of righteousness, reason and equity."

Vox Populi

If the concept of "the people" embodied in democracy was troubling, the prospect of direct "rule" was at least as bothersome for those who believed society was best governed by a few. Again dating from ancient Greece, the concept of direct rule involved the idea of free and active participation (albeit a limited franchise) by those defined as citizens. As G. Lowes Dickinson has described the Greek *polis*: "To be a citizen of a state did not merely imply the payment of taxes and possession of a vote; it implied a direct and active cooperation in all the functions of civil and military life. A citizen was normally a soldier, a judge, and a member of the governing assembly; and all his public duties he performed not by deputy, but in person." Even in the Middle Ages, when feudal relationships characterized political life, an occasional political theorist ruminated upon the benefits that direct participation might produce. Thus, for example, Marsilius of Padua wrote in the early-fourteenth century that "a law made by the hearing or consent of the whole multitude, even though it were less useful, would be readily observed and endured by every one of the citizens, because then each would seem to have set the law upon himself and hence would have no protest against it, but would rather tolerate it with equanimity."

With the settlement of the New World, a laboratory existed for putting such ideas into practice. Thus, the first political constitution to use the term democracy—Rhode Island's in 1641—meant "popular government; that is to say it is the power of the body of freemen orderly assembled, or major part of them, to make or constitute just Lawes, by which they will be regulated."

Finally, the notion of democracy entailed not only rights to participate, but the responsibilities of citizenship. The concept of "the citizen" suggested one who was able to put aside, at times, immediate and personal interests and focus on public affairs. Such a trait amounted to civic virtue, suggested by Walt Whitman's observation in 1855 that a nation the size and extent of America "were monstrous" without a citizenry of correspondingly large and generous spirit. The values associated with citizenship included a concern for the common good, the welfare of the community as a whole, willingness to honor the same rights for others that one possesses, tolerance of diverse religious, political, and social beliefs, acceptance of the primacy of the community's decisions over one's own private inclinations, and a recognition of one's obligations to defend and serve the public.

Democratic Heritage of the American Revolution

America's Founders were divided about these ideas. For most, drawing on biblical and republican traditions, the concepts of participation and civic virtue were central—though very few, indeed, imagined "citizens" as including women, slaves, or the very poor. Private property, for instance, was rarely seen as an end in itself. Even our archetypical entrepreneur, Benjamin Franklin, held that "property" is simply "the creature of Society . . . subject to the calls of that Society." The independence which small amounts of property— small farms, for example, or small stores, or artisanal skills—allowed was important in this view, in fact, because it thereby freed citizens to participate in the public life of the self-governing community, or commonwealth.

Such participation was seen as the foundation of a free society—indeed, the only way in which skills of active public life, values of communal responsibility, and consciousness of the broader common good or commonwealth could be renewed and sustained. Thus, Thomas Jefferson contrasted the Europeans who he claimed "have divided their nations into two classes, wolves and sheep," with the Indians. Groups like the Iroquois, he believed, furnished a model for self-government because of their reliance on the moral force of community opinion instead of government action to control crime and other social problems: "Controls are their manners and the moral sense of right and wrong." From such perspectives, great extremes of wealth or speculative sale of property, like the squandering of the means of one's independence, were seen in the most unfavorable light because of the clear danger that the community might be eroded or disrupted. The values prized included service to the community, frugality, hard work, independence, and self-restraint. Their opposites—extravagance, self-indulgence, idleness, and so forth—had no place in a virtuous and just republic.

For all the potency of American democratic traditions, certain flaws are unmistakable and they weakened the very movements those traditions nourished. At times, such flaws also furnished material for subsequent democratic protest, as groups excluded or marginalized by the original terms of citizenship and democracy came to point out the chasm between myth and reality.

Two Views of Freedom

America's Puritan settlers had a strongly communal sense, but in many ways it was narrow and static. Puritans saw themselves as a "saving remnant," which would redeem a wicked Europe, and feared the "chaos" outside their communities. In doctrines permeated with Calvinism, human depravity could only be checked by the strictest of controls. And the notion that human sinfulness must be checked by external law and rigid enforcements has continued throughout the American experience, shaping a long tradition of local censorship and legislation about private moral issues.

The republican tradition itself, though prizing service to the community, became fused with an eighteenth-century individual rights philosophy that emphasized the liberation of the individual from constricting traditions and communal ties. Indeed, in many ways the hallmark of American democracy became the stress upon individualism. Thus, though visions of republican community, nourished by small-town and rural experience, provided potent contrasts to large-scale, centralized institutions, the language of American republicanism took community for granted. Ralph Waldo Emerson might observe, in despair, the system of selfishness which he feared would destroy democracy: "We eat and drink and wear perjury and fraud in a hundred commodities." But his emphatic focus on the democratic *individual* held no room for acknowledgment of human interconnection. "Take away from me the feeling that I must depend upon myself, give me the least hint that I have good friends and backers there in reserve who will gladly help me, and instantly I relax my diligence and obey the first impulse of generosity that is to cost me nothing and a certain slackness will creep over my conduct of affairs."

If the democratic traditions in America contained weaknesses and flaws, however, the more conservative wing of the American Revolution had a somewhat different, but clear enough, view of democracy. They didn't like the idea. Elite perspectives instead stressed themes of radical individualism and rule by the most wealthy. For Alexander Hamilton, the nation's first Treasury secretary, "Every man ought to be supposed a knave; and have no other end in all his actions, but private interests . . . insatiable avarice and ambition." Hamilton advocated the rapid growth of a manufacturing system as the arrangement most appropriate for "sorting out" those most fit to lead. And his view—expressed with uncommon candor in a nation which has always celebrated egalitarian manners and speech—those natural leaders were never in doubt. "All communities divided themselves into the few and the many," wrote Hamilton. "The first are rich and well-born, the other the mass of the people. The people are turbulent and changing; they seldom judge or determine right. Give, therefore, to the first class a distinct, permanent share in government."

Modern Survivals — and Survivors

Though elite control and ideologies which accompany and reinforce such control have undergone constant and dynamic change throughout American history, Hamiltonian perspectives, more or less overtly, have centrally informed the views of American elites ever since. Hamilton's words resonate unmistakably with those of John Calhoun, for example, the great apologist for the slave South, who argued (in remarkably direct challenge to the Declaration of Independence) that "it is a great and dangerous error to suppose that all people are equally entitled to liberty. It is a reward to be earned, not a blessing to be gratuitously lavished on all alike." In turn, such views find contemporary expression in the positions of those such as the *Business Week* editorialist, or the current political philosopher George Gilder, who argues capitalism's great virtue is that it "exalts the few extraordinary men who can produce wealth over the democratic masses who consume it."

Directly to the point, throughout the nineteenth and twentieth centuries, these tamed, elite versions of democracy increasingly prevailed in the mainstream, as Americans came to think of an active, participatory democracy as simply a nostalgic echo from the past. The eroding faith in democratic possibility, in turn, grew from the changes that were reshaping the nation in fundamental ways.

Throughout the nineteenth century, America remained largely a "nation of villagers," in Walter Lippmann's apt phrase. Small towns and the rural landscape, organized around families, friends, churches, mutual aid societies, farm organizations, and the like, provided the matrix for most people's lives from birth to death. Moreover, the explosive growth in voluntary organizations, both male and female, contributed significantly to a broadening definition of "citizenship" and public affairs. In rural settings (with some dramatic exceptions, like slaveholding areas of the South), wealth, if not evenly distributed, did not normally produce the enormous social cleavages into rich and poor that would later characterize urban life. Neighbors knew each other, visited regularly, and helped each other out in a variety of ways—from barn raisings to quilting bees and voluntary fire departments. And an understanding of democracy that emphasized the active, continuing involvement of citizens made sense.

"Democracy" suggested New England town meetings, or more informally, decision making in religious congregations or the discussion of local affairs in voluntary groups. Government was seen in these terms, not as the primary arena of democracy but, more authentically, as the instrument of citizens joined together. Even for popular protest movements, political engagement was seen as an expression of the values and activities of community life, not as an end in itself. Thus, for instance, the nineteenth-century Knights of Labor, a movement of laboring men and women protesting the rise of giant trusts and cartels and their threat to artisan traditions, "looked to self-organized society—not to the individual and not to the state—as the redeemer of their American dream," as labor historian Leon Fink put it. "Neither ultimate antagonist nor source of salvation, the state represented a mediator in the conflict between the civil forces of democracy and its enemies."

But the developments of the late-nineteenth and early-twentieth centuries—technological change, urbanization, industrialization, waves of immigration, the growth of new professions and scientific knowledge applied to social life—radically changed the very texture of life in America. In enormous cities, one could scarcely know one's neighbors, much less those down the street or on the other side of the tracks. Waves of immigrants brought new customs, traditions, and languages. Communications technologies like the railroad, telegraph, and mass newspaper began to shatter the boundaries of the local community; technologies at work and in professions sharply eroded older patterns of craft and community tradition. Civic involvement in town meetings and voluntary groups became less and less the model of "democracy." In its place emerged corrupt big-city political machines and the manipulation of a mass electorate by techniques of public relations and sloganeering. Modernity, as Lippmann observed, "had upset the old life on the prairies, made new demands upon democracy, introduced specialization and science, had destroyed village loyalties . . . and created the impersonal relationships of the modern world."

Middle-class reformers, meanwhile, adapted to the changes with alacrity—but in ways that further eclipsed any notion of small-scale, participatory, and community-based democracy. According to the Progressive thinkers like Lippmann, *New Republic* editor Herbert Croly, Theodore Roosevelt, and others in the early-twentieth century, the erosion of local community ties and a sense of civic responsibility was more than compensated for by possibilities for broader involvement. Local community life had had positive features, sustaining values like participation, egalitarianism, and a sense of civic involvement. But the new changes had great potential, in the view of such observers, to bring in the place of small communities a far better great community that would dissolve all differences of nationality, ethnicity, religion, and region into a "melting pot."

People Taking Charge

Progressives—and those who followed in their tradition, like many liberal reformers of the New Deal—continued to advocate direct involvement of citizens in decision-making processes. But the locus of civic involvement shifted from voluntary association and community activity to government itself. Through various public agencies and electoral reforms—regulatory commissions, civil service reform, nonpartisan local elections, direct election of senators, referenda and initiative, and the like—citizens would shape the "great community" of the country. Women's suffrage, in this understanding, would be democracy's greatest realization. And democracy itself, in Croly's words, no longer meant that citizens "assemble after the manner of a New England town meeting" since there existed "abundant opportunities of communications and consultation without any meeting. . . . The active citizenship of the country meets every morning and evening and discusses the affairs of the nation with the newspaper as an impersonal interlocutor."

But the reality proved to be radically different. Aside from the new, rising middle class of professionals and white-collar workers in large private and public bureaucracies, most Americans continued to identify with their locales, their traditions, their heritages, and cultures. But their worlds seemed increasingly shaped by distant forces over which they had no control whatsoever. Corner grocers gave way to chain stores, local decisions over education were removed to state or national bureaucracies; ways of doing things—from child rearing to family home remedies—that had been passed down for generations were replaced by "expert advice" from professionals who claimed specialized knowledge.

By mid-twentieth century, political theorists celebrated the relative noninvolvement of most citizens in public life as a source of stability and order. Indeed, the *International Encyclopedia of the Social Sciences,* the 17-volume summary of social sciences containing 900-odd articles, offered nothing at all on the theme of "citizenship," a concept at the heart of active and participatory democracy. What G. B. Macpherson calls "equilibrium democracy" had largely replaced classic understandings of the word. In equilibrium democracy, a mainly passive citizenry—composed of individuals pulled in different directions by competing interests—chooses among representatives based on the attractiveness of their "consumer promises." The political system resembles a marketplace. And the point of society is not participation but "possessive individualism," where each has the right to compete, on roughly equal footing, for acquisition of material goods, status, and power.

Popular movements, it has now been widely enough documented, normally arise in defense of rights or ways of life that a changing world threatens to destroy. Examples of defensive and limited protests abound, from the nativist movements of the nineteenth century to the Ku Klux Klan and the White Citizens Council of the 1960s, from the National Union for Social Justice of the 1930s to fights against "dangerous books" in the present. Backward-looking in their central construction, such protests are in a basic sense survival efforts, aimed at returning things to "the way they were" at best, and at the least retaining whatever elements of identity, culture, and place can be salvaged.

Forward Together

Whatever the diminished sense of possibility afflicting modern thought, however, ordinary men and women have also found the courage and spirit again and again to imagine the possibility of an active, participatory democracy—to seek something radically *different,* rather than simply a "bigger piece of the pie" or a return to the way things were. From nineteenth-century farmers' populist struggles and women's fight for citizenship and suffrage to modern movements like the rise of the CIO in the 1930s, the southern civil rights struggle and the youth movement in the 1960s, and the neighborhood and citizen movements in the 1970s and 1980s, Americans have again and again articulated a broad and inclusive vision of direct participation and civic virtue that renews and enriches earlier conceptions of democracy. With varying degrees of success they have fashioned the practical skills and organizational means to seek to realize their aspirations.

The most radical challenges to conventional American politics have drawn their vocabulary and power from core issues remembered from the past. Eugene Debs, visionary spokesman for the American Socialist Party in its halcyon days of the early-twentieth century, built his denunciations of corporate greed and business concentration on the "eighteenth-century revolutionary heritage," according to his biographer, Nicholas Salvatore, "the concept that the government will rest upon the intelligence and virtue of the people." Martin Luther King, Jr., described the Civil Rights movement as "bringing the entire nation back to the great wells of democracy that were dug deep by the Founding Fathers."

There is little mysterious or unknowable about democratic movements for change. In their failure to examine the particular features that produce such endeavors, contemporary writers miss the forest for the trees. The dispossessed and powerless have again and again sought simultaneously to revive and remember older notions of democratic participation, on the one hand, and on the other have given them new and deeper meanings and applications. Democracy in these terms, then, means more than changing structures so as to make democracy possible. It means, also, schooling citizens in "citizenship"— that is, in the varied skills and values which are essential to sustaining effective participation. Democratic social movements, efforts whose goal is an enlarged democracy, are themselves vehicles for such schooling.

Sara M. Evans is professor of History at the University of Minnesota, and Harry C. Boyte directs the Project on the New Public Philosophy for the Humphrey Institute at the same university.

This essay is excerpted from the first chapter of their most recent book, Free Spaces: The Sources of Democratic Change in America. *(Copyright © 1986 by Sara M. Evans and Harry C. Boyte and reprinted by permission of Harper & Row, Publishers, Inc.)*

"A healthy public life is vital in the continuing struggle toward freedom and equality for all people. But
that movement does not begin with politics, with the
formal institutions of government. It begins with the
simple opportunities of public interaction: the chance
to meet strangers, to deal with fear and conflict, to
realize and celebrate our diversity and the unity that
lies beneath it."

The Nature and Nurture of Public Life

by Parker Palmer

Fifty years ago, John Dewey wrote that "the outstanding problem of the
Public is the discovery and identification of itself." As those words suggest,
our public life is not dead but invisible. There will always be a public, as long
as there are people in societies. The public is all around us all the time, and
each of us is always a part of it. But we lack awareness of that fact, appreciation of that opportunity, understanding of the need for conscious public
participation. So public life, which could be a force for unity, and a stimulat-
ing dimension of individual experience, lies fallow—untapped potential in a
society which concentrates its resources on cultivating private experience.

If we are to discover our life as a public and bring it into daily awareness,
we must have a working concept of public life—a concept which enables us
to see the public where it exists and to rebuild it where it has collapsed. Our
ability to see what is around us, or what might be there, depends on the concepts we carry in our heads. If we did not have a concept for "stars" we could
not see them for what they are, no matter how numerous and visible the stars
might be. Our concepts also limit our ability to act. When astronomical con-

cepts put the earth at the center of the universe, no program of space exploration would have been possible, even if the technology had existed. Our concept of public life has become so empty or narrow or deformed that we are unable to see the public accurately, to act in public creatively.

The Word "Public"

At bottom the word "public" means all of the people in a society, without distinction or qualification. A public school is a place from which no child is barred, a place where the common culture of a people can be passed along from one generation to the next. A person in public life is one whose career involves accountability to the people as a whole, who carries a public trust. Even the weaker phrase, a public figure, means a person whose life is visible to all who care to watch it. When information appears in the public press it is available to everyone; a public library collects and stores such information so it will be available to persons yet unborn. And the word is used in similar but less grandiose ways, as in the English "pub" or public house which is a gathering place for the whole community.

These uses of the word remind us of the importance of public life. In public we remember that the world consists of more than self and family and friends. We belong to a human community; we are supported by it and must support it; in this world "no man is an island." All of this and more is evoked by the idea of a public in its most general sense.

So it is puzzling that the word has come to have such a narrow meaning in our time. Today, in ordinary usage, public means "of or pertaining to government." We commonly think of the public as the body of voters whose primary function is to go to the polls, elect government officials, decide on a few referenda, and retire until the next election. Or we may speak of a public policy, meaning governmental enactments which are binding on all. When we think of a public school, we think of an institution supported by tax monies which the government collects and allocates. Or when we think of a person in public life, we picture someone whose career is in government.

Why has this word—which should evoke the common bond of a diverse people—taken on such narrow political meaning? I suspect the answer lies in an assumption which pervades the political thought of our society, the assumption that only through the processes of government can a public be created, that only through legislative enactments can the many become one.

The mainstream of our political thought has assumed that the individual, by nature, is primarily motivated by self-interest. If that is true, then a public is possible only as ways are found to correlate and control the vast diversity of self-interests. The task of government is to provide a framework of rules and penalties within which a community can be constructed out of the convergence of self-interests, with those interests which do not fit being deflected or simply denied. In this stream of political theory, the public has been reduced to an arena in which individuals compete for the most they can get with government as the referee.

This image of the public contains far less promise than an authentic public life. The regulatory powers of government, however necessary, can neither give us a vision of unity nor lead us toward community. Such powers can only provide minimal security, a level of survival without quality. The vision and reality of community come when people have direct experience of each other, experience of mutuality and interdependence unmediated by governmental sanctions and codes. The vision and reality of community come when people have a rich array of opportunities to interact in public, interactions which draw out and encourage the human impulse toward life together.

I do not deny the element of self-interest in society. Nor do I deny the need for institutions of government which limit the extent to which self-interest can be pursued. But this is a minimal vision of what is possible among people. If this is all we can say about the public life, we have traded away our birthright. And if we envision the public as nothing more than a battleground between divergent self-interests, we create a dismal self-fulfilling prophecy. Given this image, it is small wonder that fewer and fewer people venture into public without being (figuratively and literally) well armed. Small wonder that more and more people retreat from the public arena so conceived into the sanctuary of private life.

An Image of Possibilities

We need a larger and more inviting image of public possibilities, an image founded in the fact, to quote Robert Bellah, that "a society could not last a single day if its people were motivated by nothing except the maximization of self-interest." If a people lack the impulse to see themselves as one, and the chance to act out that impulse, then no government, however powerful, can hold them together.

Finally, the only limitation on self-interest is other-interest, the sense that we are members of one another for better and for worse. Other-interest comes, in part, as the result of a healthy public life. If self-interest is the dominant mood of our time, it is not because self-interest is the whole of human nature. Instead, it is partly because we lack a public life in which other interest can be evoked and nurtured.

Human nature is (to understate the case) complex and contradictory. It contains a wide range of possibilities, from the noblest self-sacrifice to the cruelest self-service, as history reveals. But these diverse tendencies of human nature will be amplified or suppressed according to the structures of encouragement, the channels of expression, available at any give time. If we had no structures for private life (e.g., private dwelling quarters, or the institution of the family) private instincts would tend to fade. And so it is with the desire for public experience.

My argument for public possibilities is based on an assumption which can be stated negatively or positively. Negatively: so long as the primary opportunities of our lives are private, our tendency to deny public relatedness will be amplified. Positively: if people are given opportunities for public experience and expression, the experience itself will evoke their willingness, interest, desire, and ability to be part of the public.

That assumption is backed by some hard data, not least the fascinating study by Richard Titmus on the way various countries collect human blood for medical uses. A voluntary system of blood donation, such as that which exists in England, gives people an opportunity to make a significant gift to the stranger; such a system nurtures the public life. But in countries like the United States, where most blood is sold to commercial establishments, what might be a gift to a stranger becomes a sale to a customer instead. Titmus demonstrates that the supply of blood is far superior, both quantitatively and qualitatively, in countries where the voluntary system predominates than it is where blood may be sold for a price. "In some countries," Titmus writes, "the commercialization of blood is discouraging and downgrading the voluntary principle. Both the sense of community and the expression of altruism are being silenced." But a structured opportunity to give a gift to the stranger encourages the impulse toward the public life.

Of course, there are some people who will always resist the public life no matter how many opportunities are offered, and most of us will find it difficult from time to time. But I believe there is an inclination, a tendency, a gravity in the human heart toward one another. We need to establish the conditions under which that tendency can find expression and gain momentum.

If that tendency does not exist in human nature, then there is nothing we can do to force a public into being. But—as Bellah suggests—the very fact that we have a functioning society means that some sort of public spirit is at work, that some forms of public life exist to evoke and channel that spirit. My question is how to widen and multiply the channels so that more of the spirit can flow.

If the public life—as I use the phrase—does not happen simply in the halls of government, and does not result simply in public policy decisions, where does it happen and what are its outcomes? As we answer those questions, we will begin to build a working definition.

Settings for Public Life

First, a brief survey of some of the places where public life occurs. The most likely place is in the public street where strangers in pursuit of private interests meet each other. No word may pass between them, but as they walk by, whether dimly aware or actively curious about each other, a public is being formed. In this encounter of strangers, an important subliminal message is being conveyed: we do not know each other, and we may look strange (even ominous) in each other's eyes, but we occupy the same territory, belong to the same human community, and we need to acknowledge that fact and learn to get along.

City parks, squares, sidewalk cafes, museums, and galleries are also settings for the public life. Here, strangers can pause, spend time in each other's presence, share common interests and pleasures, become somewhat more aware of each other, and perhaps even exchange a few words. When a city is rich in facilities such as these, the public life is more likely to thrive. Unfortunately, in most of our cities, heedless planning has made public space scarce, sacrificing it to more profitable uses.

Rallies, forums, hearings, and debates (including those conducted by means of public media) are settings in which the public interacts and becomes aware of itself. Here, strangers have an opportunity to listen and be heard, to air their differences and conflicts, to influence each other's thinking, and to move toward mutual accommodation.

But the public life is not all conflict and accommodation. It is also stimulation, celebration, and enhancement of life through the interaction of diverse people. This side of public experience is most obvious when a street musician is playing, or at carnivals, festivals, and fairs. Here people are not only entertained, but they entertain each other. Here we learn that our interdependence does not simply pose problems; it is also the source of great joy, the joy we find when we receive each other's gifts and share each other's foibles. The public life is the constant enactment of the human comedy, and when we learn to look for that and see it, life is immeasurably enriched.

The neighborhood is another important setting for the public life (though a setting which has been eroded by the trends of privatization and urbanization). The public as a whole is simply too large, too abstract, for the individual to identify with and respond to. A small world like the neighborhood gives the public a human face, a human scale. As we gain experience in the neighborhood, we increase our ability to identify with the public in its larger and more distant forms. The ability to identify with the world community itself depends on having an outward moving series of concentric public experiences, and the neighborhood is often the vital inner circle.

Voluntary associations are also settings in which strangers come together and receive training in the public life. Here we learn that it is possible for people who are neither family nor friends, people whose lives touch only tangentially, to relate within a framework of common interest, concern, commitment; to share scarce resources and make decisions about them even when disagreement exists; to take collective action even when visions differ. By gaining confidence and competence in voluntary associations (including the church) people are empowered to enter larger spheres of public activity.

A healthy public life is vital in the continuing struggle toward freedom and equality for all people. But that movement does not begin with politics, with the formal institutions of government. It begins with the simple opportunities of public interaction: the chance to meet strangers, to deal with fear and conflict, to realize and celebrate our diversity and the unity that lies beneath it.

Public Space, Psychology, and Myth

Opportunities for public interaction do not just happen. They depend on the presence of certain facilitating factors. By understanding some of these factors we will both deepen our idea of public life and get clues about practical steps toward the renewal of public experience. I want to explore three such factors here: public space, a public psychology, and a public myth.

There can be no public interaction without physical space which encourages the encounter of strangers. Historically, the primary public space has been found in the marketplace or streets where people come in pursuit of private interest (shopping, work, or simply getting from one place to another) and in the process meet as a public.

The capacity of the streets to encourage a public life is enhanced by a rich mix of private, semiprivate, and public usages within a limited area. For example, public interaction is increased if, within a few square blocks, one finds residences, shops, offices, and a square or park—for these different usages will guarantee a mix of different kinds of people moving through the space in different rhythms all through the day. But if, block after block, one finds only residences, or only places of work, the public life is undermined. In such areas persons of one kind predominate; they tend to move in and out on identical schedules, thus not mixing with each other; and they have no reason to step outside their private homes or work spaces except to travel to some distant and equally segregated office or residential area.

Our present arrangements of space do not enhance the public life, with residence here, shopping there, and employment somewhere else. By segregating these functions we have made public interaction all but impossible in many places. We go to work and disappear inside our office for the day. We go home and disappear inside the house for the night. And when we go shopping, we often go to places which may seem public but, in fact, contain far less public life than the marketplace or streets.

The Relations and Strangers

A second factor which can help or hinder the life of the public is the psychology or mind-set of the time. Richard Sennett, in *The Fall of Public Man,* has made an important contribution to our understanding of the public psychology by analyzing our sense of how we should relate to others:

> The reigning belief today is that closeness between persons is a moral good. The reigning aspiration today is to develop individual personality through experiences of closeness and warmth with others. The reigning myth today is that the evils of society can all be understood as the evils of impersonality, alienation, and coldness. The sum of these three is an ideology of intimacy: social relationships of all kinds are real, believable, and authentic the closer they approach the inner psychological concerns of each person. This ideology transmutes political categories into psychological categories. This ideology of intimacy defines the humanitarian spirit of a society without gods; warmth is our god.

Intimacy itself is not a bad thing; that is not the problem. Nor is it the case that intimacy and public life cannot coexist. Intimate private relations can obviously exist alongside the relations of strangers in public, and we sometimes know fleeting but powerful moments of intimacy even with strangers; hence, the oft-noted tendency for people to share their problems with a stranger on the train or plane, a sharing which is possible in part because the two will never see each other again. Indeed, when I argue that public life is ultimately grounded in an inward, spiritual sense of relatedness to strangers, I am rooting the public life in a kind of intimacy—the intimacy we have in God.

The problem arises when closeness and warmth become the criteria of all meaningful relations, when we reject and even fear relationships which do not yield to these standards. The problem arises when we impose the norm of intimacy (which applies primarily to private life) upon the public sphere. For within the public realm, where most relations are necessarily distant and impersonal, the demand for closeness and warmth distorts and eventually destroys the potential of public experience.

As Sennett points out, we have imposed the demand for intimacy on our public experience, but in a most ambivalent way. On the one hand, fearing the impersonality of the public realm and wanting to personalize it, we become intrigued with the personalities and private lives of public people. Thus, the success of a political candidate has as much to do with "charisma" as with his or her positions on issues. But the way in which we personalize the public life causes us to fear it even more, for we realize that if we were to enter the public ranks our own personalities and private lives would become subject to scrutiny and criticism. And so we withdraw. We are in a double bind, wanting to personalize public experience to make it less fearsome, yet simultaneously fearing the consequences of projecting our own personalities onto the public screen.

Historically, Americans have worried about the incursion of public powers into the private realm. But now we can see that there is also a problem when the psychology of private relations is forced upon the public sphere. When intimacy becomes the sole criterion for authentic human relationships, we falsify relations in public; hence, the cult of personality which has so distorted our political process. We must learn to accept and appreciate the fact that public life is fundamentally impersonal. Relations in public are the relations of strangers who do not, and need not, know each other in depth. And such relations have real virtue. The public life involves those qualities of distance and disinterest which allow us to receive from another without assuming a personal obligation, to give to another without having to make a total commitment. In fact, the public life allows us to view and listen to each other, to be edified and entertained, without forming a personal relationship of any sort. To receive full benefit from public life, one must realize that impersonal relations have a validity of their own.

"Bonded to Each Other"

A third factor which makes public life possible is the structure of myth and symbol—indeed, the theology—which defines us as a public to begin with. By "myth," of course, I do not mean a fairy tale or lie. I mean a way of looking at the world which helps explain that world and one's place in it, which tells us what is important and meaningful out of all of life's options.

Our history is full of powerful symbols of public life, symbols which allowed people to understand themselves as a public and which animated them to play a public role. The founders of this society understood themselves not as a collection of individuals but as a community, "New Israel," a "Chosen People," who had set off on an "Exodus" to establish themselves in a "New Jerusalem" or "New Canaan." England was "Egypt," King James I was the "Pharaoh," and the Atlantic Ocean was the "Red Sea." The colonists—standing in this ancient tradition—believed that they, like the first Israel, had been selected by God for a special mission in history, to be a "city set upon a hill" for the example and inspiration of others. The community they were to establish in "the promised land" had a special messianic character: it was ignited by God to give light to a world lost in the dark.

At the core of this myth, this complex of symbols, so influential in the colonial period of our society, is a master symbol, a controlling metaphor, which holds all the rest together. This is the idea of "covenant." Those who settled this country saw themselves bonded to each other in community because of their bond or covenant with God. They believed that if they were faithful to God, God would hold them together in community. Without denying that economic and political factors played an important role in the formation of colonial America, I claim only that in those early days, religion functioned exactly as the etymology of the word suggests—to bind a people together.

The secularization of public language occurred early in American history, even as early as the Declaration of Independence. Here, though God is mentioned, the language begins to "cool" in comparison with the fervent usages of the Massachusetts Bay Colony and the First Great Awakening. The Declaration speaks of "the Laws of Nature and Nature's God," of the "Creator," the "Supreme Judge," and of "Divine Providence"—all references more characteristic of a sophisticated deism than of passionate biblical faith. And as we move on to the Constitution of the United States, we find no explicit reference to God or to God's covenant with the people. Indeed, the only reference to religion is found in the so-called "wall of separation" clause, leading some observers to claim that the mentality of its writers was essentially secular, devoid of religious imagination.

But neither the Declaration nor the Constitution is a rejection of the history and religious imagery which preceded it. Instead both documents are manifestations of that history, and neither document is conceivable without the history from which it emerges. Though the Constitution does not mention "covenant," it is itself a covenant which was drafted and ratified within an ethos of covenant thought-patterns which had been building for years.

I stress this point because it is a mistake to imagine that religious symbolism is no longer capable of animating American public life. Of course, there are problems of translation; we no longer speak as the Puritans did. But the idea of covenant continues to undergird the American mind-set, no matter how far it has sunk into the unconscious realm. In fact, as psychologists tell us, that which is unconscious may have a more powerful impact on our behavior than that which is at the front of our minds. The covenant symbol is implicit, for example, in those voluntary associations still so central to American life—those little covenant groups where people join in a common commitment which, however dimly it may reflect its origins, still links us to our covenantal past. By seeing the presence of the covenant symbol in our collective unconscious, and by finding new ways to articulate it and bring it to awareness, the church could help revive the withering public myth.

Persons concerned to revive the religious grounds of public life often look with nostalgia at times when religious symbols and meanings were prominent in America's public sphere. But the process of secularization has meant driving those symbols from the public realm into the confines of private life. Perhaps, instead of bemoaning this fact, we can capitalize upon it. Perhaps the revival of America's public life will be aided most by those who learn to go deeply within, those who (as Thomas Merton did) touch the heart of God within themselves, that heart in which they are related to all other selves. Perhaps it is from such inner journeying that some will emerge with new symbols and images which can be shared in public to help create the public. The inward turn of America's religious life is fatal to the public only if it does not go far enough. The inward search, if it goes deep, will touch the One who makes us one, a source of new power for the revival of public life.

Parker Palmer is a writer and lecturer who lives in Madison, Wisconsin. This article has been adapted from his book, The Company of Strangers *(New York: The Crossroad Publishing Company, 1981).*

Reprinted by permission of the author from the Kettering Review, *Fall 1984.*

"An education for politics is necessarily an education in the practice of making choices with others who are different from us."

Civic Intelligence

by David Mathews

According to a study of college students by Alexander Astin a few years ago, only about 40 percent, far less than half of the next generation, were interested in public affairs or the great issues of the day. Only 20 percent, one out of five, were likely to become involved in helping other people in some form of community activity. The objectives of college freshmen have changed substantially in the last 15 years, Astin reported. In 1968, more than 80 percent of those surveyed identified "development of a meaningful philosophy of life" as a major objective; by 1984, less than half had that goal. More than 80 percent of the freshmen put affluence at the top of their charts.

Now perhaps that trend is being reversed. The overriding question, however, regardless of the trend, is what responsibility do colleges and universities have for the civic education of students and for their sense of social responsibility? That question is a long way from being resolved. The trend in the answers is, as it has been for a long time, that such education is a marginal responsibility of institutions of higher learning. For all the arguments over the mission of higher learning, one purpose is generally applauded: colleges and universities are responsible for the development of the human intellect. Most academics argue, and argue persuasively, that the development of the mind, of the capacity to reason, is the best guarantor of any kind of competence—civic or otherwise. They teach their discipline.

Academe lost interest in civic education centuries ago when thought was separated from action and the academic disciplines were born. It was a useful separation in some respects. Thought could be pursued for its own sake. The academic sciences flourished. The separation, however, had unfortunate side effects. All knowledge came to be judged by the standards for scientific knowledge. Academics came to prize objectivity; human perceptions and values were devalued. Consequently, education with any ethical dimension, including questions about how a political community should act, was pushed outside the walls of academe.[1]

Civic education still has a certain following but even its advocates hesitate to call it what it really is—political education. That term will probably never be decriminalized. Who wants to be accused of offering a political education? It sounds like the worst sort of indoctrination. So we are left with four alternatives for civic education.

- One approach might be described as an effort to ensure *civic literacy*. In this category, I would put teaching young people the great issues of the day—the perils of the nuclear age, the dilemmas of social welfare, etc. Most would agree that just knowing events and facts is not enough. Students cannot understand the particulars unless they understand the principles on which our political culture is based. E. D. Hirsch made that case in saying that "without appropriate tacitly shared background knowledge, people cannot understand newspapers. A certain extent of shared, canonical knowledge is inherently necessary to a literate democracy." Beyond current events as literacy there is the more persuasive argument for cultural literacy.

  In this first, general category, I would also put those who define civic literacy as knowledge about the mechanics of the political system—about what governments do, how powers are divided among the branches, how legislatures work, how bills are passed. The result is usually a course called "American Government."

- A second approach to civic education emphasizes teaching values. For example, the Society for Values in Higher Education makes a strong case for teaching values as a part of a liberal education. Their argument is familiar: education is responsible for character as well as wisdom. If the first approach to the problem of developing socially or civically responsible students can be characterized as championing civic literacy, this second approach can be fairly described as advocating an education in *civic values*.

- Advocates of a third approach emphasize *civic skills*. They often talk about "leadership." For example, there are courses on leadership at institutions from Princeton to Dartmouth to Colorado College to the University of Richmond.

- A fourth, an increasingly popular way to develop civic competence, is to encourage it through social service. Students at a number of colleges now work in all kinds of community projects. We are even considering some type of national youth service program.

These arguments all have merit. Yet they all fail to understand what civic-mindedness requires. I would emphasize the word "mind." I believe that civic competence is not just a matter of intelligence generally but of *civic intelligence*.

After all, politics was created by human beings when they moved from having their future shaped slowly by experience (usually suffering) and began to use the powers of human reason to define and secure the "good life." The Greek word for political wisdom *phronesis*, which originally meant the ability to recognize the divine order in society, was used by the fifth century B.C. to describe that aspect of human intelligence (cognition) that could be used in a methodical way to discern wise action. For the Greeks, "phronesis" was the greatest gift of all gods.[2] Politics is action or a practice. Yet, it is the kind of practice that must be instructed by thought. For some time, people have been able to distinguish the modes of thought for politics from other kinds of thought. We should know about our political culture. But political knowledge is more than knowledge *about* something. Just knowing about politics won't do. Even teaching values isn't enough; nor is sending students off campus to service programs. The development of civic intelligence, like other uses of intelligence, is very much the business of institutions of higher learning. It is implicit in the universally accepted mission of those institutions.

The most dramatic way to make the point that political thought must inform action is to look at what can happen when there is an absence of political thinking. I do not mean to overdramatize by using this example. I only intend to illustrate the connection between ways of thinking and ways of behaving politically.

The most blatant example is provided by Franz Stangl, commandant of the Treblinka death camp, whose trial gives us some insight into how a supposedly sane, educated person could order systematic murder of men, women, and children during World War II. The first question was how Stangl could commit such atrocities and live with his values or conscience. As he revealed in an interview, that was not a problem. "What I had to do," he said, "was to limit my own actions to what I—in my conscience—could answer for." That is, Stangl found a way to act that did not bother his conscience. But how? The answer was in the way he had been taught to think. In the most revealing of his comments he explained, "The only way I could live was by compartmentalizing my thinking."[3] In other words, Stangl had a way of thinking that allowed him to commit atrocities—in good conscience.

The problem with people like Stangl is rooted in how their minds work, in how they misuse their intelligence. That is the conclusion that Hannah Arendt reached when she covered the Adolph Eichmann trial. That experience led her to write about what I would call "civic intelligence" and what she called "representative thinking" and "judgment."[4]

The point becomes clearer by comparing the private uses of intelligence to the political or the civic uses of our minds. When we are using our minds for civic purposes, we have to go beyond knowing just the "facts." For example, the amount of smoke put into the air by an industry is not hard to calculate. But its effects are. The reason is not just because the biological impact is more complex a problem, but because some see the smoke as the acceptable side effect of needed jobs and others see it as unacceptable environmental damage. Being civically intelligent means having the capacity to find out both what the facts are *and* what those facts mean to *others*.

It follows that to develop civic intelligence in students, teachers need to help them move beyond the "Golden Rule" of thinking. We must do more than just think for others as we would think for ourselves. We must think with what Immanuel Kant called "enlarged mentality."[5] We must be able to understand facts *as others would understand them for themselves*—from perspectives and circumstances quite different from our own. Perhaps we should call that the "Platinum Rule" of thinking. So political thinking requires the kind of comprehension that is mutual. We have to have a shared understanding of others and the problems we face.

To understand the nature of the problems we face, our comprehension has to be comprehensive. That is, we have to be able to see more than aspects of problems, we have to see the whole of a problem. Understanding connection and interrelations is essential in political thinking. Compartmentalized thinking is disastrous. Developing the capacity to think comprehensively is very difficult, however, in a compartmentalized society. We are scientists, or lawyers, or doctors, or autoworkers. We have economic and political and social issues. And we have corresponding academic disciplines.

Most difficult of all is teaching students to understand their own, personal connectedness to the larger world around them. *Yet, being educated civically means understanding that connectedness*. Failing in that, we would be what the Greeks called "idiots." The term was not used to describe people of low intelligence but those who understand only their private worlds.

Political thinking, however, involves more than understanding one another and our problems. The practice of politics is the practice of making choices, not by ourselves but with others, about matters on which we can never be certain. And the choices we make together—the judgments—will have great consequences on those things we hold to be most valuable.

The reason politics requires what Kant called an enlarged mentality is that we have to be able to reason together. Politics is about acting together and we can't act together very well unless we can think together. The most important characteristic of political thought—which sets it apart from private thought—is that it requires public *judgment*, the essential prerequisite to making political choices. We cannot just know abstractly; we must know in order to choose, to decide. Reason, said Hannah Arendt, "requires only that I be consistent with myself." In contrast, "judgment requires that I be together with my fellow man."[6]

A political judgment requires citizens to do much the same thing judges do in courtrooms. Citizens have to be able to take the things they value, on the one hand, and the particular situation they are facing, on the other, and decide what course of action best applies their values to the issue before them. There is no authority in democratic politics to say what the correct application is. So political judgments have to be rendered in the face of unyielding uncertainty. If issues could be decided with certainty, they would not be on the political agenda.[7]

Every political issue presents us with such difficult choices. Learning to make sound judgments on those issues is what developing civic intelligence is all about. Of all that we do to teach a political culture, values, leadership, and encourage social responsibility, we rarely teach in a way that expands a student's capacity to think politically, to reason and make judgments with others.

If there is no possibility of certainty and we must deal with the varying perceptions of very different people, how then is it possible to ever know anything in politics? How can there be a common knowledge for making common decisions? That is the point at which many in academe throw up their hands and conclude that politics is a matter of individual conscience, something that cannot be instructed by someone else. Everything is relative, one person's opinion is as good as another's. One reason this problem looms so large is the individualism that prevents some from seeing any possibility for commonality. "I teach," one faculty member said, "at an institution where my colleagues do not believe that anything common is possible." That problem is insurmountable because we have no common standard for evaluating what is opined in politics. The only standard we have for judging knowledge is the standard we commonly associate with scientific knowledge—correctness.

For example, everyone measuring a piece of wood with the same ruler will come to the same conclusion about its length. Our knowledge is exact and common. Anyone who measures the wood and comes to a different conclusion is incorrect. But when it comes to the question of what we should do with the wood, no one is likely to come to the same conclusion. And there seems no basis for saying that any opinion is wrong. After all, in politics we are not dealing with exact measurement; rather, we are dealing with estimations of something's worth.

This epistemic logical barrier keeps political thinking outside the walls of academe. An exception is made for those who want to sharpen a person's critical faculties so that they can evaluate what they hear from political leaders. But the barrier remains intact. Only individual faculties are involved. We do know how to inform individual opinions. Thinking in common is another matter. That sounds like "group thinking."

Yet, thinking together so as to act together is what politics is all about. What we depend on for our survival is the quality of the decisions we make as a country and a community. Informed, individual opinions don't entirely guarantee sound public opinions. What matters is how individual opinions are joined to come to a shared conclusion. But how can we reach a shared decision if there is no common standard we can use to hold one another accountable for what is said politically? Knowing whether what is said is correct is a necessary, but not sufficient, condition.

The standard we are missing is the one that is appropriate for politics. It is the *soundness* of our opinions or judgments. Civic intelligence is for sorting out whether our estimations of the various options before us are consistent with those things we value in our common life. Do we recognize, and are we willing to accept, the consequences of our actions or what is most valuable to us as a whole? That is what we must think about together. And we can hold each other individually, and ourselves collectively, accountable for what we say by that common standard of "soundness."

Philosophically, pluralism does force people to give us the claim that any academic discipline or philosophy can provide an answer to the question of how we should live and act in a way that is valid for everyone. It does not, however, preclude the claim that ways to act together can grow out of a reasoned judgment made among the people who face the need to act together. For us to make a decision to act in a certain way, and for that decision to be sound or valid for everyone, its consequences must be acceptable to all people involved. How can people know what is acceptable? Only by thinking together. Such political thinking is necessary to reveal to us those things we can know only when we are together and never alone. That is a major distinction between political thinking and scientific logic.[8]

All of this is to say that political thinking has a claim on academe. This article is not the place for a full treatment of modes of rationality in politics. It is certainly possible to differ with the cursory treatment of the subject in the last several pages. The point being made here is that the argument that higher education is responsible for civic education is a serious one.

The reason this claim hasn't been recognized lies in the way politics is understood. The major obstacle to any change in the way we go about civic education is found in our political philosophy, not just our pedagogy. The politics we teach is not a politics in which citizens have to make hard choices about common purposes and direction. Textbooks define politics as the act of electing or influencing governments. There is no place for the formation of public judgment and so no need for thinking together. People need only advocate their favorite cause or express their preference of candidates at the ballot box. Politics is not that part of everyone's life where they work to define and build the kind of world they want to live in. It is not a specialized realm of elections, politicians, and government machinists.

Since we think of politics as a specialized realm, we provide an education *about* politics rather than an education *for* politics. That is not the way we teach other subjects. We teach both art appreciation and the skills of artistry. Yet when it comes to politics, we teach only political "appreciation." Furthermore, we define politics narrowly as market government and the competition of self-interested factions. We are reluctant to recognize that politics is a practice and, like any practice, can only be learned by experience. *An education for politics is necessarily an education in the practice of making choices with others who are different from us.* Learning politics occurs only in making real choices, ones that have direct consequences for us. The conflicts inevitable in such choices produce the necessary tension that causes people to struggle and to learn. Take away the experience of making real choices and the integrity of political education is lost. Everything turns to tapioca pudding. Because choosing is a personal experience in a shared activity, students can't learn what politics is by observing what others do in politics. Even mock exercises can be too artificial. We can't do politics in someone else's clothes, the way we do college plays.

While the major obstacle to developing civic-mindedness is in the way we understand politics, it is also in the style of pedagogy that dominates most campuses. Sitting passively in a lecture hall is ill suited to the thinking together that political choices require. So is the posturing in debate. The appropriate mode of discourse for political thinking is not argumentation. Rather, it is the open, exploratory, careful weighing of both options and the opinions of others that "deliberation" implies. Whether a choice is sound or not can't be determined in a monologue. It can only be by people talking together in a way that requires people to put themselves in one another's shoes (perspective taking must be reciprocal).[9] In order to think together, people have to talk together in a deliberative fashion. *In matters civic, talking is a way of thinking.* We cannot reason publicly unless we talk deliberatively.

Deliberative discourse serves to exercise and develop civic intelligence. It creates and reflects an "enlarged mentality." It is the kind of discourse that lends itself to recognizing the connectedness of things—and our own connectedness. It is the discourse in which we can develop the capacity to understand the structure and functioning of the *whole* social body, a capacity is essential to governing ourselves democratically.[10] Deliberative discourse allows us to discover what is common amid our differences. It is the most essential ingredient in making sound political judgments.

Pericles said it best, "instead of looking on discussion as a stumbling block in the way of action in a democracy, we teach ourselves first with discussions (*logous ...prodidaxthania*) before we act."

In sum, if colleges and universities are responsible for the development of the minds of their students, then they are certainly responsible for those particular modes of rationality that are civic. And if the civic affairs (politics) involve more than influencing governments, then that responsibility requires a reconsideration of even our best efforts to prepare the next generation for public life.

David Mathews is president of the Kettering Foundation.

Adapted from Social Education, *November/December 1985. Reprinted with the permission of the author.*

Notes

1. Richard A. Lanham, "The 'Q' Question," *South Atlantic Quarterly* (Fall 1988): pp. 653–700.

2. Christian Meier, *The Greek Discovery of Politics*, trans. by David McLintock (Cambridge, MA: Harvard University Press, 1990), pp. 129–131.

3. Gitta Sereny, *Into That Darkness*, (New York: McGraw Hill, 1974), p. 164.

4. For more on Arendt's discussion of political judgment see her *Lectures on Kant's Political Philosophy*, ed. by Ronald Beiner (Chicago: University of Chicago Press, 1982) and also her *The Life of the Mind*. (San Diego: Harcourt Brace Jovanovich, 1981).

5. Immanuel Kant, *Critique of Judgment*, trans. Werner S. Pluhar (Indianapolis: Hackett Publishing, 1987). Kant's conception of aesthetic judgment is one source of later notions of political judgment.

6. Michael Denneny, "The Privilege of Ourselves: Hannah Arendt on Judgment" in *Hannah Arendt: The Recovery of the Public World*, ed. Melvin A. Hill (New York: St. Martin's Press, 1979).

7. For further discussion of judgment see Elizabeth K. Minnich, *Transforming Knowledge* (Philadelphia, PA: Temple University Press, 1990) and Benjamin Barber, *Strong Democracy: Participatory Politics for a New Age* (Berkeley, CA: University of California Press, 1984).

8. Jürgen Habermas, *Moral Consciousness and Communicative Action*, trans. Christian Lenhardt and Shierry Weber Nicholsen (Cambridge, MA: MIT Press, 1990).

9. *Ibid.*

10. Arthur Koestler, *Darkness at Noon*, trans. Daphne Hardy (New York: Bantam Books, 1966).

"What makes mass society so difficult to bear is not the number of people involved, or at least not primarily, but the fact that the world between them has lost its power to gather them together, to relate and to separate them. The weirdness of this situation resembles a spiritualistic séance where a number of people gathered around a table might suddenly, through some magic trick, see the table vanish from their midst, so that two persons sitting opposite each other were no longer separated but also would be entirely unrelated to each other by anything tangible."

The Public Realm

by Hannah Arendt

The term "public" signifies two closely interrelated but not altogether identical phenomena: It means, first, that everything that appears in public can be seen and heard by everybody and has the widest possible publicity. For us, appearance—something that is being seen and heard by others as well as by ourselves—constitutes reality. Compared with the reality which comes from being seen and heard, even the greatest forces of intimate life—the passions of the heart, the thoughts of the mind, the delights of the senses—lead an uncertain, shadowy kind of existence unless and until they are transformed, deprivatized and deindividualized, as it were, into a shape to fit them for public appearance.[1] The most current of such transformations occurs in storytelling and generally in artistic transposition of individual experiences. But we do not need the form of the artist to witness this transfiguration. Each time we talk about things that can be experienced only in privacy or intimacy, we bring them out into a sphere where they will assume a kind of reality which, their intensity notwithstanding, they never could have had before. The presence of others who see what we see and hear what we hear assures us of the reality of the world and ourselves, and while the intimacy of a fully developed private life, such as had never been known before the rise of the modern age and the concomitant decline of the public realm, will always greatly intensify and enrich the whole scale of subjective emotions and private feelings, this intensification will always come to pass at the expense of the assurance of the reality of the world and men.

Indeed, the most intense feeling we know of, intense to the point of blotting out all other experiences, namely, the experience of great bodily pain, is at the same time the most private and least communicable of all. Not only is it perhaps the only experience which we are unable to transform into a shape fit for public appearance, it actually deprives us of our feeling for reality to such an extent that we can forget it more quickly and easily than anything else. There seems to be no bridge from the most radical subjectivity, in which I am no longer "recognizable," to the outer world of life.[2] Pain, in other words, truly a borderline experience between life as "being among men" (*inter homines esse)* and death, is so subjective and removed from the world of things and men that it cannot assume an appearance at all.[3]

Since our feeling for reality depends utterly upon appearance and therefore upon the existence of a public realm into which things can appear out of the darkness of sheltered existence, even the twilight which illuminates our private and intimate lives is ultimately derived from the much harsher light of the public realm. Yet there are a great many things which cannot withstand the implacable, bright light of the constant presence of others on the public scene; there, only what is considered to be relevant, worthy of being seen or heard, can be tolerated, so that the irrelevant becomes automatically a private matter. This, to be sure, does not mean that private concerns are generally irrelevant; on the contrary, we shall see that there are very relevant matters which can survive only in the realm of the private. For instance, love, in distinction from friendship, is killed, or rather extinguished, the moment it is displayed in public. ("Never seek to tell thy love / Love that never told can be.") Because of its inherent worldlessness, love can only become false and perverted when it is used for political purposes such as the change or salvation of the world.

What the public realm considers irrelevant can have such an extraordinary and infectious charm that a whole people may adopt it as their way of life, without for that reason changing its essentially private character. Modern enchantment with "small things," though preached by early twentieth-century poetry in almost all European tongues, has found its classical presentation in the *petit bonheur* of the French people. Since the decay of their once great and glorious public realm, the French have become masters in the art of being happy among "small things," within the space of their own four walls, between chest and bed, table and chair, dog and cat and flowerpot, extending to these things a care and tenderness which, in a world where rapid industrialization constantly kills off the things of yesterday to produce today's objects, may even appear to be the world's last, purely humane corner. This enlargement of the private, the enchantment, as it were, of a whole people, does not make it public, does not constitute a public realm, but, on the contrary, means only that the public realm has almost completely receded, so that greatness has given way to charm everywhere; for while the public realm may be great, it cannot be charming precisely because it is unable to harbor the irrelevant.

Second, the term "public" signifies the world itself, in so far as it is common to all of us and distinguished from our privately owned place in it. This world, however, is not identical with the earth or with nature, as the limited space for the movement of men and the general condition of organic life. It is related, rather, to the human artifact, the fabrication of human hands, as well as to affairs which go on among those who inhabit the man-made world together. To live together in the world means essentially that a world of things is between those who have it in common, as a table is located between those who sit around it; the world, like every in-between, relates and separates men at the same time.

The public realm, as the common world, gathers us together and yet prevents our falling over each other, so to speak. What makes mass society so difficult to bear is not the number of people involved, or at least not primarily, but the fact that the world between them has lost its power to gather them together, to relate and to separate them. The weirdness of this situation resembles a spiritualistic séance where a number of people gathered around a table might suddenly, through some magic trick, see the table vanish from their midst, so that two persons sitting opposite each other were no longer separated but also would be entirely unrelated to each other by anything tangible.

Historically, we know of only one principle that was ever devised to keep a community of people together who had lost their interest in the common world and felt themselves no longer related and separated by it. To find a bond between people strong enough to replace the world was the main political task of early Christian philosophy, and it was Augustine who proposed to found not only the Christian "brotherhood" but all human relationships on charity. But this charity, though its worldlessness clearly corresponds to the general human experience of love, is at the same time clearly distinguished from it in being something which, like the world, is between men: "Even robbers have between them [*inter se*] what they call charity."[4] This surprising illustration of the Christian political principle is in fact very well chosen, because the bond of charity between people, while it is incapable of founding a public realm of its own, is quite adequate to the main Christian principle of worldlessness and is admirably fit to carry a group of essentially worldless people through the world, a group of saints or a group of criminals, provided only it is understood that the world itself is doomed and that every activity in it is undertaken with the proviso *quamdiu mundus durat* ("as long as the world lasts").[5] The unpolitical, nonpublic character of the Christian community was early defined in the demand that it should form a *corpus*, a "body," whose members were to be related to each other like brothers of the same family.[6] The structure of communal life was modeled on the relationships between the members of a family because these were known to be nonpolitical and even antipolitical. A public realm had never come into being between the members of a family, and it was therefore not likely to develop from Christian community life if this life was ruled by the principle of charity and nothing else. Even then, as we know from the history and the rules of the monastic orders—the only communities in which the principle of charity as a political device was ever tried—the danger that the activities undertaken under "the necessity of present life" *(necessitas vitae praesentis)*[7] would lead by themselves, because they were performed in the presence of others, to the establishment of a kind of counterworld, a public realm within the orders themselves, was great enough to require additional rules and regulations, the most relevant one in our context being the prohibition of excellence and its subsequent pride.[8]

Worldlessness as a political phenomenon is possible only on the assumption that the world will not last; on this assumption, however, it is almost inevitable that worldlessness, in one form or another, will begin to dominate the political scene. This happened after the downfall of the Roman Empire and, albeit for quite other reasons and in very different, perhaps even more disconsolate forms, it seems to happen again in our own days. The Christian abstention from worldly things is by no means the only conclusion one can draw from the conviction that the human artifice, a product of mortal hands, is as mortal as its makers. This, on the contrary, may also intensify the enjoyment and consumption of the things of the world, all manners of intercourse in which the world is not primarily understood to be the *koinon*, that which is common to all. Only the existence of a public realm and the world's subsequent transformation into a community of things which gathers men together and relates them to each other depends entirely on permanence. If the world is to contain a public space, it cannot be erected for one generation and planned for the living only; it must transcend the life span of mortal men.

Without this transcendence into a potential earthly immortality, no politics, strictly speaking, no common world and no public realm, is possible. For unlike the common good as Christianity understood it—the salvation of one's soul as a concern common to all—the common world is what we enter when we are born and what we leave behind when we die. It transcends our life span into past and future alike; it was there before we came and will outlast our brief sojourn in it. It is what we have in common not only with those who live with us, but also with those who were here before and with those who will come after us. But such a common world can survive the coming and going of the generations only to the extent that it appears in public. It is the publicity of the public realm which can absorb and make shine through the centuries whatever men may want to save from the natural ruin of time. Through many ages before us—but now not any more—men entered the public realm because they wanted something of their own or something they had in common with others to be more permanent than their earthly lives. (Thus, the curse of slavery consisted not only in being deprived of freedom and of visibility, but also in the fear of these obscure people themselves "that from being obscure they should pass away leaving no trace that they have existed.")[9] There is perhaps no clearer testimony to the loss of the public realm in the modern age than the almost complete loss of authentic concern with immortality, a loss somewhat overshadowed by the simultaneous loss of the metaphysical concern with eternity. The latter, being the concern of the philosophers and the *vita contemplativa,* must remain outside our present considerations. But the former is testified to by the current classification of striving for immortality with the private vice of vanity. Under modern conditions, it is indeed so unlikely that anybody should earnestly aspire to an earthly immortality that we probably are justified in thinking it is nothing but vanity.

The famous passage in Aristotle, "Considering human affairs, one must not . . . consider man as he is and not consider what is mortal in mortal things, but think about them [only] to the extent that they have the possibility of immortalizing," occurs very properly in his political writings.[10] For the *polis* was for the Greeks, as the *res publica* was for the Romans, first of all their guarantee against the futility of individual life, the space protected against this futility and reserved for the relative permanence, if not immortality, of mortals.

What the modern age thought of the public realm, after the spectacular rise of society to public prominence, was expressed by Adam Smith when, with disarming sincerity, he mentions "that unprosperous race of men commonly called men of letters" for whom "public admiration . . . makes always a part of their reward, . . a considerable part . . . in the profession of physic; a still greater perhaps in that of law; in poetry and philosophy it makes almost the whole."[11] Here it is self-evident that public admiration and monetary reward are of the same nature and can become substitutes for each other. Public admiration, too, is something to be used and consumed, and status, as we would say today, fulfills one need as food fulfills another: public admiration is consumed by individual vanity as food is consumed by hunger. Obviously, from this viewpoint the test of reality does not lie in the public presence of others, but rather in the greater or lesser urgency of needs to whose existence or nonexistence nobody can ever testify except the one who happens to suffer them. And since the need for food has its demonstrable basis of reality in the life process itself, it is also obvious that the entirely subjective pangs of hunger are more real than "vainglory," as Hobbes used to call the need for public admiration. Yet, even if these needs, through some miracle of sympathy, were shared by others, their very futility would prevent their ever establishing anything so solid and durable as a common world. The point then is not that there is a lack of public admiration for poetry and philosophy in the modern world, but that such admiration does not constitute a space in which things are saved from destruction by time. The futility of public admiration, which daily is consumed in ever greater quantities, on the contrary, is such that monetary reward, one of the most futile things there is, can become more "objective" and more real.

As distinguished from this "objectivity," whose only basis is money as a common denominator for the fulfillment of all needs, the reality of the public realm relies on the simultaneous presence of innumerable perspectives and aspects in which the common world presents itself and for which no common measurement or denominator can ever be devised. For though the common world is the common meeting ground of all, those who are present have different locations in it, and the location of one can no more coincide with the location of another than the location of two objects. Being seen and being heard by others derive their significance from the fact that everybody sees and hears from a different position. This is the meaning of public life, compared to which even the richest and most satisfying family life can offer only the prolongation or multiplication of one's own position with its attending aspects and perspectives. The subjectivity of privacy can be prolonged and multiplied in a family, it can even become so strong that its weight is felt in the public realm; but this family "world" can never replace the reality rising out of the sum total of aspects presented by one object to a multitude of spectators. Only where things can be seen by many in a variety of aspects without changing their identity, so that those who are gathered around them know they see sameness in utter diversity, can worldly reality truly and reliably appear.

Under the conditions of a common world, reality is not guaranteed primarily by the "common nature" of all men who constitute it, but rather by the fact that, differences of position and the resulting variety of perspectives notwithstanding, everybody is always concerned with the same object. If the sameness of the object can no longer be discerned, no common nature of men, least of all the unnatural conformism of a mass society, can prevent the destruction of the common world, which is usually preceded by the destruction of the many aspects in which it presents itself to human plurality. This can happen under conditions of radical isolation, where nobody can any longer agree with anybody else, as is usually the case in tyrannies. But it may also happen under conditions of mass society or mass hysteria, where we see all people suddenly behave as though they were members of one family, each multiplying and prolonging the perspective of his neighbor. In both instances, men have become entirely private, that is, they have been deprived of seeing and hearing others, of being seen and being heard by them. They are all imprisoned in the subjectivity of their own singular experience, which does not cease to be singular if the same experience is multiplied innumerable times. The end of the common world has come when it is seen only under one aspect and is permitted to present itself in only one perspective.

Hannah Arendt, political scientist and writer, was the author of Between Past and Future, On Revolution, *and* Eichmann.

Originally published in Hannah Arendt, The Human Condition, *(Chicago: University of Chicago Press), ©1958 by the University of Chicago Press. All rights reserved. Reprinted by permission of the publisher.*

Notes

1. This is also the reason why it is impossible "to write a character sketch of any slave who lived. . . . Until they emerge into freedom and notoriety, they remain shadowy types rather than persons" (Barrow, *Slavery in the Roman Empire,* p. 156).

2. I use here a little-known poem on pain from Rilke's deathbed: The first lines of the untitled poem are: "Komm du, du letzer, den ich anerkenne, /heilloser Schmerz im leiblichen Geweb"; and it concludes as follows: "Bin ich es noch, der da unkenntlich brennt? /Erinnerungen reiss ich nicht herein./O Leben, Leben: Draussensein. /Und ich in Lohe. Niemand, der mich kennt."

3. On the subjectivity of pain and its relevance for all variations of hedonism and sensualism, see §§ 15 and 43. For the living, death is primarily disappearance. But unlike pain, there is one aspect of death in which it is as though death appeared among the living, and that is in old age. Goethe once remarked that growing old is "gradually receding from appearance" (*stufenweises Zurücktreten aus der Erscheinung*); the truth of this remark as well as the actual appearance of this process of disappearing becomes quite tangible in the old-age self-portraits of the great masters—Rembrandt, Leonardo, etc.—in which the intensity of the eyes seems to illuminate and preside over the receding flesh.

4. *Contra Faustum Manichaeum* v. 5.

5. This is, of course, still the presupposition even of Aquinas' political philosophy (see *op. cit.* ii. 2. 181, 4).

6. The term *corpus rei publicae* is current in pre-Christian Latin, but has the connotation of the population inhabiting a *res publica,* a given political realm. The corresponding Greek term *sōma* is never used in pre-Christian Greek in a political sense. The metaphor seems to occur for the first time in Paul (I Cor. 12: 12–27) and is current in all early Christian writers (see, for instance, Tertullian *Apologeticus* 39, or Ambrosius *De officiis ministrorum* iii. 3. 17). It became of the greatest importance for medieval political theory, which unanimously assumed that all men were *quasi unum corpus* (Aquinas *op. cit.* ii. 1. 81. 1). But while the early writers stressed the equality of the members, which are all equally necessary for the well-being of the body as a whole, the emphasis later shifted to the difference between the head and the members, to the duty of the head to rule and of the members to obey. (For the Middle Ages, see Anton-Hermann Chroust, "The Corporate Idea in the Middle Ages," *Review of Politics,* Vol. VIII [1947].)

7. Aquinas *op. cit.* ii. 2. 179. 2.

8. See Article 57 of the Benedictine rule, in Levasseur, *op. cit.,* p. 187: If one of the

monks became proud of his work, he had to give it up.

9. Barrow *(Slavery in the Roman Empire,* p. 168), in an illuminating discussion of the membership of slaves in the Roman colleges, which provided, besides "good fellowship in life and the certainty of a decent burial . . . the crowning glory of an epitaph; and in this last the slave found a melancholy pleasure."

10. *Nicomachean Ethics* 1177b31.

11. *Wealth of Nations,* Book I, ch. 10 (pp. 120 and 95 of Vol. I of Everyman's ed.).

Back to Basics: Which Democracy?

The selections in Part 1 alert us to various aspects of the problem of democratic political education. They call attention to what is missing in our current practices, offer reasons for this state of affairs, and indicate in broad strokes how matters might be improved. The essays in Part 2 develop a richer understanding of democracy and concomitant notions such as citizenship, civic virtue, and political education.

Democracy remains more an ideal than a reality. For that reason alone, we must always be rethinking its meaning. Since the time of Socrates, thinking about the art of government has led inevitably to thinking about the art of education, and vice versa; the two go hand in hand. In the first selection of Part Two, **Amy Gutmann** leads us along a fruitful path of reflection concerning the requirements of a theory of education for democratic political participation. To think effectively about political education, she says, we need first of all a theory about the purposes of education. That theory must be democratic and it must be focused on education. We need theory, Gutmann explains because, without it, there is no principled reason to choose one course of action over another. But theory is not enough. There are many theories. Because we differ, we must deliberate. Theories we have deliberated about will be more enlightened than alternatives. To say that democratic education must focus on education is to say that the purpose of education in a democracy is "conscious social reproduction." By that Gutmann means something more than political socialization on the one hand or public schooling on the other.

Two essays tackle the thorny issue of liberalism, our prevailing public philosophy. There are those who think that the liberal state does not need any specific kind of political education, that indeed a liberal state is defined by the absence of such collective prescriptions. **William Galston**, citing recent scholarship, denies this assumption. He argues that civic education is both "necessary and possible in a liberal state." What we share—traditions, principles, institutions—is the basis of a political education that is valid across the boundaries of our differences. These differences, of course, are important. In a liberal democracy there must be a tolerance of pluralism, respect for individual rights, limits on government, representative institutions, and room for the claims of conscience. Such liberal values are paramount, but they are not absolute; in the final analysis, the *pluribus* is limited by the *unum*. Thus Galston concludes, "despite the pluralism of liberal societies, it is perfectly possible to identify a core of civic commitments and competences whose broad acceptance undergirds a well-ordered liberal polity."

William Sullivan wishes to complement liberal values with elements of the classical republican tradition that begins with Aristotle. On the republican view, citizenship is not a private option but a public duty that is necessary for self-development, as well as for a viable community. Civic life is a shared life, a commitment to others rooted in a moral conscience. Citizenship rests upon the powerful metaphor of covenant (cf. Palmer) and its underlying notion of a common good. Sullivan proposes a philosophy of civic republicanism as an antidote to the liberal emphasis on individual values.

The classical republic tradition echoes in contemporary theories of participation, articulated and defended eloquently by **Hanna Fenichel Pitkin** and **Sara Shumer**. Democracy implies that everyone is capable of self-government, "of sharing in the deliberate shaping of common life." Pitkin and Shumer argue against three objections to participatory democracy. The first is the prevailing view that politics is necessarily a competitive struggle among self-interested individuals (the liberal posture). The second is that the size of modern societies makes widespread participation impossible. The third is that technology and participatory democracy are incompatible; the expertise demanded by the former works against the participation required by the latter.

Jane Mansbridge complains that the dominant tradition in political science reduces democracy to a mechanistic technique of aggregating self-interest. She advocates instead a "deliberative democracy" in which citizens talk together and reach decisions on the basis of shared values—"we-thinking," not merely "I-thinking." (What Mansbridge calls deliberative democracy bears a strong resemblance to Sullivan's characterization of classical republicanism.) Two schools of feminist thought throw light on the nature of deliberative democracy. One stresses women's power of nurturance and relationships. A second, more combative school concentrates on asymmetrical power relations between men and women. Both schools introduce new categories into our power-dominated political discourse: care, attentiveness, "we-thinking," relationships, "power with" (not just power over), concern for the common good, listening skills, emotional sensitivity and empathy. Both lines of feminist thought favor a more participatory democracy and constitute a fertile source of new ideas and perspectives. "Democratic theorists in search of provocative and useful new ideas," Mansbridge says in conclusion, "can find them in the constantly growing corpus of feminist theory."

As Mansbridge argues for the contribution of feminism to our thinking about democracy, so **Manuel Ramírez** and **Alfredo Castañeda** argue for the contribution of an ethnic perspective. Specifically, they propose a cultural democracy "which recognizes that the way a person communicates, relates to others, seeks support and recognition from his environment, and thinks, and learns is a product of the value system of his home and community." Equality means the right to be different, to share in a different culture, to speak a different language, to have access to a different kind of education. The melting pot model of assimilation, the authors state, has not worked well for the Hispanics. The notion of pluralism must include biculturalism. It is important, they say, "for the individual to be able to function in whichever cultural world he finds himself and at the same time to contribute to its enrichment and continued development."

Cornel West extends the argument to include all marginalized groups in American society. These groups are now energized by a new kind of consciousness and are calling for justice under the banner of a new kind of politics, what West calls a "new cultural politics of difference." This new politics, he says in his closely reasoned article, faces three formidable challenges: one, intellectual, one, existential and one, political. The intellectual challenge is to compensate for the shortcomings and failures of our cultural legacy from Europe as articulated by such spokesmen as Matthew Arnold and

T. S. Eliot and which did not include women and peoples of color or even white working-class people. Black people especially were excluded. West puts the existential challenge in the form of a question: How does one acquire the resources to survive and the cultural capital to successfully promote the new politics of difference? The political challenge, finally, "consists of forging solid and reliable alliances of people of color and white progressives guided by a moral and political vision of greater democracy and individual freedom in communities, states, and transnational enterprises."

"The most distinctive feature of a democratic theory
of education is that it makes a democratic virtue
out of our inevitable disagreement over educational
problems."

The Primacy
of Political Education

by Amy Gutmann

When citizens rule in a democracy, they determine, among other things,
how future citizens will be educated. Democratic education is therefore a
political as well as an educational ideal. Because being educated as a child
entails being ruled, "you cannot be a ruler unless you have first been ruled."[1]
Because being a democratic citizen entails ruling, the ideal of democratic
education is being ruled, then ruling. Education not only sets the stage for
democratic politics, it plays a central role in it. Its dual role poses one of the
primary moral problems of politics: Who should share the authority to influence the way democratic citizens are educated?

To answer this question, we need a democratic theory of education. But
before developing that theory, I must answer three challenges to the idea
that a democratic theory of education is worth developing. First: Why rely on
a *theory* to decide who should exercise authority over education? Second:
Why a *democratic* theory? Finally: Why focus on *education?*

Why a Theory?

"There are two human inventions which may be considered more difficult than any others—the art of government, and the art of education; and people still contend as to their very meaning."[2] We can exercise the art of education, Kant argued, either unreflectively, "without plan, ruled by given circumstances,"[3] or theoretically, with the aid of principles. Must educational policy rest on a principled theory? Why not settle for making educational policy less reflectively, as we often have in the past? Without any principled plan, we could strengthen our science and math curriculum in reaction to *Sputnik*, desegregate some schools and fund more compensatory education in reaction to the Civil Rights movement, and go "back to basics" in reaction to declining SAT scores.

Consider the recent back-to-basics movement in American education. In the absence of a theory, how might the call to go back to basics be defended? The most common and direct defense is that schools will better educate children by concentrating on reading, writing, history, mathematics, and science rather than on music, art, sex education, and so on. Having invoked the concept of a "better" education, we must ask "better" with respect to what purposes? Without a principled theory of education, an answer is not obvious. Neither, therefore, is the rationality of going back to basics.

This point is not simply academic. Consider the widely publicized recommendation by the National Commission on Excellence in Education for instituting the "New Basics." In making its recommendation, the commission noted that "if only to keep and improve on the slim competitive edge we still retain in world markets, we must dedicate ourselves to the reform of our educational system for the benefit of all—old and young alike, affluent and poor, majority and minority."[4] Although the tone of the report is set by this statement, the commission also notes that our concern for education "goes well beyond matters such as industry and commerce . . . [to include] the intellectual, moral, and spiritual strengths of our people which knit together the very fabric of our society."[5] If our educational purposes are this broad, it is not clear why the new basics do not also include art history, sex education, racial integration, and the avoidance of academic tracking. A rigorous course in high school chemistry may not contribute more to the moral and spiritual strength of students than a racially integrated classroom or an equally rigorous course in art history. The problem is not that the reforms recommended by the commission are necessarily wrong, but that we cannot judge them without a more principled understanding of our educational purposes.

The commission may have had a political reason for not engaging in a more principled analysis: the desire to achieve public consensus. The "basics" appear to provide a least common denominator for agreeing on a national agenda for education. If we agree on the basics, we can temporarily set aside our deeper disagreements on more controversial issues, such as racial integration and sex education, and get on with the work of improving our schools. But do we agree on the basics? A greater proportion of citizens may approve of teaching American history than sex education in schools (although 82 percent of the American public approves of sex education[6]), but *how* schools teach sex education and American history matters more to most citizens than *whether* schools teach these subjects, and there is no consensus on how either American history or sex education should be taught. There is, in this crucial sense, no consensus on teaching even the "basics."

Were there a consensus, it would not constitute a decisive reason for dispensing with a principled analysis of our educational problems. The charter of the commission "directed it to pay particular attention to teenage youth."[7] The report therefore focuses on high school education, yet it makes no mention (for example) of the educational problems created by a rapidly rising pregnancy rate among unmarried teenage girls[8] and, therefore, totally neglects the question of how schools might best deal with the problem. Although the teenage pregnancy rate has risen more rapidly in recent years than SAT scores have fallen, the commission concentrated exclusively on the latter problem. If public commissions put avoidance of political controversy ahead of principled analysis, they are bound to fail in the task for which they are best equipped: improving the quality of American education not directly by changing school policy, but indirectly by improving the quality of our public deliberations over education.

In a democracy, political disagreement is not something that we should generally seek to avoid. Political controversies over our educational problems are a particularly important source of social progress because they have the potential for educating so many citizens. By not taking principled positions, commissions may avoid converting some of our disagreements into full-fledged political controversies. But we pay a very high price for their avoidance: we neglect educational alternatives that may be better than those to which we have become accustomed or that may aid us in understanding how to improve our schools before we reach the point of crisis, when our reactions are likely to be less reflective because we have so little time to deliberate.

Some members of the commission may have had another reason for avoiding a principled analysis of our educational problems. They may have believed that the government's legitimate educational role does not extend to what might be called "moral education." On this view, the government should stay away from subjects such as sex education, since courses in sex education cannot possibly be neutral with regard to morality, and moral education is properly a private, not a public, concern.[9] Sex education should, therefore, be provided by parents, not by public schools. Whatever one thinks of this conclusion, it clearly presupposes a theory, a principled political theory, about the legitimate role of government in education. Unless the theory is articulated, citizens cannot assess its principled merits or its policy implications. Even a brief account of the theory suggests a problem with this rationale for the commission's recommendations. If one embraces the principle that moral education is the domain of the family rather than the state, then the basics must not include the teaching of history or biology (insofar as it includes evolution) any more than sex education or racial integration. States cannot even support schools without engaging in moral education.

All significant policy prescriptions presuppose a theory, a political theory, of the proper role of government in education. When the theory remains implicit, we cannot adequately judge its principles or the policy prescriptions that flow from them. The attractions of avoiding theory are, as we have just seen, superficial. We do not collectively know good educational policy when we see it; we cannot make good educational policy by avoiding political controversy; nor can we make principled educational policy without exposing our principles and investigating their implications.

Why a Democratic Theory?

To defend the need for a theory of education, however, is not to defend any particular theory. Why a *democratic* theory of education? It will take an entire book to defend a democratic theory in detail. But by extending the example of sex education, I can briefly explain the rationale for developing a democratic theory.

For many years, the teachers in Fairfax County, Virginia, were not permitted to discuss contraception, abortion, masturbation, homosexuality, or rape (the "Big Five," as they were called) in their classrooms. Students were required to submit any questions about these topics in writing. The policy provoked "five years of turbulent debate" in Fairfax County. In 1981, the Fairfax County School Board changed the policy by an 8-to-2 vote, authorizing the introduction of a new elective biology course that discusses the previously prohibited issues, along with other topics related to "family life." The school board's decision gave parents "the right to choose whether their children will take either the new sex education course or one or two other courses designed as alternatives" (which do not discuss the "Big Five"). The controversy over sex education in Fairfax County has not ended, but a school survey found that 75 percent of parents and an even-greater majority of students favored the new elective course.[10]

Existing theories of education suggest different reactions to this example that either neglect the problem of authority that it poses or denigrate the democratic authority that it exemplifies. Conventional philosophical approaches typically neglect the problem of authority. Utilitarianism, which assumes that the purpose of education is to make the mind "as far as possible, an operative cause of happiness," provides an indeterminate standard for deciding whether sex education is conducive to the pursuit of happiness.[11] Rights theories can more straightforwardly support sex education as a means of preparing children for choice among competing conceptions of the good life, although they have difficulty accounting for the greater value we typically accord to quality rather than quantity of choice.[12] Conceptual approaches, which derive standards (such as rationality, openness to criticism, and so on) from the very meaning of the term "education," can defend sex education courses insofar as they are, properly speaking, educational, and criticize opponents of such courses as opposed not just to sex education but to education per se.[13] These philosophical approaches can aid us in articulating a moral ideal or a conceptual understanding of education,[14] but they give us no guidance in answering the question of who should make educational policy.

Conventional political approaches often give us the wrong guidance. Conservative theories of education object, in principle, to courses on sex education on grounds that the state should stay out of those aspects of moral education that directly affect the private realm of the family.[15] Because parents are the appropriate educational authorities in that realm, they should decide how their children are sexually educated. What if a majority of parents want public schools to teach their children about sex, as apparently was the case in Fairfax County, at least in 1981? The conservative position on parental authority must then support a more expansive role for democratic authority, even over sex education, than is commonly acknowledged, provided the majority does not force students to take courses against their parents' wishes (as the Fairfax County School Board did not). Conservative theories of education therefore cannot consistently support the view that a *democratic* state must stay out of moral education, even as it directly affects the family. This apparent inconsistency in conservative theories of education points toward the need for a more subtle specification of the realm of legitimate democratic authority.[16]

Liberal theories of education, which aim at developing individual autonomy, would criticize just that part of the new policy of the Fairfax County School Board that conservatives could applaud.[17] Under the new policy, parents are permitted to restrict what their children learn about sex in school. By liberal standards, the School Board should have voted to give *all* teenagers, not just those who received parental permission, the opportunity "to begin to assume responsibility for the course of their own lives, and to understand that responsibility goes far further than the pleasures of the moment."[18] If all future citizens must be taught to assume responsibility for their lives, sex education courses should not be limited to only those students whose parents approve of it or to only those schools whose boards are educationally enlightened.

The federal government should mandate the permissive policy for all students in all schools, public and private. When liberals authorize the federal government to make educational policy for local communities if, but only if, its views are right, they do not take democracy seriously, at either the local or the federal level.

Liberal political theories might become more philosophical, and simply avoid the question of authority, arguing only for the best educational policy "in principle" or the policy most recommended "by reason." Liberal theories may thereby guide individuals in formulating their own educational ideals, but they cannot give adequate guidance to communities in deciding what educational policies to pursue. The more philosophical liberal theories become, the less they face up to the facts of life in our society: that reasonable people disagree over what forms of freedom are worth cultivating and, therefore, over what constitutes the best education, in principle as well as in practice.[19]

Functionalist theories of education pride themselves on facing up to the facts of social reproduction. One of the most prominent functionalist theories suggests that schooling in a capitalist society serves to reproduce the social inequalities necessary to maintain the capitalist mode of production.[20] Viewed in this theoretical light, the Fairfax County School Board's new policy (that made sex education an elective course, based on parental preference) is one among several educational means to reproduce existing class divisions, in this case, between middle-class women, who must defer child-bearing to compete in the professional work force, and working-class women, who must bear children early to maintain the reserve army of the unemployed. Functionalist theories do not claim that educational authorities intended these outcomes, nor do they specify the mechanism by which the unintended outcomes are produced.[21] The primary evidence supporting the claims of functionalism is the stability of the system (in this case, capitalism) that educational policy (intentionally or unintentionally) supports.

. . . In contrast to these theories, a democratic theory faces up to the fact of difference in our moral ideals of education by looking toward democratic deliberations not only as a means to reconciling those differences, but also as an important part of democratic education. The most distinctive feature of a democratic theory of education is that it makes a democratic virtue out of our inevitable disagreement over educational problems. The democratic virtue, too simply stated, is that we can publicly debate educational problems in a way much more likely to increase our understanding of education and each other than if we were to leave the management of schools, as Kant suggests, "to depend entirely upon the judgment of the most enlightened experts."[22]

The policies that result from our democratic deliberations will not always be the right ones, but they will be more enlightened—by the values and concerns of the many communities that constitute a democracy—than those that would be made by unaccountable educational experts.

The primary aim of a democratic theory of education is not to offer solutions to all the problems plaguing our educational institutions, but to consider ways of resolving those problems that are compatible with a commitment to democratic values. A democratic theory of education provides principles that, in the face of our social disagreements, help us judge (a) who should have authority to make decisions about education, and (b) what the moral boundaries of that authority are.

. . . A democratic theory of education recognizes the importance of empowering citizens to make educational policy and also of constraining their choices among policies in accordance with those principles—of nonrepression and nondiscrimination—that preserve the intellectual and social foundations of democratic deliberations. A society that empowers citizens to make educational policy, moderated by these two principled constraints, realizes the democratic ideal of education.

Why Focus on Education?

The ideal helps define the scope of a democratic theory of education. A democratic theory of education focuses on what might be called "conscious social reproduction"—the ways in which citizens are or should be empowered to influence the education that, in turn, shapes the political values, attitudes, and modes of behavior of future citizens. Since the democratic ideal of education is that of *conscious* social reproduction, a democratic theory focuses on practices of deliberate instruction by individuals and on the educative influences of institutions designed at least partly for educational purposes.

Education may be more broadly defined to include every social influence that makes us who we are. The inclusiveness of the broad definition is intellectually satisfying. Almost every major political philosopher, who wrote about education, began with the broad definition, but few, if any, employed it in their subsequent analysis.[23] When one begins with the broad definition, it is much easier to extol the significance of education than it is to say anything systematic about it.[24]

Most political scientists who write about education subsume it under the concept of political socialization. Political socialization is typically understood to include the processes by which democratic societies transmit political values, attitudes, and modes of behavior to citizens.[25] Since many of these processes are unintended, political socialization studies tend to focus on what might be called "unconscious social reproduction." The focus of political socialization studies makes sense as long as their aim is to explain the processes by which societies perpetuate themselves. If one's aim is instead to understand how members of a democratic society should participate in consciously shaping its future, then it is important not to assimilate education with political socialization.[26] When education is so assimilated, it is easy to lose sight of the distinctive virtue of a democratic society—that it authorizes citizens to influence how their society reproduces itself.

On the other hand, when education is distinguished from political socialization, it is hard to resist the temptation to focus entirely on schooling, since it is our most deliberate form of human instruction. I try to resist this temptation without succumbing to the opposite, even more troubling one, of regarding schools as an insignificant part of what American education is or should be. Among the many myths about American education in recent years has been the view that schooling does not matter very much—except perhaps for the pleasure it gives children while they experience it—because it makes little or no difference to how income, work, or even intelligence gets distributed in our society. Like most myths, this one has no apparent author but a lot of social influence.[27] Unlike some myths, the myth of the moral insignificance of schooling distorts, rather than illuminates, our social condition. Its prophecy—of inevitable disillusionment with even our best efforts to educate citizens through schooling—is self-fulfilling because it pays exclusive attention to the question of whether schools *equalize*, and neglects the question of whether they *improve* the political and personal lives of citizens.

We can appreciate the centrality of schooling to democratic education and still recognize that there is much more to democratic education than schooling. Institutions other than schools—libraries, for example—can contribute to democratic education, and other institutions—television, for example— can detract from it. This much may be obvious, although the implications of the obvious are often avoided for the sake of making discussions of education more manageable. By focusing our inquiry, beyond schooling, on the central political question of how authority over educational institutions should be allocated in a democratic society, we can avoid perpetuating the false impression that democratic education ends with schooling.

Political Education

. . . Although we cannot conclude that democratic politics has causal primacy over democratic education, we can conclude that "political education"—the cultivation of the virtues, knowledge, and skills necessary for political participation—has moral primacy over other purposes of public education in a democratic society. Political education prepares citizens to participate in consciously reproducing their society, and conscious social reproduction is the ideal not only of democratic education but also of democratic politics, as I shall argue in a moment.

At the level of primary schooling, the primacy of political education supplies a principled argument against tracking, sexist education, racial segregation, and (narrowly) vocational education. Even when these practices improve the academic achievement of students, they neglect the virtues of citizenship, which can be cultivated by a common education characterized by respect for racial, religious, intellectual, and sexual differences among students. The moral primacy of political education also supports a presumption in favor of more participatory, over more disciplinary methods of teaching. Participatory methods are often the best means of achieving the disciplinary purposes of primary schooling. But even when student participation threatens to produce some degree of disorder within schools, it may be defended on democratic grounds for cultivating political skills and social commitments.

The primacy of political education reorients our expectations of primary schooling away from the distributive goals set by standard interpretations of equal opportunity (such as educating every child for choice among the widest range of good lives) and toward the goal of giving every child an education adequate to participate in the political processes by which choices among good lives are socially structured. The most devastating criticism we can level at primary schools, therefore, is not that they fail to give equally talented children an equal chance to earn the same income or to pursue professional occupations, but that they fail to give all (educable) children an education adequate to take advantage of their political status as citizens.

At the level of higher education, the primacy of political education points away from a singular conception of the university—as an ivory tower, a multiversity, or a community of learning—toward a more pluralistic conception, which accommodates the associational freedoms of a wide variety of universities, all of which uphold academic freedom. Universities serve democracy both as sanctuaries of nonrepression and as associational communities. They also serve as gatekeepers of valuable social offices and, as such, they should give priority to the democratic principle of nondiscrimination over efficiency in their admissions procedures.

When we turn our attention away from schools, the idea of the primacy of political education integrates the educational purposes of cultural, economic, and political institutions into a coherent democratic vision. The primary educational purpose of the mass media, industry, and government, like that of schools, is to cultivate the knowledge, skills, and virtues necessary for democratic deliberation among citizens. What distinguishes primary schools, universities, and programs of adult education from the mass media, industry, and other political institutions is that the educational purpose of the former is also their primary social purpose. By contrast, the educational purposes of the mass media, industry, and political institutions are by-products of their other social purposes, the precise content of which are properly subject to democratic determination.

The view that political education is primary—its purpose being to foster the capacities for democratic deliberation essential to conscious social reproduction—does not commit us to considering every outcome of democratic deliberations as correct. Nor does it commit us to accepting democratic authority over every form of education. Rather, it commits us to accepting nondiscriminatory and nonrepressive policies as legitimate even when they are wrong, and to viewing children as neither the mere creatures of their parents nor the mere creatures of a centralized state. Democratic education is best viewed as a shared trust, of parents, citizens, teachers, and public officials, the precise terms of which are to be democratically decided within the bounds of the principles of nondiscrimination and nonrepression.

Democratic Education and Democratic Theory

How does the ideal of democratic education fit into a democratic theory? If my understanding is correct, our concern for democratic education lies at the core of our commitment to democracy. The ideal of democracy is often said to be collective self-determination. But is there a "collective self" to be determined? Are there not just so many individual selves that must find a fair way of sharing the goods of a society together? It would be dangerous (as critics often charge) to assume that the democratic state constitutes the "collective self" of a society, and that its policies, in turn, define the best interests of its individual members.

We need no such metaphysical assumption, however, to defend an ideal closely related to that of collective self-determination—an ideal of citizens sharing in deliberatively determining the future shape of their society. If democratic society is the "self" that citizens determine, it is a self that does not define their best interests. There remain independent standards for defining the best interests of individuals and reasons for thinking that individuals, rather than collectivities, are often the best judges of their own interests. To avoid the misleading metaphysical connotations of the concept of collective self-determination, we might better understand the democratic ideal as that of conscious social reproduction, the same ideal that guides democratic education.

The convergence of democratic ideals is not coincidental. Democratic education supplies the foundations upon which a democratic society can secure the civil and political freedoms of its adult citizens without placing their welfare or its very survival at great risk. In the absence of democratic education, risks—perhaps even great risks—will still be worth taking for the sake of respecting the actual preferences of citizens, but the case for civic and political freedom and against paternalism is weaker in a society whose citizens have been deprived of an adequate education (although not as weak as Mill suggested). Democracy thus depends on democratic education for its full moral strength.

The dependency, however, is reciprocal. Were we not already committed to democratic principles, our ideal of education might take a very different form, similar perhaps to that practiced for thirteen centuries in Imperial China, where a centralized state supported schools and designed a highly intricate and seemingly thorough system of examinations that determined access to all state offices. When working at its best, the Chinese educational system allowed for considerable social mobility. Children of rich, well-educated families who could not pass the rigorous examinations lost the high social status of their parents. Lowly peasant children climbed up the academic "ladder of success" to become rich and highly esteemed.[28] The Chinese educational system thus supported a widespread belief in what one scholar describes as an "academic Horatio Alger myth."[29] Such an educational system would rightly be subject to devastating criticism in our society, but not primarily because the academic Horatio Alger myth would distort social reality as much as did the original, economic version of the Horatio Alger story. The more devastating criticism due such a system would be that a centralized, nondemocratic state usurps control of what rightly belongs to citizens: decisions concerning how the character and consciousness of future citizens take shape outside the home. Democratic sovereignty over education thereby follows at the same time as it reinforces our fundamental political commitments.

Families do not belong to citizens, yet they profoundly affect democratic education, often in adverse ways—when parents predispose their children to violence, religious intolerance, racial bigotry, sexism, and other undemocratic values. Because we so highly value the intimacy of family life and because regulation of parental behavior (within broad bounds) would interfere with that intimacy in repressive ways, the ideal of democratic education does not permit political regulation of the internal life of families. The authority of parents, therefore, constrains democratic sovereignty over education, although not as absolutely as advocates of the state of families argue.

Respect for the intimacy of the family is consistent with democratic authorization of policies that facilitate changes in the structure of families. Subsidized day care and flexible time for working parents are examples of such policies. By encouraging more egalitarian gender relations, these policies are likely to lead to more democratic education within the family. To the extent that unequal gender roles predispose women to political passivity or deference to men, the ideal of democratic education recommends policies that encourage gender equality, even though it does not permit direct political interference to create more egalitarian families. The ideal of democratic education thus may be morally demanding even when it cannot be politically authoritative. Far from treating the family as a haven in a heartless world, the ideal of democratic education subjects the family to moral scrutiny—but not to political repression. Although political education has primacy among the purposes of public education, public education is bounded by the (private) educational authority of parents.

"The prospect of a theory of education," Kant argued, "is a glorious ideal, and it matters little if we are not able to realize it at once." Kant went on to warn that "we must not look upon the idea as chimerical, nor decry it as a beautiful dream, notwithstanding the difficulties that stand in the way of its realization."[30] Political philosophers are likely to be more receptive to Kant's warning than are policymakers, but we might issue ourselves a parallel warning: that we must not look upon education as a realm ideally to be separated from the tumult of democratic politics. By heeding such a warning, we may develop a less glorious but better grounded theory of both democratic education and democracy.

Amy Gutmann is Mellon Professor of Politics and director of the program in Political Philosophy at Princeton University. She is the author of Liberal Equality *and the editor of* Democracy and the Welfare State.

Originally published in Amy Gutmann, Democratic Education *(Princeton: Princeton University Press, 1987: 3–10, 11, 14–16, 287–291), ©1987 by Princeton University Press. Reprinted by permission of the publisher.*

Notes

1. Aristotle, *The Politics of Aristotle*, trans. Ernest Barker (London: Oxford University Press, 1971), p. 105 (1277b).

2. Immanuel Kant, *Kant on Education (Ueber Padagogik)*, trans. Annette Churton (Boston: D. C. Heath and Co., 1900), p. 12.

3. *Ibid.*, p. 13.

4. National Commission on Excellence in Education, *A Nation At Risk: The Imperative for Educational Reform* (Washington, D.C.: U.S. Government Printing Office, April 1983), p. 7.

5. *Ibid.*

6. Reported in Joel H. Spring, *American*

Education: An Introduction to Social and Political Aspects (New York: Longman, 1985), p. 133.

7. *A Nation at Risk*, p. 2.

8. For a discussion of the dimensions of the problem, see Hyman Rodman, Susan Lewis, and Saralyn Griffith, *The Sexual Rights of Adolescents* (New York: Columbia University Press, 1984).

9. See, for example, "Sex Education in Public Schools?—Interview with Jacqueline Kasun": "Q: Why shouldn't schools teach about sexual choices? A: Because such choices pertain to values, and schools should leave the teaching of values to the

family and the church." *U.S. News and World Report,* vol. 89, no. 14 (October 1980): 89.

10. *Washington Post,* May 15, 1981, pp. A1, A28.

11. W. H. Burston, ed., *James Mill on Education* (Cambridge: Cambridge University Press, 1969), p. 41. For a contemporary utilitarian approach to education, see R. M. Hare, "Opportunity for What? Some Remarks on Current Disputes about Equality in Education," *Oxford Review of Education,* vol. 3, no. 3 (1977): 207–216.

12. For a more thorough critique of utilitarian and rights theories of education, see Amy Gutmann, "What's the Use of Going to School? The Problem of Education in Utilitarian and Rights Theories," in Amartya Sen and Bernard Williams, eds., *Utilitarianism and Beyond* (Cambridge: Cambridge University Press, 1982), pp. 261–77.

13. The purest conceptual approach is John Wilson, *Preface to the Philosophy of Education* (London: Routledge and Kegan Paul, 1979). See also P. H. Hirst and R. S. Peters, *The Logic of Education* (London: Routledge and Kegan Paul, 1970); R. S. Peters, *Ethics and Education* (London: Allen and Unwin, 1966); R. S. Peters, ed., *The Concept of Education* (London: Routledge and Kegan Paul, 1967); P. H. Hirst, "Liberal Education and the Nature of Knowledge," in *Education and the Development of Reason,* ed. R. F. Dearden, P. H. Hirst, and R. S. Peters (London: Routledge and Kegan Paul, 1972), pp. 391–414.

14. There is, for example, a large but perhaps not very fruitful debate between conceptual and normative analysis. One need not claim that a conceptual analysis of education is wrong to recognize that it is not enough to invoke the concept to criticize (so-called) educational practices that are repressive. One must argue the case for why such practices should not be repressive, and why repressive practices should not be authorized, even by (otherwise) legitimate political authorities.

15. Some conservatives focus on the specific objections of the parents who oppose the courses. Parents who oppose sex education often argue that it encourage[s] pregnancies by implying that sexual activity is acceptable. *(Washington Post,* May 15, 1981, p. A28.)* There is no empirical evidence to support this claim and some evidence to doubt it. I, therefore, concentrate on the more plausible and principled version of conservative theory.

16. See Chapter Four on "Sex Education and Sexist Education."

17. For such a theory, see Bruce Ackerman, *Social Justice in the Liberal State* (New York and London: Yale University Press, 1980), esp. pp. 139–67.

18. *Washington Post,* May 15, 1981, p. A28.

19. Liberal theories can also become more democratic and defend those educational policies for a community that are necessary for democratic deliberation. Such a liberal theory, fully developed, would converge with the democratic theory that I shall defend. For a suggestion of such a theory, see Israel Scheffler, "Moral Education and the Democratic Ideal," in *Reason and Teaching* (London: Routledge and Kegan Paul, 1973), p. 142.

20. See Samuel Bowles and Herbert Gintis, *Schooling in Capitalist America: Educational Reform and the Contradictions of Economic Life* (New York: Basic Books, 1976); e.g., p. 48: "The educational system serves—through the correspondence of its social relations with those of economic life—to reproduce economic inequality and to distort personal development. . . . It is precisely because of its role as producer of an alienated and stratified labor force that the educational system has developed its repressive and unequal structure. In the history of U.S. education, it is the integrative function which has dominated the purpose of schooling, to the detriment of the other liberal objectives." See also Joel H. Spring, *Education and the Rise of the Corporate State* (Boston: Beacon Press, 1972), esp. p. 151: "Schools tend to reinforce and strengthen existing social structures and social stratification." Other functionalist analyses of schools include Colin Greer, *The Great School Legend* (New York: Basic

Books, 1972); Clarence Karier, Paul Violas, and Joel H. Spring, *Roots of Crisis: American Education in the Twentieth Century,* (Chicago: Rand McNally, 1973); and Michael B. Katz, *Class, Bureaucracy, and Schools: The Illusion of Educational Change in America* (New York: Praeger, 1971).

21. For a general critique of functionalism, see Jon Elster, "Marxism, Functionalism, and Game Theory," *Theory and Society,* vol. 11 (1982): 453–82; and Elster, *Sour Grapes: Studies in the Subversion of Rationality* (Cambridge: Cambridge University Press, 1983), pp. 101–108. For a more specific critique of functionalist analyses of schools, see David K. Cohen and Bella H. Rosenberg, "Functions and Fantasies: Understanding Schools in Capitalist America," *History of Education Quarterly* (Summer 1977): 113–37. For two recent sympathetic critiques of Bowles and Gintis, see Ira Katznelson and Margaret Weir, *Schooling for All: Class, Race, and the Decline of the Democratic Ideal* (New York: Basic Books, 1985), esp. pp. 17–23, 46–48; and Martin Carnoy and Henry M. Levin, *Schooling and Work in the Democratic State* (Stanford, CA: Stanford University Press, 1985), esp. pp. 18–22.

22. Kant, *Kant on Education,* p. 17.

23. For example, see Rousseau's understanding in *Emile,* cited at the beginning of Chapter One. A contemporary example is Israel Scheffler, "Moral Education and the Democratic Ideal," in *Reason and Teaching,* pp. 139–40.

24. But systematic analysis is not impossible. Historians of American education have made significant contributions to our understanding of the educative role of institutions other than schools, especially after Bernard Bailyn's critique of "an excess of writing along certain lines and an almost undue clarity of direction" in historical writing about schooling. See Bernard Bailyn, *Education in the Forming of American Society* (New York: Vintage, 1960), p. 4. Education, according to Bailyn, is "the entire process by which a culture transmits itself across the generations. . . ." (p. 14). Compare Lawrence Cremin (who has probably written more extensively and systematically about American education than any other contemporary historian): education is "the *deliberate,* systematic, and sustained effort to transmit, evoke, or acquire knowledge, attitudes, values, skill, or sensibilities, as well as any outcomes of that effort." (Emphasis added.) Lawrence A. Cremin, *Traditions of American Education* (New York: Basic Books, 1977), p. 134.

25. Because its subject is so vast, the literature on political socialization defies simple summary. For a broad definition and overview of the field, see Fred I. Greenstein, "Socialization: Political Socialization," *International Encyclopedia of the Social Sciences* (New York: Macmillan, 1968), 14: 551–55. See also Richard E. Dawson and Kenneth Prewitt, *Political Socialization* (Boston: Little, Brown and Co., 1969); Kenneth P. Langton, *Political Socialization* (New York: Oxford University Press, 1969); and Roberta S. Sigel, *Learning About Politics: A Reader in Political Socialization* (New York: Random House, 1970).

26. For another reason not to assimilate education and socialization, see David Nyberg and Kieran Egan, *The Erosion of Education: Socialization and the Schools* (New York: Teachers College Press, 1981), pp. 2–5.

27. The two works most often identified with this view are Christopher Jencks et al., *Inequality: A Reassessment of the Effect of Family and Schooling in America* (New York: Basic Books, 1972); and James S. Coleman et al., *Report on Equality of Educational Opportunity* (Washington, D.C.: U.S. Government Printing Office, 1966). See esp. Jencks, pp. 29, 256.

28. See Ping-Ti Ho, *The Ladder of Success in Imperial China: Aspects of Social Mobility, 1368–1911* (New York: Columbia University Press,1962), esp. pp. 257–62.

29. *Ibid.,* p. 262.

30. Kant, *Kant on Education,* p. 8.

> "At some point the attenuation of civic spirit and competence will create pathologies with which liberal institutions, however perfect their technical design, simply cannot cope. The viability of liberal society depends on its ability to conduct civic education."

Civic Education and the Liberal State

by William Galston

There is a tradition of Mandevillean argument that liberal politics do not need—indeed, are distinctive in not needing—civic education directed to the formation of liberal citizens because social processes and political institutions can be arranged so as to render desired collective outcomes independent of individual character and belief. Albert Hirschman has traced the emergence in seventeenth- and eighteenth-century social thought of the thesis that republican government could best be secured not through civic virtue but through the liberation of the commercial-acquisitive "interests" of the middle class in opposition to the politically destructive "passions" of the aristocracy.[1] The most famous of the *Federalist Papers* (*10* and *51*) contain memorable formulations of the need to counteract interest with interest and passion with passion. Immanuel Kant, who was at once the most profound moral philosopher and the most devoted liberal theorist of his age, argued vigorously for the disjunction between individual virtue and republican government. A liberal government that fully protects individual rights "is only a question of a good organization of the state, whereby the powers of each selfish inclination are so arranged in opposition that one moderates or destroys the ruinous effect of the other. The consequence . . . is the same as if none of them existed, and man is forced to be a good citizen even if not a morally good person."[2]

The proposition that liberal societies are uniquely able to do without the fruits of civic education has been sharply challenged, however. Recent interpretations of the liberal theoretical tradition have emphasized the copresence of institutional and character-based arguments, as have rereadings of the *Federalist.*[3] Recent explorations of public policy problems—crime, drugs, dependency—have focused on the formation of character and belief as well as on the manipulation of incentives.[4] Historical inquiries into American public education have documented the driving role played by the perceived need for a civic pedagogy that could turn immigrants into citizens.[5] Groups across the political spectrum have reemphasized their belief that a refurbished civic education is an urgent necessity: "Democracy's survival depends upon our transmitting to each new generation the political vision of liberty and equality that unites us as Americans. . . . Such values are neither revealed truths nor natural habits. There is no evidence that we are born with them. Devotion to human dignity and freedom, to equal rights, to social and economic justice, to the rule of law, to civility and truth, to tolerance of diversity, to mutual assistance, to personal and civic responsibility, to self-restraint and self-respect—all these must be taught and learned."[6]

Common experience buttresses what history and argument suggest: that the operation of liberal institutions and the functioning of liberal society are affected in important ways by the character and belief of individuals (and leaders) within the liberal polity. At some point the attenuation of civic spirit and competence will create pathologies with which liberal institutions, however perfect their technical design, simply cannot cope. To an extent difficult to measure but impossible to ignore, the viability of liberal society depends on its ability effectively to conduct civic education.

The Possibility of Liberal Democratic Civic Education

Liberal democratic civic education may be necessary, but is it possible? In the same way that the religious diversity of liberal society makes it impossible to reach a religious consensus suitable for public endorsement, so too, the moral and political diversity of the liberal polity might seem to undermine the possibility of a unitary civic pedagogy acceptable to, and binding on, all groups. Indeed, the movement from the religious neutrality of the liberal state to a wider moral and political neutrality is one of the defining characteristics of liberal theory in our time, a development with roots in the opinions of urban-based social elites.

This generalization of liberal neutrality is neither necessary nor wise. To the extent that we accept a shared citizenship, we have something important in common—a set of political institutions and principles that underlies them. What we share, beyond all our differences, provides the basis for a civic education valid across the boundaries of our differences.

Some of the virtues needed to sustain the liberal state are requisites of every political community: the willingness to fight on behalf of one's country; the settled disposition to obey the law; and loyalty—the developed capacity to understand, to accept, and to act on the core principles of one's society. Some of the individual traits are specific to liberal society—independence, tolerance, and respect for individual excellences and accomplishments, for example. Still others are entailed by the key features of liberal democratic politics. For citizens, the disposition to respect the rights of others, the capacity to evaluate the talents, character, and performance of public officials, and the ability to moderate public desires in the face of public limits are essential. For leaders, the patience to work within social diversity and the ability to narrow the gap between wise policy and popular consent are fundamental. And the developed capacity to engage in public discourse and to test public policies against our deeper convictions is highly desirable for all members of the liberal community, whatever political station they may occupy.[7]

A leading contemporary theorist of civic education, Amy Gutmann, has reached conclusions parallel to, but divergent from, the theses just sketched. Her point of departure is democracy, and her argument is that our civic pedagogy should be oriented toward democratic virtue: "the ability to deliberate, and hence to participate in conscious social reproduction,"[8] In my view, this is a piece—but only a piece—of the civic education appropriate to our situation, and it becomes a distortion when it is mistaken for the whole.

Let me begin with a methodological point. The adequacy of a conception of civic education cannot be determined in the abstract, but only through its congruence with the basic features of the society it is intended to sustain. To depart significantly from those features is to recommend a conception of civic education suitable for some society other than the one at hand. Differently put, it is to endorse a politics of transformation based on a general conception of the political good external to the concrete polity in question. I do not wish to deny the possibility or appropriateness of such theoretical practices. But I do not want to distinguish between them and the task of fitting pedagogical practices to existing communities.

It is, at best, a partial truth to characterize the United States as a democracy in Gutmann's sense. To begin with the obvious: in a liberal democracy the concern for individual rights and for what is sometimes called the private sphere entails limits on the legitimate power of majorities, and it suggests that cultivating the disposition to respect rights and privacies is one of the essential goals of liberal democratic civic education. In Gutmann's account, the power of the majority is limited by the requirement of "nonrepression" and "nondiscrimination," but these limits are themselves derived from the conception of a democratic society all of whose members are equipped and authorized to share in ruling.[9] These considerations are not robust enough to generate anything like a liberal account of protections for individuals and groups against the possibility of majority usurpation.

A second liberal reservation against Gutmann's democracy is the distinction between momentary public whim and the settled will—that is, the considered judgment—of the community. This distinction is what underlies the liberal effort to construct a framework of relatively stable institutions partially insulated from shifting majorities. It is, in short, one of the motives for constitutions as distinct from acts of legislation as well as for processes that complicate the task of forging legislative majorities, at least for certain purposes. A form of pedagogy more fully appropriate than Gutmann's to a liberal democratic constitutional order would incorporate an understanding of these limitations on "conscious social reproduction."

Third, in liberal democracies representative institutions replace direct self-government for many purposes. A civic education congruent with such institutions will emphasize, as I have suggested, the virtues and competences needed to select representatives wisely, to relate to them appropriately, and to evaluate their performance in office soberly. These characteristics are related to, but in some respects quite distinct from, the traits needed for direct participation in political affairs. Perhaps it would be fairer to say that the balance between participation and representation is not a settled question, in either theory or practice. A civic pedagogy for us may rightly incorporate participatory virtues. It may even accommodate a politics more hospitable to participation than are our current practices. But it is not free to give participatory virtues pride of place or to remain silent about the virtues that correspond to representative institutions.

Finally, in liberal democracies certain kinds of excellences are acknowledged, at least for certain purposes, to constitute legitimate claims to public authority. That is, in filling offices and settling policy, equalities of will and interest are counterbalanced by inequalities of training and accomplishment. Examples include the technical expertise of the public health official, the interpretive skill of the judge, and even the governance capabilities of political leaders. As paradoxical as it may appear, a tradition of political theory extending back to Aristotle has understood the selection of public officials through popular elections as significantly aristocratic in its effect. In American thought, some of our greatest democrats have embraced this view. Thomas Jefferson once wrote John Adams: "there is a natural aristocracy among men. The grounds of this are virtue and talents. . . . May we not even say, that that form of government is best, which provides the most effectively for a pure selection of these natural *aristoi* into the offices of government? . . . I think the best [way of doing this] is exactly that provided by all our constitutions, to leave to the citizens the free election and separation of the *aristoi* from the *pseudo-aristoi.*"[10]

To put this point more broadly: the problem that liberal democracy sets itself is to achieve the greatest possible conjunction between good judgment and virtue, on the one hand, and participation and consent on the other. Democratic processes, suitably refined, may hold out the best prospects for accomplishing this goal. But they are not ends in themselves; they are to be judged by their fruits. Liberal democratic civic education must therefore aim to engender, not only the full range of public excellences, but also the widest possible acceptance of the need for such excellences in the conduct of our public life. Populist rancor against the claims of liberal democratic excellence is understandable, and even at times a useful counterweight to arrogance and usurpation. But it cannot be allowed to obliterate the legitimacy of such claims.

Civic Education versus Liberal Privacy

Civic education poses a special difficulty for liberal democracy. Most forms of government, classical and contemporary, have tacitly embraced the Aristotelian understanding of politics as the architectonic human association to which all others—family, tribe, economic groupings, even religion—are rightly subordinated. For all such political communities the government's authority to conduct civic education is unquestioned, because conflicts between political and subpolitical commitments are resolved by the belief that the political enjoys a principled primacy. In liberal societies, by contrast, the resolution of such conflicts is far less clear-cut. Reservations against public authority in the name of individual autonomy, parental rights, and religious conscience are both frequent and respectable. The liberal tradition is animated by the effort to carve out spheres that are substantially impervious to government—an effort set in motion by the historical lesson that the attempt to impose religious uniformity through public fiat undermines civil order as well as individual conscience. Thus, even if liberal theories, or public authorities moved by such theories, succeed in specifying a core of habits and beliefs supportive of the liberal polity, individuals and groups may nonetheless object to civic education that tries to foster these habits and beliefs universally.

Yet while the liberal tradition is sensitive to the claims of individual conscience, early liberal theorists were equally mindful of the dangers and limits of those claims. John Locke, for example, refused to expand his doctrine of religious tolerance into an inviolable private sphere of conscience. On the contrary, he insisted that in cases of conflict, civil authority takes precedence over conscience or faith, however deeply held. The key criterion is the maintenance of civil order. Opinions that threaten the peace of society may be legitimately opposed or even suppressed: "No opinion contrary to human society, or to those moral Rules which are necessary to the preservation of Civil Society, are to be tolerated by the Magistrate." Nor did toleration preclude affirmative public discourse on behalf of those necessary rules. Locke distinguished between coercion and persuasion. The fact that the sovereign cannot legitimately command adherence to a specific belief does not mean that civil authority cannot offer systematic arguments for, or instruction in, that belief.[11] Thus, although Locke thought that in practice civic education would occur in families rather than through state mechanisms, his theory leads directly to the legitimation of the conduct of such education through public means, individual conscience to the contrary notwithstanding.

Two other lines of argument bolster this conclusion. In practice, the private sphere within which conscience is exercised can only be defined within civil society. In the classic American formulation, government is instituted "to secure these rights." It follows that individuals must be willing to surrender whatever portion of these rights must be sacrificed to the requirements of public order and institutional perpetuation. Individuals who seek to exercise, without compromise, the totality of their presocial rights will quickly find that conflict with other rights-bearers impedes the attainment of their ends and the security of their liberty. Even if we begin with a robust conception of individual rights defined theoretically rather than historically or politically, we are forced to conclude that public authority may legitimately restrict those rights in the name of maximizing their effective exercise. In particular, government may properly teach those beliefs and habits needed to bolster the institutions that secure liberal rights, and citizens of liberal politics who resist this civic education would be irrationally contradicting their own self-interest, rightly understood.

The second argument follows hard on the heels of the first. If citizenship means anything, it means a package of benefits and burdens shared, and accepted, by all. To be a citizen of a liberal polity is to be required to surrender so much of your own private conscience as is necessary for the secure enjoyment of what remains. To refuse this surrender is in effect to breach the agreement under which you are entitled to full membership in your community.

Now, it is perfectly possible to petition your community for special relief from the burdens accepted by your fellow citizens: "My conscience makes it impossible for me to fight in battle/pledge allegiance to the flag/whatever." Public authority may then make a prudential determination as to whether granting your request will or won't impose unacceptable costs on public aims and institutions. If you are part of a small minority, and if the grounds on which you seek exemption from shared burdens are so narrow and idiosyncratic as to suggest that others are unlikely to follow suit, then it may be possible to grant the exemption. But if the facts suggest that acceding to you will open the floodgate for many others, then it would be rational for public authorities to reject your plea. The issue, to repeat, is one of concrete practice rather than general principle.

A variant of this problem arises when individuals or groups are willing to take the next step, abjuring the benefits of citizenship in order to gain release from its burdens. This is, in effect, to request a kind of resident alien status within one's community: you remain subject to basic laws of civil order, but you are no longer expected to attain the character, beliefs, and competences needed for effective political membership. Your real desire is simply to withdraw, to be left alone. Here again, as before, the issue is practical. If there is reason to believe that granting this request will generate significant ripple effects, there is a rational basis for public authority to resist it. Alternatively, it might be argued that withdrawal is an untenable halfway house between citizenship and actual physical exit. As long as your group remains located within the domain of wider community, it necessarily interacts with, and affects, that community in many ways. While some free-rider problems could be addressed through taxation, other difficulties would prove far less-tractable. It is not clear that the political community could afford to remain indifferent to the example you might set for other potential withdrawers. (This is not intended as an argument against the right of physical exit, which rests on quite different foundations and raises different issues. The Soviets have improperly used arguments parallel to those in this paragraph to thwart the emigration of disaffected groups.)

Perhaps the most poignant problem raised by liberal civic education is the clash between the content of that education and the desire of parents to pass their way of life on to their children. Few parents, I suspect, are unaware of, or immune to, the force of this desire. What could be more natural? If you believe that you are fit to be a parent, you must also believe that at least some of the choices you have made are worthy of emulation by your children, and the freedom to pass on the fruits of those choices must be highly valued. Conversely, who can contemplate, without horror, totalitarian societies in which families are compelled to yield all moral authority to the state?

Still, your child is at once a future adult and a future citizen. Your authority as a parent is limited by both these facts. For example, you are not free to treat your child in a manner that impedes normal development. You may not legitimately starve or beat your child or thwart the acquisition of basic linguistic and social skills. The systematic violation of these and related norms suffices to warrant state intervention. Similarly, you are not free to impede the child's acquisition of a basic civic education—the beliefs and habits that support the polity and enable individuals to function competently in public affairs. In particular, you are not free to act in ways that will lead your child to impose significant and avoidable burdens on the community. For example, the liberal state has a right to teach all children respect for the law, and you have no opposing right as a parent to undermine that respect. Similarly, the liberal state has a right to inculcate the expectation that all normal children will become adults capable of caring for themselves and their families.

Thus far, the argument is reasonably strong and uncontroversial. But how much farther may the liberal state go? Amy Gutmann argues that children must be taught both "mutual respect among persons" and "rational deliberation among ways of life," and that parents are unlikely to do this on their own. It is precisely because communities such as the Old Order Amish are morally committed to shielding their children from influences that might weaken their faith that the state is compelled to step in: "The same principle that requires a state to grant adults personal and political freedom also commits it to assuring children an education that makes those freedoms both possible and meaningful in the future. A state makes choices possible by teaching its future citizens respect for opposing points of view and ways of life. It makes choice meaningful by equipping children with the intellectual skills necessary to evaluate ways of life different from that of their parents."[12]

I do not believe that this argument can be sustained. In a liberal democratic polity, to be sure, the fact of social diversity means that the willingness to coexist peacefully with ways of life very different from one's own is essential. Further, the need for public evaluation of leaders and policies means that the state has an interest in developing citizens with at least the minimal conditions of reasonable public judgment. But neither of these civic requirements entails a need for public authority to take an interest in how children think about different ways of life. Civic tolerance of deep differences is perfectly compatible with unswerving belief in the correctness of one's own way of life. It rests on the conviction that the pursuit of the better course should be (and in many cases can only be) the result of persuasion rather than coercion—a classic Lockean premise that the liberal state *does* have an interest in articulating. Civic deliberation is also compatible with unshakable personal commitments. It requires only that each citizen accept the minimal civic commitments, already outlined, without which the liberal polity cannot long endure. In short, the civic standpoint does not warrant the conclusion that the state must (or may) structure public education to foster in children skeptical reflection on ways of life inherited from parents or local communities.

It is hardly accidental that Gutmann takes the argument in this direction. At the heart of much modern, liberal democratic thought is a (sometimes tacit) commitment to the Socratic proposition that the unexamined life is an unworthy life, that individual freedom is incompatible with ways of life guided by unquestioned authority or unswerving faith. As philosophic conclusions, these commitments have much to recommend them. The question, though, is whether the liberal state is justified in building them into its system of public education. The answer is that it cannot do so without throwing its weight behind a conception of the human good unrelated to the functional needs of its sociopolitical institutions and, at odds with, the deep beliefs of many of its loyal citizens. As a political matter, liberal freedom entails the right to live unexamined, as well as, examined lives—a right whose effective exercise may require parental bulwarks against the corrosive influence of modernist skepticism. I might add that, in practice, there is today a widespread perception that our system of public education already embodies a bias against authority and faith. This perception, in large measure, is what underlies the controversy over "secular humanism" that is so incomprehensible to liberal elites.

It is not difficult to anticipate the objections that will be raised against the argument I have just advanced. There are, after all, three parties to the educational transaction: children, their parents, and the state. Perhaps the state has no direct right to shape public education in accordance with the norms of Socratic self-examination. But doesn't liberal freedom mean that children have the right to be exposed to a range of possible ways of life? If parents thwart this right by attempting, as we would say, to "brainwash" their children, doesn't the state have a right—indeed, a duty—to step in?

The answer is no on both counts. Children do have a wide range of rights that parents are bound to respect and that government is bound to enforce against parental violation. As I argued earlier, parents may not rightly impede the normal physical, intellectual, and emotional development of their children. Nor may they impede the acquisition of civic competence and loyalty. The state may act *in loco parentis* to overcome family-based obstacles to normal development. And it may use public instrumentalities, including the system of education, to promote the attainment by all children of the basic requisites of citizenship. These are legitimate, intrusive state powers. But they are limited by their own inner logic. In a liberal state, interventions that cannot be justified on this basis cannot be justified at all. That is how liberal democracies must draw the line between parental and public authority over the education of children, or, to put it less confrontationally, that is the principle on the basis of which such authority must be shared.[13]

But, doesn't this position evade the emotional force of the objection? Does it legitimize parental brainwashing of children, which is a terrible thing? Again, the answer is no, for two reasons. First, the simple fact that authority is divided means that, from an early age, every child will see that he or she is answerable to institutions other than the family—institutions whose substantive requirements may well cut across the grain of parental wishes and beliefs. Some measure of reflection—or at least critical distance—is the likely result. Second, the basic features of liberal society make it virtually impossible for parents to seal their children off from knowledge of other ways of life. And, as every parent knows, possibilities that are known, but forbidden, take on an allure out of all proportion to their intrinsic merits.

To these points I would add a basic fact of liberal sociology: the greatest threat to children in modern liberal societies is not that they will believe in something too deeply, but that they will believe in nothing very deeply at all. Even to achieve the kind of free self-reflection that many liberals prize, it is better to begin by believing something. Rational deliberation among ways of life is far more meaningful (I am tempted to say that it can *only* be meaningful) if the stakes are meaningful—that is, if the deliberator has strong convictions against which competing claims can be weighed. The role of parents in fostering such convictions should be welcomed, not feared.

Despite the pluralism of liberal societies, it is perfectly possible to identify a core of civic commitments and competences whose broad acceptance undergirds a well-ordered liberal polity. The state has a right to ensure that this core is generally and effectively disseminated, either directly, through public civic education, or indirectly, through the regulation of private education. In cases of conflict this civic core takes priority over individual or group commitments (even the demands of conscience), and the state may legitimately use coercive mechanisms to enforce it.

But the liberal state must not venture beyond this point. It must not throw its weight behind ideals of personal excellence outside the shared understanding of civic excellence, and it must not give pride of place to understandings of personal freedom outside the shared understanding of civic freedom. For if it does so, the liberal state prescribes, as valid for and binding on all, a single debatable conception of how human beings should lead their lives. In the name of liberalism, it becomes totalitarian. It betrays its own deepest—and most defensible—principles.

William A. Galston is a professor in the School of Public Affairs at The University of Maryland at College Park.

Originally published in Liberalism and the Moral Life, *Nancy L. Rosenblum (ed.) (Cambridge, MA: Harvard University Press),* ©1989 *by the President and Fellows of Harvard University. Reprinted with permission of the publisher.*

Notes

1. Albert Hirschman, *The Passions and the Interests* (Princeton: Princeton University Press, 1977).

2. Immanuel Kant, "Perpetual Peace," in Lewis White Beck, ed., *Kant on History* (Indianapolis: Bobbs-Merrill, 1963), pp. 111–112.

3. See especially Rogers Smith, *Liberalism and American Constitutional Law* (Cambridge, MA: Harvard University Press,

1985); Nathan Tarcov, *Locke's Education for Liberty* (Chicago: University of Chicago Press, 1984); Harvey Mansfield, Jr., "Constitutional Government: The Soul of Modern Democracy, *The Public Interest* 86 (Winter 1987): 53–64.

4. James Q. Wilson, "The Rediscovery of Character: Private Virtue and Public Policy," *The Public Interest* 81 (Fall 1985): 3–16.

5. Charles Glenn, Jr. *The Myth of the Common School* (Amherst: University of Massachusetts Press, 1988).

6. "Education for Democracy: A Statement of Principles," (Washington, D.C.: American Federation of Teachers, 1987), p.8.

7. This paragraph summarizes the central argument of my "Liberal Virtues," *American Political Science Review* 82 (December 1988): 1277–1290.

8. Amy Gutmann, *Democratic Education* (Princeton, NJ: Princeton University Press, 1987), p. 39.

9. Ibid., pp. 44–46.

10. Alphaeus Mason, ed., *Free Government in the Making,* 3rd ed. (New York: Oxford University Press, 1965), p. 385.

11. See William Galston, "Public Morality and Religion in the Liberal State," *PS* 19 (Fall 1986): 807–824.

12. Gutmann, *Democratic Education,* pp. 30–31.

13. For a very different way of drawing this line, see Bruce Ackerman, *Social Justice in the Liberal State* (New Haven: Yale University Press, 1980), chap. 5.

"Those who read the American spirit as so dominantly individualistic that private comfort and competitive achievement define a monochrome of national traits are both dangerously distorting our past and threatening our future, because they are closing off a sense of that living civic tradition which has been and continues to be vital for our national life."

A Renewal of Civic Philosophy

by William Sullivan

Contemporary American problems reveal the orthodox liberal conception of society and politics as considerably less than the self-sustaining whole it proclaims itself to be. Liberalism has boasted that it could uphold human dignity and respect for the individual while simultaneously encouraging each individual to adopt a self-seeking, instrumental stance toward others. It freed individuals from having to guide and restrain their behavior in common with others, replacing both traditional morality and discussion in common with hopes for self-regulating social machinery. Liberal thinkers rightfully decry the encroachment on individual life of the administrative state, and, though less often, the bureaucratic corporation and mass media. But they see no relationship between willful abnegation of an ethics of mutual concern, announced as freedom, and weakening of social solidarity outside those encroaching structures. Yet, as some thinkers sympathetic to the liberal vision have come to see, if personal dignity and self-determination are to survive the constraints and potentiality for social control found in modern society, it can only be through the political action of citizens joined in active solidarity.[1] That turnaround requires tapping a sense of purpose and possibility different from the ones liberalism has invoked. There is a circle here, though not a vicious one.

Conserving America's deepest founding values will require, ironically, a substantial change in the structure and direction of American society, and that will require development of a new civic consciousness. While a renewal of civic spirit seems possible only if there remain aspects of social and cultural life from which movements for social change can draw strength, political history suggests that those social and cultural potentials will fully come to light only dynamically, as part of the successful development of such movements. That there is an experimental and participational aspect to any renewal of civic politics seems inescapable. The articulation of the conceptual resources of the civic republican heritage is a necessary aspect of our effort to cope with our present.

The great tradition of modern social thought, from Montesquieu and Rousseau onward, has been a working out of the meaning of the transformation effected by seventeenth-century thinkers in the Western understanding of life. This tradition, which includes the American Federalists, has at the same time attempted to devise a functional replacement for the integrating conception of man as political being, the *zoon politikon* and *animal rationale* of the classical and medieval theorists. The development of this replacement has been a central preoccupation of modern culture as a whole, similar in stature to the efforts at devising a secular counterpart to the idea of authority transmitted by biblical religion.

Yet, the classical notion of citizenship from which so much modern social thought has drawn its strongest nourishment has been a singularly long-lived and, in purely pragmatic terms, amazingly successful ideal. Citizenship as a symbol has evolved a whole understanding of human nature, of the good life, of authority, of man's place in the world. And like all genuinely emblematic symbols, that of the citizen in the commonwealth has remained powerful in part because of its compactness. It has, at times, evoked stirring loyalties, harkening back to the idealized classic ages of Greece and Rome, yet enabling generations of medieval jurists, Renaissance humanists, American and French revolutionaries, Hegelians and Marxists to sum up their very diverse understandings of the ideal of a public life. Through these varied channels it continues to provide us with vital images.

Even on a cursory inspection the classical notion of citizenship strikingly sums up a vision of life that is also a moral idea. The tradition of republican citizenship stretching from Plato and Aristotle to the makers of the American Revolution links power and authority within the state with the social, economic, psychological, and religious realms.[2] By contrast, modern discussions of citizenship that operate under largely liberal assumptions are far more abstract. The mechanisms of governance, the delineation of the institutions of the state as compared to those of society, the contractual relationship of citizens to each other, the ideas of authority and legitimacy all appear to float in a kind of Cartesian ether. Setting classical and modern views side by side, the troubling sense that there have been large losses, as well as gains, creeps upon us unavoidably. The principal loss is identifiable immediately. It is a loss of any relationship among political, social, economic, and psychological theorizing and the concreteness of citizenship as a way of life.

The contemporary starting point for understanding the classical conception of the citizen must be the recovery of a sense of civic life as a form of personal self-development. The kind of self-development with which the theorists of the civic life have been concerned is, in many ways, the antithesis of contemporary connotations of the notion of self-development in a "culture of narcissism."[3] Citizenship has traditionally been conceived of as a way of life that changes the person entering it. This process is essentially a collective experience. Indeed, the notion of *citizen* is unintelligible apart from that of *commonwealth,* and both terms derive their sense from the idea that we are by nature political beings. Self-fulfillment and even the working out of personal identity and a sense of orientation in the world depend upon a communal enterprise. This shared process is the civic life, and its root is involvement with others: other generations, other sorts of persons whose differences are significant because they contribute to the whole upon which our particular sense of self depends. Thus, mutual interdependency is the foundational notion of citizenship. The basic psychological dynamic of the participants, in this interdependent way of life, is an imperative to respond and to care.

From the viewpoint of modern liberalism such a civic vision seems a distinct overvaluing of the political. Whatever loss may be incurred in finding public life to be only an impersonal mechanism of profit and loss is, for the liberal, offset by the room thereby created for a rich private life free of state tyranny. Indeed, the notions of mutual dependency and care do sound more like private than public values, as liberal culture makes that division. But— putting aside Tocqueville's revelations of the coercive effects of public conformity which liberal capitalist society seems condemned to generate—it is clear that no liberal regime actually operates without large doses of civic spirit.

Still, the cultivation of a more than instrumental citizenship is seen as a private matter. And, cut off from collective scrutiny and discussion as they are, the responses of individuals and groups to their social setting often have become as hostile, defensive, and self-serving as one might fear. Awareness of the interdependency of citizens and groups is basic to the civic vision because it enlightens and challenges these disparate parties about their mutual relations. The citizen comes to know who he is by understanding the web of social relationships surrounding him. This realization is not only cognitive, it requires experience, finding one's way about and thus coming to know, in practice, who one is.

However, it is important to see that the civic tradition does not simply romanticize public participation. The dangers of misguided, fanatical, and irresponsible civic involvement have been well documented, and some of the most eloquent warnings of those dangers have come from the classical theorists of citizenship. The point, rather, is that the notion of involved concern within an interdependent community provides the image for a collective enterprise in self-transformation. The civic ideal is thus alluring and disquieting, at once delicately fragile and morally consuming in the responsibility it demands.

As the questioning of the liberal assumptions of contemporary public policies for managing interests becomes progressively more fundamental, the self-confidence of the governing groups in America continues to weaken. The much-decried turning away from politics by many is surely related to these developments. However, the tremendous rise of interest in psychological and religious movements, the apparent national obsession with healing wounds, real or imagined, in the self are first of all social events. They undoubtedly reveal something of what the current American crisis of values is about. Instrumentalist, liberal politics is being abandoned not only because it is seen as ineffective, it is also being deserted because it is seen as corrupting and empty of a genuine sense of orientation. That political activity ought to be rooted in moral conscience, that politics is in an important way related to the search for a meaningful life—these themes, which were powerfully reenunciated in the movements of the sixties, have not disappeared. Instead, they seem to have become at least partially embedded in much apparent privatism. Part of the meaning of the current American retreat to privatism is a continuing search for what counts in life, a hunger for orientation that neither the dynamics of capitalist growth nor the liberal vision of politics provides.

For this reason, the resources of the civic republican tradition are especially well suited to speak to our situation. Those who read the American spirit as so dominantly individualistic that private comfort and competitive achievement define a monochrome of national traits are both dangerously distorting our past and threatening our future, because they are closing off a sense of that living civic tradition which has been and continues to be vital to national life.[4]

The language of civic republicanism addresses directly the craving of the human self for a life of inclusion in a community of mutual concern. The civic tradition addresses the public value of exploring and developing those qualities of life that go beyond competitive success and economic well-being. It does this not by abstracting from social inequalities and economic needs but by addressing them as human, moral, personal realities rather than simply as the technical and distant issues of liberal understanding. In the imagination of great speakers for this tradition, as Martin Luther King, Jr. spoke for it, social and economic relations become translated into the moral and personal meaning they have for members of the polity. Poverty and unemployment cease to be unfortunate side effects of capitalist economic growth, to be neglected benignly, or tidied up managerially. They appear in their full reality as institutionalized denials of dignity and social participation, glaring failures of communal responsibility. As such, these issues emerge as painful spurs to challenge and change the shares of power and the institutions of collective coordination. The logic of King's republican understanding of politics led him to broaden the civil rights struggle to challenge institutions that perpetuate poverty. Finally, just before his assassination, he was advocating a coalition that would join opposition to the Indochina war and the military-industrial priorities to a broad struggle for economic and social democracy.

The great power of the civic vision, as contrasted with the liberal view, lies in its fundamental philosophic commitments. These entail the realization that the personal quest for a worthwhile life is bound up with the reality of interdependency and, so, with power. Large-scale social processes cannot remain merely technical issues but must be understood as part of the texture of personal living, just as personal life is woven into the patterns of collective organization.

Thus, the fundamental language and symbols of the American civic tradition link private and public, personal and collective sensibilities in synoptic form. American patriotism is not a nationalism based upon immemorial ties of blood and soil, but neither is it, in practice, simply a kind of commercial contract. As observers, from Tocqueville on, have reported, the underlying conception that animates patriotism in America is a moral, even a religious, one: the notion of civic covenant.[5] Unlike the liberal idea of contract, which emphasizes mutual obligations within clearly defined limits, a civic covenant is a bond of fundamental trust founded upon common commitment to a moral understanding.

Covenant morality means that as citizens we make an unlimited promise to show care and concern to each other. It is the commitment to such a trust that is summed up in the mutual pledge of loyalty which concludes the American Declaration of Independence. Within the civic perspective, the business of politics at its highest is to fulfill these covenantal promises within the changing flow of events. In practice, which is almost never politics at its highest, the civic understanding provides the sense of conscience and idealism against which the institutions and the conduct of our collective life have to be judged. Again, Martin Luther King, Jr.'s relentless campaign for justice was a prime example of the practical efficacy of the civic imperative to care for the common good.

But what could the common good be? As a liberal would see it, the institutions of our society, the government, corporations, even the cities in which people live and work are all variations on the model of a business enterprise. Political, even social, vitality and progress are measured according to economic criteria. The public good, seen that way, becomes the utilitarian sum of individual satisfactions. A common interest can be presumed to lie only in ensuring advantageous conditions of general exchange—what is called, more realistically, a "good business climate." Beyond that, interest in mutually advantageous exchanges, the civic language of a common good sounds to the liberal somehow darkly mystical or at least unnecessarily grandiose. Justice, as John Rawls makes clear, can be, at most, a matter of regulating these exchanges so that no one benefits unfairly. Why press further in confusing language, when it is likely to "overload" the political system, to encourage malcontents to assuage private wants, illegitimately, through public policy or mass movements?

To take this position is to fail to understand that the conception of the common good, with its long history in the civic tradition, is part of a language that articulates a way of living. In any practical context, language functions as more than the purely descriptive vehicle which is the ideal of analytic science. A political philosophy is always more than a neutral description; it is also, and more importantly, a proposal and a vision. Political philosophies propose to evoke an experience of a kind of living. Indeed, it is the important peculiarity of liberal political theory that political language should be shorn of its evocative dimensions. That opinion is, seen in larger context, itself a proposal to think and experience life in a certain way. Now, all forms of life, especially those that have been consciously cultivated for generations, are rich with highly charged, compact phrases and gestures which serve to evoke a whole scheme of meaning.[6] In the civic tradition, *common good* is one of these phrases.

Thus, it is not surprising that such an emblematic phrase would cause puzzlement when heard from within an alien scheme of meaning such as liberal utilitarianism. But if we grant to the civic tradition the possibility that its language points to a way of life which is meaningful in its own terms, then our imagination can rise to a new possibility. This new possibility is the idea of a civic life. To understand this requires at first, in Wittgenstein's phrase, coming "to feel our way around" in its characteristic language. Such an adventure may enable us to see the contemporary morass of liberal capitalist politics in a fresh way.

A virtue of the civic republican tradition is that its language provides an understanding of the social conditions upon which it depends. The chief of these conditions is an interpretation of psychic and moral development importantly different from the liberal account. The immediate merit of this alternative is that it offers an understanding of what liberal theory cannot provide: an explanation for the missing connections in its own interpretation of social life.

How, then, is a civic life possible? That is to ask, how can we conceive of individual fulfillment as realized through mutual commitment to a common good? The answer the civic tradition provides is clear: civic life is possible because human nature is naturally disposed to find its fulfillment in what is called a life of virtue. This statement immediately calls up for us—partly as a kind of prophylaxis against a suspected tyranny—the proud ideal of freedom, the "core symbol" of liberalism. Leaving aside the confusions and controversies that continue to rage about the notion of freedom, in particular its relation to the other great liberal value of equality,[7] the civic conception of virtue becomes clearer when contrasted with liberal freedom.

In important respects, in fact, freedom is virtue's ambiguous child. For the republican tradition, civic virtue is the excellence of character proper to the citizen. It *is* freedom in a substantive sense, freedom understood as the capacity to attain one's good, where *goodness* describes full enjoyment of those capacities which characterize a flourishing human life. Since humans are by nature social beings, living well requires a shared life, and a shared life is possible only when the members of a community trust and respect one another. To participate in such a shared life is to show concern for, and reciprocity to, one's fellows, and to do so is simultaneously fulfilling for the individual. Thus, the individual's true good must consist not in attaining a sum of satisfactions but in showing in himself, and sharing as a participant, an admirable and worthwhile form of life.

Modern liberalism isolates the act of free volition, the will as self-assertion, and emphasizes the individual struggling against constriction. The classical image of freedom as virtue, however, is quite different. It focuses upon the exhibition of form as the flowering of potential powers. From the Promethean standpoint of modern culture it is easy to mistake this ideal for mere static completion or passivity, but, in fact, it is neither static nor passive or, rather, the categories of civic language propose a way of seeing life that is different from the utilitarian. This language suggests that what makes life worth living is not simple pleasure but the peculiarly human satisfaction of feeling oneself to be a significant member of an ongoing way of life that appeals because of its deep resonances of beauty and meaning. (Curiously, modern advertising, that most ostensibly utilitarian of capitalist institutions, grasps this point profoundly, if narrowly. What else is most advertising but the rhetorical association of a commodity, such as a car or a cigarette, with a symbol of a commonly desired way of life or admired character ideal: the Beautiful People or, *de gustibus*, the Cowboy?)

The task of civic intelligence is to bring these inchoate appeals to clarity, to find and to weave a harmony among the various threads of significance embodied in family life, in the various skills and crafts, in religious and artistic traditions. In its most general formulation, the civic sense of virtue as freedom is captured in the idea of human dignity. Medieval natural-law theorists brought Christian theological commitments to bear on Greek and Roman notions of a common humanity in their statement that the fundamental natural end or purpose of political life is to provide dignity for all.

Notice that it is consistent in this context to speak of the political community as natural because it is a necessary condition for, indeed is an essential manifestation of, a dignified human life. This dignity is the most basic, general, even ontological aspect of the flourishing of human nature. Practically, it is the reality that Martin Luther King, Jr. called the sense of "somebodyness." Dignity is thus the realization of freedom. It is the evidence of the full development of civic virtue.

The idea of "free institutions" (which bulks large in American political discourse), while a phrase much used in liberal thought, has its roots in the same civic conception of dignity and virtue. When Montesquieu and other early liberals looked for positive qualities in the republics of the ancient world, they saw above all free, as opposed to despotic, regimes. By this, they meant that the structure and powers of the state derived from no force outside the citizens themselves. Neither occupying army, nor dictator's mercenaries, nor isolated elite maintained the practices of life, the laws, the defenses of those cities; rather, their strength came from the concerted spirit of their citizens.

It seemed to the early liberals, living in an age of monarchy and the Old Regime, amazing that the ancients could sustain, even for brief periods, the public spirit of Periclean Athens or Republican Rome, for it was evident from the descriptions and discussions of the classical theorists that maintenance of a self-governing polity required a generally high degree of identification, on the part of the citizen, of his own good with the well-being of the community.[8] Given the liberal assumptions of the early modern theorists, they had little trouble accounting for the "corruption" and decline of ancient republics into despotic empires. Indeed, as self-seeking competition weakened the bonds of the commonwealth, those thinkers were proposing the liberal order as a way to engineer correctly, what they took as the natural human gravitation toward competitive egoism. What seemed astonishing, and really hardly credible at all, was the notion of civic spirit, of civic acts as such.[9] Yet, the sheer weight of historical testimony forced them to accept its reality.

Holding to our intention to extend to the civic tradition a presumption of experiential validity, it is clear that citizenship is taken by republicanism as the natural fulfillment of human powers, not as an extreme feat of moral athleticism. However rare the truly excellent examples may be, citizenship remains the common vocation and the proper object of moral education.

We may shed light on the matter by trying to describe a civic act, as opposed to a merely private one. In modern electoral politics, candidates frequently try to persuade citizens to cast their votes because their interests will be advanced by so doing. While the civic philosophers would agree with this reasoning, the "interests" to be advanced would be rather differently defined. Indeed, the premise of public discussion of policy even in a liberal regime is not only to enlighten all interested parties as to what they stand to gain or lose in the event that a certain course of action is taken. When that is all or the greatest part of the public debate, little "policy" results; instead there is a watering-down of choices to please everyone. Where the issue is simply a proposal to choose one kind of private enrichment over another, the arts of bargaining and political compromise are not inappropriate, tempered by a concern for fairness, like John Rawl's theory of justice, as a kind of rational and self-interested choice. But what about political decisions about making war, or the kinds of economic growth which should be pursued, or about use and care for the natural environment? Because these political decisions so affect the kinds of life that will prevail, public debate is critical for developing a shared understanding of the consequences of policy choices, of hidden costs and benefits to the whole community. Indeed, it is the general discussion of interdependency that brings a "public" into being. Public discussion aims to bring before the whole civic community an understanding of the "externalities" of policy choices—to use the language of liberal economics—precisely in terms of what pursuing these options will mean for the situation of various groups.

Voting to endorse a policy or candidate, were the choices really clear (which is another extremely critical matter), is a public, a civic act, because it carries with it responsibility for changing or maintaining the social, and often the natural, environment shared by all. Thus, to reduce such an act to a simple reflex of self-interest is fundamentally to misconceive the actual interdependence of citizens in a commonwealth. It is to imagine that the polity is a self-balancing mechanism—a familiar enough misassumption. But it is also to fail to take seriously the complicated web of interactions that ties together the lives of even the most private citizens. It is here that the liberal penchant for modeling political questions on economic choices in a marketplace shows its most dangerous and morally irresponsible side. Against the liberal claim that free institutions, in Montesquieu's sense, can be sustained merely by concentration upon an expanding market system, civic republican insight and historical experience strongly suggest that such a course is folly, because it rests on a misconception of politics and, finally, on too narrow an understanding of the reality of social life.

The strange utopian side of liberalism shows up clearly here. Confronted with the overwhelming fact of social interdependence, the liberal retreat to the mechanism of market choice is cloaked as humility! After all, one hears the argument, actually to make public decisions about the kinds of communities we should have, the kinds of lives people ought to lead, is moral arrogance and presumption. Let the ideal market choices mediate. Then if consenting adults wish to commit capitalist or communalist acts, that is their private matter. But notice: this "value-neutral" position assumes that all humanly relevant goods can somehow be exchanged through the market, and that the moral qualities of respect and fairness can be developed in private life alone. Highly questionable assumptions indeed: not even the early modern liberal philosophers held such sanguine views.

To the early liberals, the utopian element of classical republican morality was not the fact of interdependence and mutual responsibility but the expectation and requirement that citizens act in an appropriately responsible way in practice. For them, the key problem in the civic vision was the idea that self-interested motives could actually be transformed through a public culture to the extent that genuinely civic acts became widely practiced. Now, our present situation differs from theirs in one critical respect. We cannot fall back on the optimistic hope that an improved social mechanics will produce a functional equivalent of civic virtue by harnessing private egoism. Indeed, the viability of any self-governing institution is threatened by the failure of those dreams. We need to look closely at the civic tradition because, if democracy is to survive, we have no other option.

So, again, what conditions make civic life possible? Classical political philosophy understood the life of civic or moral virtue to stand in opposition to the life of self-interest which they called economic, meaning that the latter aimed at private satisfaction. Since economic life is concerned with wants that are in principle limitless, the motivation in dealings with others is always the expectation of gain. This is the marketing orientation familiar from utilitarian theory. By contrast, moral virtue represents a higher integration of the powers of the self. This integration was conceived as at once the goal and the effect of participation in civic life. Virtue, the *arete* ("excellence") of the Greek theorists, describes the disposition of a person whose conduct is guided by a shared value or principle rather than by private needs and desires. This kind of excellence, moreover, is a personal ideal as well as a collective one, in that it describes a personality sufficiently integrated both to live up to commitments and to cooperate with others to achieve common values. In traditional language such an integration of the personality was described as *courage*, the ability to sum oneself up in word and action, and *temperance*, or self-control, an ordering of the person so that the higher values consciously affirmed can predominate over merely private impulses and desires.

The civic life has intrinsic value, then, because it is necessary for human maturation. The teleological conception of human nature, which the civic tradition long maintained, places the achievement of mature personhood within a context of interdependence and mutual concern. The great modern ideal of the autonomous self who is also respectful of others, as reflected in contractarian liberalism, is in reality a kind of echo of civic virtue. For the modern theorists of obligation, only autonomy is isolated from sociability, just as the modern theorists' state of nature locates man outside social relations. Given their assumption of the primacy of analytical reason, this conclusion appeared quite natural and obvious to the liberal thinkers. Again we see the tight connection among an understanding of politics, a theory of human nature, and a conception of reason. By contrast with liberalism, classical teleological reason situates achievement of an integrated self capable of self-reflection, and so of responsible action, within a continuity of life which is both social and natural.

What enabled classical thinkers to argue that a prudential reasoning, based upon a cultivated moral sense, could in fact be trusted to promote the good of the community? It was their vision of autonomy as always developing in tension with care for others in a particular shared situation. The whole classical notion of a common *paideia*, or moral-civic cultivation, rested on the assertion that growth and transformation of the self toward responsible mutual concern is the realistic concern of public life.

William Sullivan, associate professor of Philosophy at LaSalle College, is the coeditor of Interpretive Social Science: A Reader *and a coauthor of* Habits of the Heart.

Excerpted from William Sullivan's Reconstructing Public Philosophy, *Berkeley and Los Angeles: University of California Press, © 1982 by the Regents of the University of California. Reprinted with the permission of the publisher.*

Notes

1. This insight is developed with varying degrees of clarity in the recent works of social analysis discussed in Chapter One.

2. See J. G. A. Pocock's *The Machiavellian Moment: Florentine Political Thought and the Atlantic Republican Tradition* (Princeton, New Jersey: Princeton University Press, 1975). For the transformation of that tradition during the course of the American Revolution and its aftermath see Gordon S. Wood, *The Creation of the American Republic: 1776–1787* (Chapel Hill: University of North Carolina Press, 1969).

3. This term has been popularized by Christopher Lasch in his *The Culture of Narcissism: American Life in an Age of Diminishing Expectations* (New York: W. W. Norton, 1979). Richard Sennett has pro-

pounded an important interpretation of the same phenomenon as a defensive response to the failure of Western societies to maintain a vital public life during the social turmoil generated by industrialization: see Richard Sennett, *The Fall of Public Man: The Social Psychology of Capitalism* (New York: Knopf, 1977).

4. The most influential presentation of that position is by the so-called neoconservatives, especially those gathered around the journal *The Public Interest*. For example, see Nathan Glazer and Irving Kristol, eds., *The American Commonwealth—1976* (New York: Basic Books, 1976).

5. Robert N. Bellah, among others, has powerfully rearticulated this theme. See his *The Broken Covenant: American Civil Reli-*

gion in Time of Trial (New York: Seabury Press, 1975). See also John Schaar, "The Case for Patriotism," *New American Review No. 17* (New York: Bantam Books, 1972), pp. 59–99.

6. Herbert Fingarette describes these compact symbols in the context of personal psychodynamics as "cue phrases." The meanings they call up are as important as the information they convey. See Herbert Fingarette, *The Self in Transformation: Psychoanalysis, Philosophy and the Life of the Spirit* (New York: Harper and Row, 1963), pp. 23–26.

7. Alexis de Tocqueville organized his monumental work on American society around what he took to be the opposition between liberty and equality. See his *Democracy in America,* translated by George Lawrence (Garden City, New York: Doubleday Anchor, 1969), esp. vol. II, pt. II, chs. 1–20 and IV, chs. 1–6. compare Isaiah Berlin, *Four Essays on Liberty* (New York: Oxford University Press, 1969). Ronald Dworkin dissents from the notion that liberty and equality are opposed by arguing that it is possible to provide a coherent account of a right to equality but not of a presumed "right to liberty." See Ronald Dworkin, *Taking Rights Seriously* (Cambridge, Massachusetts: Harvard University Press, 1977), ch. 12. Charles Taylor provides a critical analysis of the nihilistic implications of the notion of radical freedom of the will as an absolute value in his *Hegel* (London: Cambridge University Press, 1975), pp. 546–69.

8. See Baron de Montesquieu, *The Spirit of Laws,* translated by Thomas Nugent (New York: Hafner, 1949), bk. III, chs. 3, 7; bk. IV, ch. 2. Compare Thomas L. Pangle, *Montesquieu's Philosophy of Liberalism* (Chicago: University of Chicago Press, 1973).

9. For example, see Adam Smith's deflation of traditional heroism as pride: Adam Smith, *The Theory of the Moral Sentiments* (New York: A. M. Kelley, 1966), pp. 405–9, 420–21. Tocqueville expresses similar sentiments: *Democracy in America,* translated by George Lawrence (Garden City, New York: Doubleday Anchor, 1969), p. 497.

"Only public deliberation and political action allow citizens to realize their dignity and powers as responsible agents and judges."

On Participation

by Hanna Fenichel Pitkin and Sara M. Shumer

Of all the dangerous thoughts and explosive ideas abroad in the world today, by far the most subversive is that of democracy. Taken seriously, the idea of democracy threatens every established elite of privilege or power, all hierarchy and deference, the legitimacy of virtually every government in the world. It undermines the ideological support of bureaucratic state capitalism as much as that of bureaucratic state socialism. That is why governing and privileged strata everywhere seek to suppress the least sign of a genuinely democratic movement, and why those who would fight against oppression must take the idea most seriously. At first glance, democracy may seem a battle long won, but that is only because we pay lip service to the term without thinking about its meaning, let alone trying to live by its implications. The idea of democracy is the cutting edge of radical criticism, the best inspiration for change toward a more humane world, the revolutionary idea of our time.

The basic idea is simple: people can and should govern themselves. They do not need specially bred or anointed rulers, nor a special caste or class to run their affairs. Everyone has the capacity for autonomy, even quite ordinary people—the uneducated, the poor, housewives, laborers, peasants, the outsiders and castoffs of society. Each is capable not merely of self-control, of privately taking charge of his own life, but also of self-government, of sharing in the deliberate shaping of their common life. Exercising this capacity is prerequisite both to the freedom and full development of each, and to the freedom and justness of the community.

Implicit in that simple democratic creed is a more complex understanding of what it means to be human, simultaneously both creature and creator of history. We are the species that makes itself, collectively, through the gradual accretion of technology, custom, and civilization. We are all involved in that process, but our individual contribution is minute and, for the most part, the inadvertent by-product of our intentional activities. The opportunities available to each and the limits on the private freedom to pursue personal goals are set by social conditions, which are humanly produced and sustained, yet not in our control.

It is only in political activity that we sometimes can recognize those conditions as human creations, take charge of our history making, deliberate about what we are doing, and set policy for ourselves. Only public deliberation and political action allow citizens to realize—both to make real and to become aware of—their dignity and powers as responsible agents and judges. And only thus can a community achieve justice. Through participation, the needs of all and the unique perspective of each are taken into account.

We shall not advocate this creed, but presume it. We address those who already share it, or would share it if only they could persuade themselves of its contemporary relevance, its feasibility under modern conditions. The latter group, we suspect, is large, for we have all been schooled to a prudent resignation in this matter: the voices consigning democracy to a golden but irretrievable past are legion, and they come as much from the left as from the right. Participatory democracy, they say, may have made sense long ago in small and simple societies whose citizens met under the village oak, but it is irrelevant to governing or mobilizing masses in a modern nation-state with its huge population, mass communications, nationally and internationally organized economic structures, and enormous technical complexity. Here only hierarchy, centralization, bureaucracy, and expertise make sense. Even those who would redirect society in radical ways must adapt to these requirements. Mass apathy can only be countered by disciplined organization; establishment technocrats must be matched by radical experts, established ideology by radical propaganda.

Genuine and serious obstacles do challenge the realization of democracy today. But the notion that it is impossible is an illusion, largely self-induced among would-be democrats; conceding it makes it self-fulfilling. The conviction of democracy's irrelevance has many origins, but surely one is the unthinking acceptance of a conceptual framework formulated by the enemies of democracy and derived from a tradition that has, on the whole, sought to prevent rather than encourage participation. Even on the left, our understanding of democracy is captive to the currently dominant liberal conception of politics as a competitive struggle among self-interested individuals over who will make the rules allocating "values." Politics concerns "who governs," which means determining "who gets what, when, how." For all but a few professionals, it is a remote, disagreeable, strictly instrumental activity. So democracy is assimilated into representation by way of the division of labor: professionals take care of politics so that the rest of us are free for more gratifying and gainful activities. Even radicals, sharing these assumptions, often seek to mobilize power in the interest of the oppressed, rather than involving them directly in democratic political action. In this perspective, fellow citizens are at best useful means, more often competitors and obstacles; and the public good is simply an aggregation of individual interests.

But this liberal perspective also offers a traditional countertheme, familiar from grade-school civics classes and patriotic ceremonies but taken seriously by almost no one. This minor theme insists that there is indeed a public good to which all are obligated, duty requiring the subordination of personal preference and private interest. Here, citizenship is less a privilege than a burden: the civic duty to vote, keep informed, pay taxes, obey the law, even to "lay down one's life in the service of his country."

This countertheme is ostensibly opposed, yet actually complementary to the dominant understanding. The one construes politics in terms of self-interest, the other in terms of self-sacrifice. Yet both assume that politics is disagreeable; neither takes it as intrinsically gratifying or valuable, or recognizes its radical potential. Democracy is bound to be distorted when viewed through these lenses. If politics is simply the pursuit of self-interest, active citizen participation will seem so potentially disruptive of order and communal ties that only a unanimously harmonious community can afford it. If politics is self-sacrifice, democratic participation will seem a burden to be reluctantly accepted or cynically dodged, and the public good will seem external to the self. Unless an alternative is found to this dilemma, participatory democracy cannot be achieved.

One day, as Albert Camus puts it, "a slave who has been taking orders all his life suddenly decides that he cannot obey some new command," and he says "No more!"[1] So one begins, and others join in; together they try to take charge of their lives. Historically, such popular empowerment has appeared both on the large, dramatic scale of revolution, and on the small, everyday, and local scene. It appeared in the sections of the Paris Commune and the "popular societies" and political clubs of the French Revolution, in the soldiers' and workers' soviets of the Russian Revolution, the "fanshen" assemblies of the Chinese Revolution, in the Committees of Correspondence of the American Revolution. Still visible to Tocqueville in the America of the 1830s, it reappeared in the Populist mobilization of the 1880s and 1890s. But it can also be found in Swiss cantons and Yugoslavian factories, in early Israeli kibbutzim, in the "Prague Spring," the literacy campaign of the Nicaraguan Revolution, the struggles of Japanese peasants to oppose expansion of the Tokyo airport, at times in the labor movement, the Civil Rights movement, the women's movement. It can begin in some local incident (a bus in Montgomery or a shipyard in Gdansk) and spread to mobilize most of a nation. It can occur among colonized people, among slaves, among the subjects of a ruthless dictator. It is no mere fantasy or utopian absolute, but a relatively familiar recurrent phenomenon, a persistent struggle pursued in the widest variety of ways, under the most diverse and inhospitable circumstances. People find ways of being citizens even when they are excluded from the formal institutions of power.

The romantic, abstracted, and thoroughly unpolitical image of participation offered by recent theorists needs to be corrected by such a list of historical examples, showing that democracy is no dim and distant chimera, confined to the Greek city or the idealistic affinity group, remote from people's needs or presupposing automatic harmony, but a very real, practical human enterprise of the greatest possible political significance, repeatedly undertaken by ordinary people. Such a list of historical examples is, of course, motley, mixing rebellion and revolt with democratic movements, democratic societies, democracy as an established form of government. Few of the instances listed can be said unambiguously to have succeeded. Historically, such efforts have not only aimed at democratizing their societies, but also themselves provided the democratic experience for their participants. At what point and in what ways shall we say that such a movement has failed or ended? Certainly many "failed" movements left both the world and their members significantly transformed in democratic directions.

Nor is it obvious what might be proved by a record of democratic defeats. It might, for instance, be taken as confirming the thesis that democracy is dangerous: as soon as such a movement gives any signs of succeeding, all the resources of established power and privilege will be brought to bear "to destroy it, divert it, buy it, or try in any way to gain effective control over it," as Lawrence Goodwyn has written.[2] Or the record might be taken as indicating how often democrats are misled by bad theoretical formulations, failing to nurture and preserve within their own groups the democracy they seek for their polity as a whole.

Certainly such a review of historical examples reminds us that hope—and the democratic impulse—springs eternal, even in the face of the most forbidding circumstances; and that from small, seemingly harmless beginnings, great and genuinely radical movements can grow. Much of the history of democracy has taken place within movements struggling to transform societies that were themselves far from democratic. The power and radical nature of those movements grew specifically from the liberating, transforming capacity of political action. So the decision of a tired black woman to sit in the front of the bus can become a national drive for human dignity and equality;

a self-help cooperative providing credit for poor farmers can become a democratizing national movement; sections of the Paris Commune can, in demanding cheap bread, simultaneously begin developing "a new type of political organization" that will enable people to be "participators in government."[3]

Democratic movements become stronger and potentially more radical as they diversify and reach out to other groups: when workers join with peasants, antinuclear ecologists join with nuclear plant workers and the unemployed, civil rights activists join with blue-collar workers and feminists. Not only do they acquire new members and allies, but they grow more political, and more just. As the group becomes more inclusive, members move beyond scapegoating toward increasing sophistication about the true social causes of their pain, and toward a more principled justification of who should pay what price to relieve it. So members discover their connectedness—and forge new connections—with others, with principle, and with their own capacities. Democrats must be as committed to fostering participatory politics within their movements as they are to the intrinsic value of participation in democratic government.

When people say that democracy is "obviously" not suitable for a large population, they fall captive to an abstract notion of assembling more and more people in one place: "no room can hold them all." But that is not how democratic movements grow, nor how real democratic politics function. Consider the America Tocqueville discovered in the 1830s, a people deeply engaged in democratic self-government: their "most important business" and their greatest pleasure. Take away politics from the American, Tocqueville said, and you rob him of half his existence, leaving a "vast void in his life" and making him "incredibly unhappy."[4] Yet Tocqueville's America was no city-state, nor could its citizens assemble in one place. If size was no bar then to so lively a democratic engagement, it need not be now.

Face-to-face citizen assemblies are indeed essential to democracy, but one single assembly of all is not. Representation, delegation, cooperation, coordination, federation, and other kinds of devolution are entirely compatible with democracy, though they do not constitute and cannot guarantee it. Disillusioned democrats from Robert Michels to Frances Fox Piven and Richard A. Cloward have argued that any large organization and any differentiated leadership necessarily must take the life out of democracy, rigidifying into bureaucratic hierarchy. But formless, spontaneous mobs in the streets disrupting an established order cannot by themselves be a source of enduring change or even enduring challenge. Even if ossification were ultimately inevitable for any democratic engagement, surely the democrat's task still would be to prolong and revitalize the early, militant stage of popular involvement. The point is not to eschew all organization and all differentiated leadership, confining democracy to the local and spontaneous, but to develop those organizational forms and those styles of authority that sustain, rather than suppress, member initiative and autonomy. From historical examples we know that such forms and styles exist; it has sometimes been done.

Democrats need to think hard—both historically and theoretically—about the circumstances and the institutions by which large-scale collective power can be kept responsible to its participatory foundations. In the new American states, for example, after the disruption of British rule, radicals insisted on unicameral legislatures, weak or collective executives, frequent elections, rotation in office to prevent formation of a class of professional politicians. Most important, representatives were elected by participatory town or country meetings, thus by political bodies with an identity and some experience in collective action, rather than by isolated voters. Consequently, dialogue between representatives and their constituencies was frequent and vigorous; representatives were often instructed and sometimes recalled. But there are many possibilities for vital and fruitful interaction between the local and the national community. Recent resolutions on nuclear disarmament passed by New England town meetings are a promising experiment. All such devices, however, depend ultimately on the character of the citizenry, their love of and skill in exercising freedom; and these, in turn, rest mainly on the direct experience of meaningful local self-government.

Tocqueville argued that what made the American nation democratic was the vitality of direct participation in small and local associations. Face-to-face democracy was the foundation—not a substitute—for representative institutions, federalism, and national democracy. In direct personal participation, Tocqueville observed, people both learn the skills of citizenship and develop a taste for freedom; thereafter, they form an active rather than deferential, apathetic, or privatized constituency for state and national representation, an engaged public for national issues. Size is not an insurmountable problem. On the basis of local, face-to-face politics, all sorts of higher and more distant structures of representation and collective power can be erected without destroying democracy—indeed, they can enhance it. Lacking such a basis, no institutional structures or programs of indoctrination can produce democracy.

From the question of size, turn next to that of technology. Has the technological complexity of modern society, requiring specialized expertise, rendered democracy obsolete? Here, it is useful to remember that while the technological society may be new, the claims for expertise against democracy are very old, at least as old as Plato's *Republic*. The idea that ordinary people are incompetent to deal intelligently with the issues affecting their lives rests now, as it always has, on an overly narrow idea of what constitutes politically relevant knowledge, and a confusion between knowledge and decision.

First off, stupidity knows no class. Maybe most people are foolish, but foolishness is found in all social strata. Education removes some kinds of ignorance, but may entrench or instill others. The cure is not to exclude some but to include as diverse a range of perspectives and experience as possible in political deliberation. Second, expertise cannot solve political problems. Contemporary politics is indeed full of technically complex topics, about which even the educated feel horribly ignorant. But on every politically significant issue of this kind, the "experts" are divided; that is part of what makes the issues political. Though we may also feel at a loss to choose between them, leaving it to the experts is no solution at all.

Finally, while various kinds of knowledge can be profoundly useful in political decisions, knowledge alone is never enough. The political question is what we are to *do;* knowledge can only tell us how things are, how they work, while a political resolution always depends on what we, as a community, want and think right. And those questions have no technical answer; they require collective deliberation and decision. The experts must become a part of, not an alternative to, the democratic political process.

Technology as such is not the problem for democracy; the problems here are popular deference to experts, and the belief in technology as an irresistible force, an "imperative" beyond human control. Since such deference and fatalism originate in people's experience, which is rooted in social conditions, they may be fought wherever they arise; and that is reason for hope and perseverance. The apathetic oppressed constitute an enormous pool of potential democratic energy. And as the historical examples remind us, even the most oppressed people sometimes rediscover within themselves the capacity to act. Democrats today must seek out and foster every opportunity for people to experience their own effective agency: at work, at school, in family and personal relations, in the community. Democratic citizenship is facilitated by democratic social relations and an autonomous character structure; dependency and apathy must be attacked wherever people's experience centers. Yet such attacks remain incomplete unless they relate personal concerns to public issues, extend individual initiative into shared political action. A sense of personal autonomy, dignity, and efficacy may be requisite for, but must not be confused with, citizenship.

And so we return to the need for direct, personal political participation. As Tocqueville already made clear, not just any kind of small or local group can provide the democratic experience: the point is not gregariousness but politicization. To support democracy, face-to-face groups must themselves be internally democratic in ways already discussed, must deal with issues that really matter in their members' lives, and must have genuine power to affect the outcomes of those issues. One can experience freedom or learn citizenship no better in a "Mickey Mouse" group where nothing of importance is at stake than in a hierarchical organization.

Tocqueville's America was already big, but many important matters could still be addressed and resolved on the small scale. Confronting the realities of large-scale private power and social problems today requires national and even international organization. Such organization can be democratic, we have argued, if it rests on active, engaged citizenry. Technology, too, can be democratically handled by such a citizenry. But such a citizenry emerges only from *meaningful* small-scale participation. Is that still a realistic possibility in a society such as ours?

To answer that crucial question, one must distinguish between short- and long-run requirements. In the long run, if we truly want full democracy, there is no doubt that we shall have to change our society and economy in fundamental ways. But in the short run, the right means toward that goal are participatory democratic movements. That such movements can still occur was shown in the 1960s; nothing fundamental has changed since then. Today's democrat must hope that in the brief experience of active participation that follows a flaring up of the democratic impulse, ordinary people, discovering the connections between local problems and national structures, coming up against the repressive power of established privilege, will themselves discover the need for more fundamental changes. We must be prepared to use the impulses toward, and the experience of, democracy, where they occur and while they last, to produce the social and economic changes that will further facilitate democracy. Each time it is, one might say, a race between the radicalizing and liberating potential of political action, and the dispiriting and paralyzing effects of the repression and political defeat likely to follow.

Confronting this most central and difficult problem, we need to recall not only Tocqueville and revolutionary America, but also the movements of the 1960s, to build on their achievements and learn from their mistakes. On the whole, these movements did not see themselves as building participatory alternatives, nor as engaged in a long-term transformation of consciousness and social conditions to make possible a more democratic America. They looked for immediate changes on specific issues, mobilized people for short-term successes, and saw their own internal organization largely in instrumental terms. Even the Students for a Democratic Society, which did begin with a larger vision and did value internal democracy, eventually became absorbed in ending the Vietnam War. Neglecting democratic organization for immediate policy changes, the 1960s movements failed in what Goodwyn has called "democratic patience," the capacity to sustain democratic momentum for the long haul.[5] Yet they left behind a changed America, and many less conscious yet active neighborhood groups, and radical opposition groups in unions, the professions, and among consumers.

A democratic movement for our time must come out of such groups, out of local organizing around the grievances and aspirations people now feel. It must encourage local autonomy, ways of doing for ourselves and doing without, so as to cut loose from the system. Yet it must also encourage a widening perspective on the issues, their connections with the larger social structures of private power; it must foster alliances and debate among such groups. People must organize in ways that constantly enlarge rather than suppress movement members' active engagement, independent judgment, and preparedness for continued struggle.

Such local and ad hoc beginnings by no means preclude a commitment to radical systemic social and economic change. In the long run, democracy's full realization might well entail abolishing the joint-stock limited-liability corporation; or abolishing private ownership of the means of production; or even abandoning the Faustian dream of mastering and exploiting nature to gain infinitely expanding wealth.

But that is to get ahead of ourselves. For surely the privileged elites of corporate power will not permit such radical changes today or tomorrow, nor are our fellow citizens ready to fight on such grounds. We must not postpone the practice of participatory democracy until after such changes are achieved, nor expect it to emerge automatically from them. Democracy is our best means for achieving social change and must remain our conscious goal. Then the vicious circle of social process, in which democracy seems to presuppose the conditions that only democracy can bring about, can become ground for hope: wherever we do cut into the circle, we thereby transform all the rest of its course. We can begin where we are.

Hanna Fenichel Pitkin, professor of Political Science at the University of California at Berkeley, is the author of Fortune Is a Woman: Gender and Politics in the Thought of Niccolo Machiavelli. *Sara M. Shumer is a professor of Political Science at Haverford College.*

Originally published in Democracy 2 (Fall 1982): 43–54. Reprinted by permission of the authors.

Notes

1. Albert Camus, *The Rebel*, trans. Anthony Bower (New York: Random House, 1956), p. 13.

2. Lawrence Goodwyn, "Organizing Democracy: The Limits of Theory and Practice," *Democracy* Vol. I, no. 1 (January 1981), p. 47.

3. Hannah Arendt, *On Revolution*, p. 247.

4. Alexis de Tocqueville, *Democracy in America*, ed. J. P. Mayer (Garden City, NY: Doubleday and Co., 1969), p. 243.

5. Lawrence Goodwyn, "Organizing Democracy: The Limit of Theory and Practice," *Democracy* Vol. I, no. 1 (Jan. 1981), p. 47.

"Cultural democracy states that an individual can be bicultural and still loyal to American ideals."

Toward a Cultural Democracy

by Manuel Ramírez and Alfredo Castañeda

The American ideology of assimilation embodied in the theory of the melting pot as a basis for educational policy is vividly illustrated by the following reproduction reflecting the "No Spanish Rule" adopted by many districts in the Southwest until very recently.

```
VIOLATION SLIP—SPANISH DETENTION
_____ was speaking
(Student's name and classification)
Spanish during school hours. This pupil must report to Spanish
Detention in the Cafeteria on the assigned day. (The teacher report-
ing should place the date on this slip.)
_____
   (Dates to report)          (Teacher reporting)
Return this slip to Mr. _____ or Mr. _____
before 3:30 p.m. 9/66
```

As reported by the United States Civil Rights Commission (1972), the violation slip reproduced here was used to place children in "Spanish Detention Class" in a school district in Texas. Although the survey reported in this Civil

Rights Commission Report did not uncover instances in which school officials admitted to administering physical punishment for speaking Spanish, allegations concerning such punishment were heard by the commission at its hearing in San Antonio (1968). Moreover, other forms of punishment are revealed in the following excerpts from the themes of one class of seventh-grade, Mexican-American students in Texas. They were written as part of an assignment to describe their elementary school experiences and their teachers' attitudes toward speaking Spanish in school.

> If we spoke Spanish we had to pay 5 cents to the teacher or we had to stay after school.
>
> In the first through the fourth grade, if the teacher caught us talking Spanish we would have to stand on the "black square" for an hour or so.
>
> When I was in elementary they had a rule not to speak Spanish but we all did. If you got caught speaking Spanish you were to write three pages saying, "I must not speak Spanish in school."
>
> In the sixth grade, they kept a record of which if we spoke Spanish they would take it down and charge us a penny for every Spanish word. If we spoke more than 1,000 words our parents would have to come to school and talk with the principal.
>
> If you'd been caught speaking Spanish you would be sent to the principal's office or given extra assignments to do as homework or probably made to stand by the wall during recess and after school [U.S. Commission on Civil Rights: Mexican-American Study Report III: *The Excluded Student*, May 1972, pp. 18, 19].

In this same report, an interview with a school principal revealed that he would "fight teaching Spanish past the third grade because it destroys loyalty to America [p. 20]." This assertion, in our opinion, reflects an unfounded fear, a fear that reinforces the ideology of the Anglo conformity view of acculturation. This fear may explain in part why American public education struggles to keep alive the principles of political and economic democracy, and yet has ranged from ambivalence to open antagonism toward the child's struggle to remain identified with his or her own home and community socialization experiences.

It is to this issue that the Office of Civil Rights, Department of Health, Education and Welfare, attempts to speak via posters which contain the faces of Mexican-American children with the following inscriptions:

> *Yo tengo derecho a mi idioma y mi
> cultura.*
> I have a right to my own language and
> culture.

*Saber me idioma y mi cultura me ayuda a
    ser un buen ciudadano.*
Knowing my language and my culture will
    help me to become a good citizen.

*El Acta de los Derechos Civiles de 1964
    protege mis derechos de poder hablar
    mi idioma y de continuar mi cultura.*
The Civil Rights Act of 1964 protects my
    right to speak my language and
    continue to identify with my culture.

Cultural Democracy

The implications of the Civil Rights posters refer to the legal rights of an individual to be different while at the same time be a responsible member of a larger society. More specifically, cultural democracy, as we define it, states that an individual can be bicultural and still be loyal to American ideals. Cultural democracy is a philosophical precept which recognizes that the way a person communicates, relates to others, seeks support and recognition from his environment (incentive motivation), and thinks and learns (cognition) is a product of the value system of his home and community. Furthermore, educational environments or policies that do not recognize the individual's right, as guaranteed by the Civil Rights Act of 1964, to remain identified with the culture and language of his cultural group are culturally undemocratic.

Whatever its intention, any educational policy (such as those based on the Anglo conformity view of acculturation) that keeps a Mexican-American child from learning or valuing Spanish or Mexican-American cultural values creates painful psychological problems for the child. The school's rejection of the Spanish language or of anything in his life which is related to Mexican-American culture implies rejection of the child himself. Instead of providing the opportunity to establish a bicultural identity, such policies exert pressure on the child to make a choice at a time in his life when the values that he has acquired at home are not consciously articulable by the child. Consequently, one of the basic principles of democracy, that of conscious choice, is being violated by such policies.

The philosophy of cultural democracy requires that the school refrain from making the choice for the child. A culturally democratic learning environment is a setting in which a Mexican-American child can acquire knowledge about his own culture and the dominant culture; the learning, furthermore, is based on communication, human-relational, incentive-motivational, and learning patterns that are culturally appropriate. The goal of such an environment is to develop biculturalism with regard to communication, human relations, motivation, and learning. The educational goal is to help children learn to function competently and effectively in, as well as to contribute more to, more than one cultural world.

Cultural Pluralism and Cultural Democracy

Historical Origins

The concept of cultural democracy has its roots in an alternative ideology that emerged in reaction to the Anglo conformity view of acculturation. The threat to cultural diversity posed by this conformity view spurred the development of a new line of thought designed to promote cultural diversity in the United States: Under the general term "cultural pluralism," ideas designed to counteract or moderate the impact of the Anglo conformity view of acculturation became part of the national dialogue shortly after the turn of the century.

In a two-part essay entitled *Democracy versus the Melting Pot,* Kallen (1915) rejected the melting pot theories and the Anglo conformity views of acculturation as models of what was actually transpiring in American life. Observing a vigorously continuing ethnic existence in many different parts of the United States, Kallen felt that America stood at a kind of cultural crossroads. America could persist in policies implied by the melting pot or encourage its ethnic groups to develop democratically by way of each emphasizing its own deep-rooted culture. Kallen (1924) argued for the possibility of a democratic commonwealth as implied in the following:

> Its form would be that of the federal republic; its substance a democracy of nationalities, cooperating voluntarily and autonomously through common institutions in the enterprise of self-realization through the perfection of men according to their kind. The common language . . . of its great tradition, would be English, but each nationality would have for its emotional involuntary life its own peculiar dialect or speech, its own individual and inevitable esthetic and intellectual forms. The political and economic life of the commonwealth is a single unit and serves as the foundation and background for the realization of the distinctive individuality of each *natio* that composes it and of the pooling of these in harmony above them all [p. 124].

Kallen (1915) fundamentally believed that:

> . . . the United States are in the process of becoming a federal state not merely as a union of geographical and administrative unities, but also as a cooperation of cultural diversities, as a federation or commonwealth of national cultures [p. 116].

Kallen proposed this to be the more or less inevitable consequence of democratic ideals since individuals constitute groups, and democracy for theindividual must, by implication, also mean democracy for the group. Thus, Kallen interpreted the term "equal" as it appears in the Declaration of Independence, and the Preamble and the Amendments to the Constitution, as affirmation of the right to be different. While Kallen's writings, in which he coined the term "cultural pluralism," have many aspects, his theme of a "federation of nationalities," with its implication for the creation of geoethnic states, as well as the suggestion that the individual's fate is predetermined by his ethnic group membership, caused some distress among the ranks of the cultural pluralists.

Cultural Pluralism and the Democratic Idea of Choice

Kallen's emphasis on the individual's right to retain his ethnic identity brought about considerable discussion among other cultural pluralists who were concerned with the democratic theme or principle of freedom of choice. Specifically, Berkson (1920) and Drachsler (1920) adopted the position that different ethnic groups should have the right to maintain an ethnic identity and even proposed a variety of ways this might be done; e.g., the creation of ethnic communal centers, or after-public-school-hour ethnic schools. They both favored efforts by the ethnic community to maintain its communal and cultural life, providing a rich and flavorful environment for its successive generations; and they felt that the government should institute in the public schools a program emphasizing knowledge and appreciation of the various cultures. Drachsler argued, however, that whether or not some groups continued to maintain their separate communal existence would be a course legitimately sanctioned by democratic values, since the choice of whether to fuse or to remain separate, either for the group or the individual, should be a free one. This choice, which Drachsler felt should be added to the older American ideas of political and economic democracy, he labeled "cultural democracy."

At the abstract, philosophical level, in both Drachsler's and Berkson's ideas, an important question arose: Cultural pluralism may be democratic for groups, but how democratic is it for individuals? The choice of whether or not to "melt" should be a free one. In his more recent book, *Assimilation in American Life*, Gordon (1964) summarizes this issue:

> The system of cultural pluralism . . . has frequently been described as "cultural democracy," since it posits the right of ethnic groups in a democratic society to maintain their communal identity and their own subcultural values . . . however, we must also point out that democratic values prescribe free choice not only for groups but also for individuals. That is, the individual, *as he matures and reaches the age where rational decision* is feasible, should be allowed to choose freely whether to remain within the boundaries of communality created

by his birthright ethnic group, to branch out into multiple interethnic contacts, or even to change affiliation to that of another ethnic group should he wish to do so. . . . If, to the contrary, the ethnic group places such heavy pressures on its birthright members to stay confined to ethnic communality that the individual who consciously wishes to "branch out" or "move away" feels intimidated or subject to major feelings of personal guilt and, therefore, remains ethnically enclosed, or moves but at a considerable psychological cost, then we have, in effect, cultural democracy for groups but not for individuals. Realistically, *it is probably impossible to have a socialization process for the child growing up in a particular ethnic group that does not involve some implicitly restrictive values; nevertheless, the magnitude and intensity of such restrictive norms must be kept within bounds if we are not to be left with a system which provides cultural democracy for groups but enforced ethnic enclosure for individuals* [pp. 262–263; emphasis added].

Biculturalism and the Concept of Choice

Gordon's analysis contains, from our own perspective, the dilemma of choice which has permeated most views on cultural pluralism. This dilemma is in part due to a persisting view of personality development which contains *mono-* rather than *bi-* or *multi-*cultural orientations. Thus, Gordon's (1964) statement appears to be more concerned with the abstract philosophical democratic principle of "freedom of choice."

> . . . the individual, as he matures and reaches the age where rational decision is feasible, should be allowed to choose freely whether to remain within the boundaries of communality created by his birthright ethnic group, to branch out into multiple interethnic contacts, or even to change affiliation to that of another ethnic group should he wish to do so [p. 263].

We note, however, that Gordon's analysis, with the term "branch out into multiple interethnic contacts," appears to restrict or exclude other potential options involved in choice as it relates to cultural matters. As with other interpretations of cultural democracy, it appears to us that Gordon's interpretation raises the issue of choice as being of the either-or category: the individual either chooses to remain ethnic or chooses to acculturate. This interpretation of cultural democracy appears to assume an *unresolvable conflict or incompatibility* between the "dominant" sociocultural system and other sociocultural systems.

The form of cultural pluralism we wish to describe more fully concentrates on the *bicultural* reality of many Mexican-American children living in the United States today. On the one hand, at the time these children enter school, they are products of the sociocultural system characteristic of their homes and communities. They are now confronted, on the other hand, with being required to acquire the characteristics inherent in the sociocultural system of the school which, we have indicated, is more compatible with the Anglo-American sociocultural systems. The basic educational issue in our interpretation of cultural democracy concerns the need for providing Mexican-American children with the educational experiences necessary to enhance their right to be able to function in *both* cultural worlds, the cultural world of the Mexican-American as well as the cultural world of the Anglo-American. In one sense *both* the Anglo conformity views of acculturation and older interpretations of cultural pluralism have failed to appreciate this psychological necessity on the part of the child. Within the melting pot framework, Mexican-American children have been forced to make the type of choice implied in Gordon's statement and at times in their lives when the ability to make such a "rational choice" has been least developed and the psychological costs of making such a choice considerable.

The writings of many cultural pluralists have placed a major emphasis on the preservation of the language, heritage, and cultural values of the ethnic group. Perhaps this concern has been historically necessary in that the Anglo conformity view of acculturation has been inimical to any notion implying preservation of cultural differences. The basic theme in our interpretation of cultural pluralism is not this preservation as such, but the ability to function in both cultural worlds, whatever their characteristics at any given point in time. The cultural worlds of both the Mexican-American and the Anglo-American have undergone and are undergoing modification and change and, from an educational point of view, it is important for the individual to be able to function in whichever cultural world he finds himself and, at the same time, to contribute to its enrichment and continued development.

Manuel Ramírez is professor of Psychology at the University of Texas at Austin. Alfredo Castañeda, Ph.D. in Clinical Psychology, was professor of Bilingual and Multicultural Education at Stanford University until his death in 1981.

Published originally in M. Ramírez and A.Castañeda, Cultural Democracy, Bicognitive Development, and Education. *(Chapter 2, "Cultural Education"), ©1974 Academic Press, Inc. Reprinted by permission of the publisher and authors.*

"The quality of deliberation makes or breaks a democracy."

Democracy, Deliberation, and the Experience of Women

by Jane Mansbridge

For centuries, while men ran governments and wrote political philosophy, the experience of women had little influence on democratic practice or thought. Recently, however, feminist ideas have been at the center of an emerging debate about the nature of democratic politics.

The dominant tradition in political science sees democracy primarily as a method of summing up individual desires rooted in self-interest. The tradition's critics emphasize that any workable democracy requires that its citizens and representatives think not only as "I," but also as "we." Democracy involves public discussion of common problems, not just a silent counting of individual hands. And when people talk together, the discussion can sometimes lead the participants to see their own stake in the broader interests of the community. Indeed, at its best, the democratic process resolves conflict not only by majority will, but by discovering answers that integrate the interests of minorities. Thus a "deliberative democracy" does not simply register preferences that individuals already have; it encourages citizens to think about their interests differently.

Two strands of feminist writing illuminate the debate on deliberative democracy. One strand, which celebrates women's greater nurturance, modifies and enriches the deliberative framework by providing images and models of practice from women's experience. In this view, women's socialization and role in child rearing, among other causes, makes them especially concerned to transform "I" into "we" and to seek solutions to conflict that accommodate diverse and often suppressed desires. In our society women are usually brought up to identify their own good with that of others, especially their children and husbands. More than men, women build their identities through relationships with friends. As Jennifer Nedelski puts it, the female self has more "permeable" boundaries. Feminist writers propose this capacity for broader self-definition as a model for democratic politics.

Yet, as feminists are also well aware, the very capacity to identify with others can easily be manipulated to the disadvantage of women. A second strand of feminist thought, which focuses on male oppression, warns against deliberation serving as a mask for domination. Permeability, Andrea Dworkin demonstrates, is the avenue for invasion as well as intimacy. The transformation of "I" into "we" brought about through political deliberation can easily mask subtle forms of control. Even the language people use as they reason together usually favors one way of seeing things and discourages others. Subordinate groups sometimes cannot find the right voice or words to express their thoughts and, when they do, they discover that they are not heard. Feminists who focus on the inequality of power between men and women point to the ways women are silenced, encouraged to keep their wants inchoate, and heard to say "yes" when they mean "no." These same insights help us to grasp other forms of domination, such as those based on wealth, that can also infect the deliberative process.

So, as political theorists turn to thinking about democracy as deliberation, feminist thought lends both encouragement and caution. Feminists bring to the new stress on deliberation, experiences of a self accustomed to encompassing others' welfare in its own and achieving that common welfare more by persuasion than by power. Yet feminists also bring a vivid recognition of the capacity of a dominant group to silence or ignore voices it does not wish to hear.

Democracy as Deliberation

Democracy originally meant deliberative democracy. Aristotle, while not a democrat, still concluded that the people in their deliberative capacity could come to better decisions on many matters than could an expert—"just as a feast to which many contribute is better than one provided by a single person." The great writers on democracy in the eighteenth and nineteenth centuries saw democracy as primarily a way of reasoning together to promote the common good. James Madison thought that factions pitted against one another could cancel each other out, allowing men of public virtue the space to deliberate and make wise decisions. John Stuart Mill argued that the most important business of a representative assembly was "talk," bringing to bear different perspectives on the public's interests. Before World War II, Ernest Barker, the great translator of Aristotle's *Politics*, defined democracy not, in its essence, as a matter of voting, but rather as "a method of government by laying heads together, in a common debate in which all share, to attain a result which as many as possible are agreed in accepting."

The political thought that emerged from World War II reversed this emphasis on deliberation and the common good, demanding the recognition of power and conflict. Schools of thought as disparate and mutually contradictory as those of Marx, Freud, Arthur Bentley (founder of the group conflict view of politics), and neoclassical economics all assumed a political world based on self-interest, power, and competing interests.

In 1942, the economist Joseph Schumpeter formalized a deeply influential theory that recast democracy as a marketplace. In democracy, as Schumpeter understood it, there is no common good or public interest. Voters pursue their individual interests by making demands on the political system in proportion to the intensity of their feelings. Politicians, also pursuing their own interests, adopt policies that buy them votes, thus ensuring accountability. To stay in office, politicians act like entrepreneurs and brokers, looking for formulas that satisfy as many interests as possible. The decisions that emerge from the interchange between self-interested voters and self-interested brokers come as close as possible to a balanced sum of individual interests. In politics as marketplace, candidates are commodities, selling themselves or being sold.

For a generation in American political science, Schumpeter's formulation underlay the dominant understanding of democratic practice. It also seemed to many to represent a democratic ideal. The study of pluralism, interest groups, and who gets what, where, when, and how typically assumed that citizens (and their representatives) were self-interested and that interests would conflict. Most of those who criticized the American polity, whether from the right, the mainstream, or the left also agreed with these underlying assumptions about politics as power.

Ten years ago, the tide began to turn again. A few political scientists began to point out that some legislative actions were inexplicable unless representatives cared about good public policy as well as re-election. Legislators in the House and Senate, for example, voted in the late 1970s and early 1980s to deregulate the airline and trucking industries, a move they thought would benefit the public. They did so against strong lobbying by both the unions and the industries, which had close relations with the regulatory commissions. Political scientists now also noticed that citizens took stands on issues like Vietnam and busing, less because the policy they favored would benefit them than because they thought that policy was right.

In small towns, the concern of citizens for the common good was, if anything, even stronger. My own study of a small New England town and a collectively run workplace convinced me that the implicit theory of democracy in these small polities differed sharply from Schumpeter's marketplace model. Schumpeter handled conflict, in theory, by counting and weighing preferences. The members of the communities I came to know assumed that on many issues there was a common good and that reasoning together—deliberation—could let them discover or create that good.

When recent democratic theorists reject the conception of democracy as only a mechanism for aggregating conflicting and self-interested preferences, they draw on several independent philosophical traditions. J. G. A. Pocock and Garry Wills have demonstrated that the framers of the American Constitution, far from reflecting only Lockean individualism, wanted to promote both public spirit and benevolence. Pocock traces the concern for public spirit to Machiavelli's writing on the corruption of republican virtue in Florence; Wills traces the concern for benevolence to the Scottish Enlightenment. Cass Sunstein argues that the United States Supreme Court has never countenanced a theory of democracy based purely on aggregating preferences. Although the Court will generally not look beneath the rationale that legislators present, it has always insisted in principle that legislation be guided by a public interest. Jurgen Habermas, writing on public spaces and the characteristics of an ideal "speech situation," has inspired many to ask what institutions and structures of power are most hospitable to public deliberation.

The new deliberative theorists have suggested various institutional changes to renew the democratic process.

The quality of deliberation makes or breaks a democracy. Good deliberation produces, along with good solutions, the emotional and intellectual resources to accept hard decisions. Active participation in decisions makes it easier to bear—and understand the reasons for—the losses some decisions entail. The manipulation of participation generates cynicism both in the factory and the polity. Deliberation that accords respect to all participants and rests outcomes on reasons and points of view that stand up under questioning generates outcomes that even opponents can respect.

Theorists who promote deliberation, however, sometimes conflate deliberation and the common good. The language not only of Mill and Barker but also of more recent theorists like Benjamin Barber and Joshua Cohen suggests that deliberation must be deliberation on the common good. Deliberation, in this view, must be framed in terms of "we"; claims of self-interest are invalid. Yet ruling self-interest out of order makes it harder for any participant to sort out what is going on. In particular, the less powerful may not find ways to discover that the prevailing sense of "we" does not adequately include them. Deliberation, and the political process more broadly speaking, ought to make participants more aware of their real interests, even when those interests turn out to conflict.

Deliberative theorists also sometimes forget power. When, as often happens, no policy will benefit everyone, democracies require some way of legitimating a process by which one group of people makes another do something that it does not want to do. To avoid giving too much weight to the status quo, democracies must facilitate some exercise of power. They can legitimate the coercion by, in theory, giving each citizen equal power in the process. The system succeeds where each loses on some issues but wins on others. Feminism, in both its nurturant and antioppression strands, can correct the vision of both the unrealistically "hard-nosed" political scientists who insist that politics is nothing but power and the deliberative theorists who either reject power altogether or overlook the ways the powerful often use to their advantage the openness of deliberation, its procedures, and the orientation of many participants toward the common good.

Nurturance: A Politics without Power?

Politics without domination is an ideal with a long ancestry on both its paternal and maternal sides. Claude Henri de Saint-Simon, an early prophet of socialism, and Edward Bellamy, the nineteenth-century American utopian, both wanted to replace the government of men by the administration of things. Karl Marx envisioned the withering away of "political power properly so-called," that is, class domination. John Stuart Mill and Ernest Barker replaced crude power not with administration but with deliberation. Yet when women arrived at their own understanding of politics without domination, their language often carried overtones of their experiences as mothers. The outcome was not quite the same. Nurturance, a particular form of making the other's good your own—invaded the political sphere.

In 1818, Hannah Mather Crocker, an early feminist, argued in almost the same breath that God had "endowed the female mind with equal powers and faculties" to those of men and that "it must be the appropriate duty and privilege of females, to convince by reason and persuasion." One hundred years later, the suffragists used the same formula of equality with difference. Strategically, the suffragists relied on persuasion because they had little political power. Yet many also believed that women would bring virtue into politics by extending the stance of motherhood to the public sphere, substituting persuasion for power, and replacing party politics with Progressive good government.

In *Herland,* a feminist utopian novel published six years before women won the suffrage, Charlotte Perkins Gilman painted a society peopled only by women, where domination had no place. Of the three men who stumble on this utopia, the most aggressive aches to fight, tries to "master" the women, and glorifies competition. The women return patient understanding, meting out no punishments and experiencing no competitive feeling stronger than "a mild triumph as of winning some simple game."

Without Gilman's explicit concern for nurturance, Mary Parker Follett, an organizational theorist writing a generation later, also argued against "domination" ("a victory of one side over the other"). She even opposed "compromise" ("each side gives up a little in order to have peace"), in favor of "integration," which allows neither side "to sacrifice anything." Follett often gave as an example of integration, how one day sitting in a library she had wanted a window shut, while another reader had wanted it open.

Instead, they opened the window in an unoccupied adjacent room. "There was no compromise," she wrote, "because we both got all we really wanted."

What we would now call "win-win" solutions, like those Follett proposed, pose a necessary corrective to politics as a battle of wills. Yet it is easy in some feminist visions to mistake the corrective for the whole story, or to mistake the stress on nurturance or empathy for the conclusion that all of human relations can be encompassed in nurturance.

It is also easy to confuse the normative claim that nurturant or attentive approaches to relationships are good in themselves (or promote other values good in themselves) with the empirical claim that women are more likely than men to adopt these approaches. Whether or not women differ from men in nurturance or attentiveness, the moral claims should stand on their own. We should be able to find the language to make a persuasive case for any claim without appeal to gender. Yet because persuasion rests on experience and some experiences are more socially salient to women (whether or not they have actually had the experience of, say, motherhood itself), the persuasive images that come most easily to women will not always strike a responsive chord in men. Some claims will have to take shape within a community that shares the relevant experiences and later be "translated" for other audiences.

As early as 1968 and 1969, for example, in almost the same moment as discovering themselves as a "class," with separate and sometimes conflicting interests to those of men, women discovered they had a distinct and in some ways superior "culture." For non-separatist strands in feminist thought, the problem became how to integrate the nurturance, listening, and emotional sensitivity of this culture into the politics that women had inherited from men. This project now finds allies among political theorists promoting deliberative democracy.

Feminist Theories of Power

Consider the "femaleness" of nurturance. Some feminists have reacted to the prevailing definition of politics as only power, and power as only domination, by elaborating what Nancy Hartsock calls "the feminist theory of power." Adopting Mary Parker Follett's distinction between "power over" and "power with," they have portrayed power not only as dominance but also as "energy, capacity, and effectiveness." In 1980, Sara Ruddick became the first academic theorist to bring maternal ideals into politics. Arguing against the conjunction of power and powerlessness in the received understanding of motherhood, Ruddick stated as her project "the construction of an image of maternal power which is benign, accurate, sturdy, and sane," suggesting that women bring to the public world a culture and tradition embodied in the ideal of "maternal thinking," with its characteristics of "humility, resilient good humor, realism, respect for persons, and responsiveness to growth." Kathy Ferguson soon urged that in creating new forms of organization, women draw upon values "structured into women's experience—caretaking, nurturance, empathy, connectedness." Virginia Held pointed out that the relation between "mothering parent" and child provides an understanding of power that does not involve bending another to one's will: "The mothering person seeks to empower the child to act responsibly. She wants neither to wield power nor to defend herself against the power wielded by the child." When they are physically weakest, as in infancy and illness, children can "command" the greatest amount of attention and—care because then their needs are so serious.

Neither Ruddick, nor Ferguson, nor Held, nor any of the many theorists now writing in this vein are trying to replace a political vocabulary based on power with one based on care or intimacy. Their aim is to integrate into political thought a rich but neglected vocabulary and set of experiences—neglected because usually allocated to the domestic realm and defined as private, nonpolitical, or even antipolitical. This project of integration requires some subtlety. It requires maintaining useful distinctions between the governmental and nongovernmental, and between the particularism of one-to-one empathy and the universalism of solidarity with all humankind. The project does not require merging the public with the private. But it does require seeing relations formed in the private, domestic, and particular realm as reasonable models for, or the first steps toward, some forms of public spirit. The step the ancient Greeks took in using "philia," or friendship, as "civic friendship," the basis of the state, does not differ in form from the suffragists' step, in "social motherhood," of applying the maternal relation to the larger polity.

Taking motherhood seriously, for example, reveals the radical limitations political theories based on a misplaced analogy to the marketplace. When Robert Nozick suggests that individuals have a primordial right to own and sell what they produce, Susan Okin replies that, in that case, mothers own and have a right to sell their children. Mothers' relations with their children usefully undermine neoclassical models of independent individuals, rights, contracts, or owning and selling.

Listening and Democratic Deliberation

Attentiveness to relationships is not the same as "nurturance." Nancy Chodorow has proposed that boy children may be required, in a society where women give the most care in early childhood, to separate themselves more firmly and oppositionally than girls from their mothers. Thus, in later relationships, men may feel less intrinsically connected with others. Whether for this reason or for reasons derived from a history of subordination, girls and women in the United States do seem to value relationships more than do boys and men. Girls' games, at least in white middle-class communities, take place in small, relatively homogeneous groups and deemphasize the rules and competition that characterize boys' games. Girls and women are better than men at interpreting facial expressions and other interpersonal cues. Women speak less in public than men do, and listen more. As Marlene Dixon put it in 1970, "Women are trained to nuances, to listening for the subtle cues which carry the message hidden under the words. It is part of that special skill called 'intuition' or 'empathy' which all female children must learn if they are to be successful in manipulating others to get what they want and to be successful in providing sympathy and understanding to their husbands and lovers." While the "all" in her sentence undoubtedly exaggerates, it is true that generations upon generations of women have been taught to be good listeners. As early as the fifth century B.C., Sophocles said, "Silence is a woman's crown."

The skills of listening—though not of silence—do seem to produce better decisions. The laboratory experiments of social psychologists suggest that the best group decisions (those most likely to produce a "correct" answer or a creative solution) come when members solicit the opinions of individuals who are initially in a minority. When an experimenter instructs a group to consult every member, the group makes more correct decisions than without these instructions. When leaders facilitate the emergence of minority opinion, their groups perform better than leaderless groups. Organizational consultants have learned from the psychologists the useful though rather jarring phrase, "I hear you saying. . . ." To say those words, you need to have listened, and others have a chance to correct what you think you've heard. Without this jargon, feminists teach the same lesson—listening.

Along with promoting an ethic of care and skill in listening, feminist thinkers have also suggested a critical role for the emotions in deliberation. Emotions help tell us who we want to be. Good deliberation is not fostered by "keeping emotion out of it." Rather, "integrative" or "win-win" solutions often require the emotional capacity to guess what others want, or at least to ask in a genuinely curious and unthreatening way. It takes emotional ability to elicit from people in conflict the sometimes subconscious sentiments and unobserved facts that can help create an integrative solution.

Union members sometimes strike in support of another union's demands; some childless property owners vote for higher taxes to improve the schools. Such actions are based not only on a rational commitment to maxims that one would will to be universal or on a belief in achieving the greatest good for the greatest number, but also on a process that has evoked empathy, solidarity, or the commitment of one's identity and actions to a principle. The presence of others with interests different from one's own makes it hard, rightly or wrongly, to insist on claims based on pure self-interest. When people with competing claims come face to face, the conflict not only creates selfish competitiveness; it also often becomes emotionally clearer how self-interested behavior can harm others. When individuals are capable of principled commitment or solidarity, engaging the emotions helps create the self-transformations necessary to think "we" instead of "I."

Overcoming the Subtle Forms of Power

But who is the "we" in a deliberation? "We" can easily represent a false universality, as "mankind" used to do. Even if spoken and believed by the subordinate, "we" may mask a relationship that works against the subordinate's interests. Women's experience of silence, of unexplored wants, of words that do not mean (and are not heard to mean) what they say, and of subtle forms of domination generalize beyond gender to alert both theorists and practitioners to the pitfalls of unequal power in deliberation.

Silence, on its positive side, permits listening. On the negative side, a history of relative silence makes women political actors more likely to understand that when deliberation turns into theater, it leaves out many who are not, by nature or training, actors. When deliberation turns into a demonstration of logic, it leaves out many who cannot work their emotionally felt needs into a neat equation. When many voices compete for the deliberative floor, the sample that gets heard is not representative.

Many shy men are quiet, but the equivalent percentage of shy women is increased by learning silence as appropriate to their gender. So, too, it is the human condition, not just a gendered condition, not to know what one wants. But over and above the human condition, women were taught—at least as I was growing up—not to have too strongly defined wants. Boys wondered, as early as "soldier, sailor, Indian chief," which kinds of work they were suited for. Middle-class boys wondered what careers they would choose. Girls like myself wondered, instead, what kind of man they would marry. My mother, always practical, increased my range of options in the best way she knew how. She brought me up with an array of skills, she told me more than once, so that I might marry either "a prince or a pauper."

Training to be chosen, rather than to choose, includes not allowing one's wants to become too definite. Keeping one's wants indefinite makes it even harder than usual for one's intellect to learn the signs the self emits of wanting one thing rather than another. Knowing how easy it is to keep one's wants indefinite makes women realize that deliberative assemblies must work actively at helping participants discover and create what they truly want. Preferences themselves, let alone interests, are not given. They must be tentatively voiced, tested, examined against the causes that produced them, explored, and finally made one's own. Good deliberation must rest on institutions that foster dissent and on images of appropriate behavior that allow for fumbling and changing one's mind, that respect the tentativeness of this process. Only such safeguards can help participants find where they themselves want to go.

Words are the very stuff of deliberation. But women traditionally have been trained not to say what they mean. Carole Pateman directs us to the last chapter of Rousseau's *Emile*, the first handbook of progressive education, designed to produce a virtuous and naturally healthy man and woman. After all the brave first chapters, where Emile is raised to emotional honesty and to despise the hypocrisy of the city and the court, it comes as a shock, when Rousseau turns to Sophie, to have him teach her to say "no" when she means "yes," and teach Emile, in response, to act as if she had said "yes," not "no." In the very paragraph where Rousseau puts forth the radical doctrine that all sexual intercourse, even in marriage, must be based on mutual desire, he states that men must disregard verbal signs of nonconsent to read consent in women's looks.

As rapes increase across the United States, but it becomes gradually illegal, state by state, to have intercourse with one's wife against her will, women have particular reason to want their "no" taken to mean "no" and not "yes," and to want women taught, like men, to say "no" when they mean "no."

It is not hard to see how deliberation is distorted when subordinates say "yes" ("Yes, boss") when they mean "no." The convolutions of mismeaning embedded in men's and women's dance of domination and subordination reveal other layers, and other types of distortion, of which both parties may be unaware, and in which the larger culture is complicit.

It has been the decade of deconstruction, semiotics, and Foucault. As deconstruction picks apart a piece of literature to see what lies behind, as semiotics sees every pause, word, or nonword as a signifier, as Foucault uncovers power in the interstices of every social act, these currents have served as allies, often consciously unwanted, in the feminist enterprise of unmasking, and guarding against, subtle forms of domination.

An important example of this enterprise, on the theoretical plane, is Andrea Dworkin and Catharine MacKinnon's analysis of the domination implicit in the act of intercourse. Dworkin and MacKinnon suggest that in the average act of sexual intercourse the fact that one person penetrates and the other is penetrated, one thrusts and the other receives, encodes a pattern of domination and subordination, reinforced in some cases by top versus bottom position, initiator versus initiate, and other reflections or coy reversals of external structures of power. Feminists have brought out the power imbalances inherent in many subtle acts—the clothing the two genders use, the hairstyle, makeup, laughter, and attitudes toward food or one's own body.

Women, more than most oppressed groups, have come to learn the covert as well as the overt faces of power. Many women, no matter how active as feminists, have loved their fathers, sons, sometimes their male lovers or husbands. And many men have loved women, sometimes (at least in the modern era) with a strong conscious commitment to creating in the social world, or at least their intimate relations, the equality they perceive "underneath." Because this love and commitment to equality are also bound up tightly with conscious and unconscious forms of domination, women have had to begin learning to parse out the confused grammars of love and power.

Sensitivity to subtle forms of power pervaded the egalitarianism and commitment to consensus of the early radical women's movement. It continues today to inspire the National Women's Studies Association's experiments with equalizing power, like its caucuses for constituencies who feel they have a less-than-equal voice. Mainstream women's organizations share the same concerns. The League of Women Voters from its beginning has made decisions by what the organization calls "consensus," namely "agreement among a substantial number of members, representative of the membership as a whole, reached after sustained study and group discussion." The aim is deliberation, and decision through persuasion. Throughout the 1970s and 1980s state and local branches of the National Organization for Women fought inequalities in power among their members, suggesting in Massachusetts in

1972, for example, a rotating president because "they didn't want to have a star system."

Used indiscriminately, practices aimed at ensuring equality and consensus can undermine deliberation, not advance it. We need laboratories, which feminist practice abundantly provides, to assess which forms work and which do not.

"Difference" as a Political Strategy

To say that feminists can add something new to political theory through their understanding of women's experience does not require believing that women are "essentially" different. It requires only that certain experiences be distributed unequally between men and women. A fairly small difference in experience can become a large difference in self-image and social perception. If one group is dominant, as men are, they typically take pains to avoid the language and images attributed to the subordinates. The subordinate group, on the other hand, is torn between pride in its own language and images and a desire to emulate the dominant group.

Empathy—the quality of being able to put oneself emotionally in another's place, may serve as an example. Women are typically seen, and see themselves, as more empathetic than men. Research on empathy, however, shows gender difference to vary dramatically depending on how empathy is measured. In experimental studies simulating emotional situations, few differences between men and women show up in physiological reactions or reports of feelings of sympathy or concern. But when asked on questionnaires to respond to items such as "I tend to get emotionally involved with a friend's problems," girls and women score much higher on empathy than do boys and men. The social reputation for difference is as important as any difference in behavior. For it suggests an alternative model—an ideal type of behavior valued by the subordinate group.

In some parts of their lives, women and men do have dramatically different experiences. Women give birth, nurse, and are socialized for child rearing. They are far more likely to be raped, battered, and the victims of incest, or to have to plan their lives around the fear of rape. They are more likely to become secretaries, nurses, or elementary school teachers, to have interrupted careers, and to experience poverty. But not every women has given birth or been raped. Some manage to avoid the pervasive fear of rape. A few arrange job trajectories much like those of men.

In many other respects, men's and women's experiences overlap greatly. Since on many psychological, social, and political measures the means between the two sexes are so close, almost half the men in any group have had a certain "female" experience or trait more often than half the women. The same is true of women in regard to "masculine" traits and experiences.

Because socialization to gender is not merely a passive response to punishment and reward but rather the result of an active, engaged building of the personality, and because healthy people tend to like and want to be who they are, children probably value being a boy or a girl long before they know what that means. As children create themselves, they learn that gender is a salient identifying characteristic and adopt the traits their social milieus associate with women or men. Even in the future, when I expect the significance of gender to diminish greatly, biological sex will continue to be sexy.

Whenever we learn, as adults or children, that certain features of human personality or action are socially salient, we become more conscious of those features, perhaps even exaggerating them in our minds, as we absorb them into our self-image. Social images grow in much the same way. When a distinction makes a difference in a culture, we build those distinctions into schemas, or stories, that explain the world. The mirror of society magnifies emotions and behavior already enlarged in the mirror of the self.

These magnified distinctions influence our ways of knowing. Ways of knowing associated with women can be scorned as "soft," ways of knowing associated with men praised as "hard." The nature of inquiry itself can become part of an overall pattern of domination. When the subordinate classes fight back, they can expose the power relations inherent in the dominant paradigm. Fighting as women for women's ways of knowing binds women closer in sisterhood, reinforcing common experience. It also shoots adrenaline into the collective intellectual system, helping to see the world differently, and sometimes more clearly.

Out of this process can come critical intellectual tools. Take Carol Gilligan's distinction between the "male" emphasis on rights versus the "female" emphasis on relationships. Differences between men and women do appear both on Kohlberg's scales of moral development (in which women often appear at a "lower" stage of development) and on Carol Gilligan's and her colleagues' more recent measures of orientation to rights and relationships. These differences are often so small that they do not show up in every study or reach statistical significance when the cases are few in number. But even if there were no differences between men and women on these dimensions in actual behavior, if the differences persisted in social image they would help us understand how one way of looking at moral questions—a "different voice" that stresses relationships rather than rights—could have been passed over in the development of moral theory.

That different voice is by no means unanimously female. Gilligan herself points out that many men also speak with a different voice. But by signaling that the previously overlooked and discredited perspective is typically, if only by a small margin, a woman's perspective and can easily be perceived, through the lens of self and social image, as a woman's perspective, she not only explains its previous subordination, she also mobilizes to fight for it as a legitimate perspective in its own right. Reading Gilligan's A *Different Voice* angers women. It helps explain why whole disciplines have devalued what "women" do, and it gives women the energy to fight back, with their sisters, the next time it happens. As they fight back, the men who also adopt a "different voice" benefit, too. And so, with luck, does the larger human analytic enterprise.

A focus on women's differences from men goes a long way toward building feminist solidarity. However, for the purpose of changing mainstream— that is—male practices and ideas, the strategy is double-edged. Any idea should be persuasive in its own right. Harnessing that idea to women's differences from men assures it the automatic attention given anything related to sex. At the same time, yoking the idea to the age-old "war between the sexes" will work for or against it, depending on the audience. There are costs to such a strategy—in possibly neglecting nongendered arguments for the idea, in seeming to diminish its scope, in seeming to suggest that the differences between men and women are large, innate, or ineradicable, in eliminating potential audiences, in discounting the experiences of the many, both men and women, whose feelings are not congruent with gendered social expectations, and in tapping emotional sources of intellectual activity that can blind as well as clarify. There are also benefits—in generating the idea in the first place, getting people to think about it, explaining previous denigration, and providing through the connection with gender the language and additional perspectives that help the idea make sense.

In the next decades, feminism is bound to be a fertile source of insight not only into its main subject of gender relations, but also into most other human relations that involve inequalities of power or making another's good one's own. Regardless of the strategy chosen, feminists need allies when their goal is improving mainstream political practice and thought. In the near future feminists can find allies in the political theorists and empirical political scientists who are newly concerned with the quality of deliberation. And when democratic theorists are in search of provocative and useful new ideas, they can find them in the constantly growing corpus of feminist theory.

Jane Mansbridge is professor of Political Science and Sociology, and member of the research faculty at the Center for Urban Affairs and Policy Research, Northwestern University. She is author of Beyond Adversary Democracy *and* Why We Lost the ERA, *both published by the University of Chicago Press.*

Originally published in The American Prospect, *Spring 1990: 126–139. Reprinted with permission of the author.*

"We have now reached a new stage in the perennial struggle for freedom and dignity."

The New Cultural Politics of Difference

by Cornel West

In these last few years of the twentieth century, there is emerging a significant shift in the sensibilities and outlooks of critics and artists. In fact, I would go so far as to claim that a new kind of cultural worker is in the making, associated with a new politics of difference. These new forms of intellectual consciousness advance reconceptions of the vocation of critic and artist, attempting to undermine the prevailing disciplinary divisions of labor in the academy, museum, mass media, and gallery networks, while preserving modes of critique within the ubiquitous commodification of culture in the global village. Distinctive features of the new cultural politics of difference are to trash the monolithic and homogeneous in the name of diversity, multiplicity, and heterogeneity; to reject the abstract, general, and universal in light of the concrete, specific, and particular; and to historicize, contextualize, and pluralize by highlighting the contingent, provisional, variable, tentative, shifting, and changing. Needless to say, these gestures are not new in the history of criticism or art, yet what makes them novel—along with the cultural politics they produce—is how and what constitutes difference, the weight and gravity it is given in representation and the way in which highlighting issues like exterminism, empire, class, race, gender, sexual orientation, age, nation, nature, and region at this historical moment acknowledges some discontinuity and disruption from previous forms of cultural critique. To put it bluntly, the new cultural politics of difference consists of creative responses to the precise circumstances of our present moment—especially those of marginalized First World agents who shun degraded self-representations, articulating instead their sense of the flow of history in light of the contemporary terrors, anxieties, and fears of highly commercialized North Atlantic capitalist cultures (with their escalating xenophobias against people of color, Jews, women, gays, lesbians, and the elderly). The thawing, yet still rigid, Second World excommunist cultures (with increasing nationalist revolts against the legacy of hegemonic party henchmen) and the diverse cultures of the majority of inhabitants on the globe, smothered by international communication cartels and repressive postcolonial elites (sometimes in the name of communism, as in Ethiopia), or starved by austere World Bank and IMF policies that subordinate them to the North (as in free-market capitalism in Chile) also locate vital areas of analysis in this new cultural terrain.

The new cultural politics of difference is neither simply oppositional in contesting the mainstream (or *male*stream) for inclusion, nor transgressive in the avant-gardist sense of shocking conventional bourgeois audiences. Rather, they are distinct articulations of talented (and usually privileged) contributors to culture who desire to align themselves with demoralized, demobilized, depoliticized, and disorganized people in order to empower and enable social action and, if possible, to enlist collective insurgency for the expansion of freedom, democracy, and individuality. This perspective impels these cultural critics and artists to reveal, as an integral component of their production, the very operations of power within their immediate work contexts (i.e., academy, museum, gallery, mass media). This strategy, however, also puts them in an inescapable double bind—while linking their activities to the fundamental, structural overhaul of these institutions, they often remain financially dependent on them (so much for "independent" creation). For these critics of culture, theirs is a gesture that is simultaneously progressive *and* co-opted. Yet without social movement or political pressure from outside these institutions (extraparliamentary and extracurricular actions like the social movements of the recent past), transformation degenerates into mere accommodation or sheer stagnation, and the role of the "co-opted progressive"—no matter how fervent one's subversive rhetoric—is rendered more difficult. There can be no artistic breakthrough or social progress without some form of crisis in civilization—a crisis usually generated by organizations or collectivities that convince ordinary people to put their bodies and lives on the line. There is, of course, no guarantee that such pressure will yield the result one wants, but there is a guarantee that the status quo will remain or regress if no pressure is applied at all.

The new cultural politics of difference faces three basic challenges—intellectual, existential, and political. The intellectual challenge—usually cast as methodological debate in these days in which academicist forms of expression have a monopoly on intellectual life—is how to think about representational practices in terms of history, culture, and society. How does one understand, analyze, and enact such practices today? An adequate answer to this question can be attempted only after one comes to terms with the insights and blindnesses of earlier attempts to grapple with the question in light of the evolving crisis in different histories, cultures, and societies. I shall sketch a brief genealogy—a history that highlights the contingent origins and often ignoble outcomes—of exemplary critical responses to the question. This genealogy sets forth a historical framework that characterizes the rich, yet deeply flawed, Eurocentric traditions which the new cultural politics of difference build upon, yet go beyond.

The Intellectual Challenge

An appropriate starting point is the ambiguous legacy of the Age of Europe. Between 1492 and 1945, European breakthroughs in oceanic transportation, agricultural production, state-consolidation, bureaucratization, industrialization, urbanization, and imperial dominion shaped the makings of the modern world. Precious ideals like the dignity of persons (individuality) or the popular accountability of institutions (democracy) were unleashed around the world. Powerful critiques of illegitimate authorities—of the Protestant Reformation against the Roman Catholic church, the Enlightenment against state churches, liberal movements against absolutist states and feudal guild constraints, workers against managerial subordination, people of color and Jews against white and gentile supremacist decrees, gays and lesbians against homophobic sanctions—were fanned and fueled by these precious ideals refined within the crucible of the Age of Europe. Yet the discrepancy between sterling rhetoric and lived reality, glowing principles and actual practices loomed large.

By the last European century—the last epoch in which European domination of most of the globe was uncontested and unchallenged in a substantive way—a new world seemed to be stirring. At the height of England's reign as the major imperial European power, its exemplary cultural critic, Matthew Arnold, painfully observed in his *Stanzas From the Grand Chartreuse* that he felt some sense of "wandering between two worlds, one dead / the other powerless to be born." Following his Burkean sensibilities of cautious reform and fear of anarchy, Arnold acknowledged that the old glue—religion—that had tenuously and often unsuccessfully held together the ailing European regimes could not do so in the mid-nineteenth century. Like Alexis de Tocqueville in France, Arnold saw that the democratic temper was the wave of the future. So he proposed a new conception of culture—a secular, humanistic one—that could play an integrative role in cementing and stabilizing an emerging bourgeois civil society and imperial state. His famous castigation of the immobilizing materialism of the declining aristocracy, the vulgar philistinism of the emerging middle classes, and the latent explosiveness of the working-class majority was motivated by a desire to create new forms of cultural legitimacy, authority, and order in a rapidly changing moment in nineteenth-century Europe.

As an organic intellectual of an emergent middle class—as the inspector of schools in an expanding educational bureaucracy, Professor of Poetry at Oxford (the first noncleric and the first to lecture in English rather than Latin) and an active participant in a thriving magazine network—Arnold defined and defended a new secular culture of critical discourse. For him, this discursive strategy would be lodged in the educational and periodical apparatuses of modern societies as they contained and incorporated the frightening threats of an arrogant aristocracy, and especially of an "anarchic" working-class majority. His ideals of disinterested, dispassionate, and objective inquiry would regulate this new secular cultural production, and his justifications for the use of state power to quell any threats to the survival and security of this culture were widely accepted. He aptly noted, "Through culture seems to lie our way, not only to perfection, but even to safety."

This sentence is revealing in two ways. First, it refers to "our way" without explicitly acknowledging who constitutes the "we." This move is symptomatic among many bourgeois, male Eurocentric critics whose universalizing gestures exclude (by guarding a silence around), or explicitly degrade, women and people of color. Second, the sentence links culture to safety—presumably the safety of the "we" against the barbaric threats of the "them"; i.e., those viewed as different in some debased manner. Needless to say, Arnold's negative attitudes toward British working-class people, women, and especially Indians and Jamaicans in the Empire clarify why he conceives of culture as, in part, a weapon for bourgeois male European "safety."

For Arnold, the best of the Age of Europe—modeled on a mythological mélange of Periclean Athens, late Republican/early Imperial Rome and Elizabethan England—could be promoted only if there was an interlocking affiliation among the emerging middle classes, a homogenizing of cultural discourse in the educational and university networks, and a state advanced enough in its policing techniques to safeguard it. The candidates for participation and legitimation in this grand endeavor of cultural renewal and revision would be detached intellectuals willing to shed their parochialism, provincialism, and class-bound identities for Arnold's middle-class-skewed project: ". . . Aliens, if we may so call them—persons who are mainly led, not by their class spirit, but by a general *humane* spirit, by the love of human perfection." Needless to say, this Arnoldian perspective still informs much of the academic practices and secular cultural attitudes today—dominant views about the canon, admission procedures, and collective self-definitions of intellectuals. Yet Arnold's project was disrupted by the collapse of nineteenth-century Europe—World War I. This unprecedented war brought to the surface the crucial role and violent potential not of the masses Arnold feared, but of the state he heralded. Upon the ashes of this wasteland of human carnage—some of it the civilian European population—T. S. Eliot emerged as the grand cultural spokesman.

Eliot's project of reconstituting and reconceiving European highbrow culture—and thereby regulating critical and artistic practices—after the internal collapse of imperial Europe can be viewed as a response to the probing question posed by Paul Valéry in *The Crisis of the Spirit* after World War I,

> This Europe, will it become what it is in reality; i.e., a little cape of the Asiatic continent? or will this Europe remain rather what it seems; i.e., the priceless part of the whole earth, the pearl of the globe, the brain of a vast body?

Eliot's image of Europe as a wasteland, a culture of fragments with no cementing center, predominated in postwar Europe. And though his early poetic practices were more radical, open, and international than his Eurocentric criticism, Eliot posed a return to and revision of tradition as the only way of regaining European cultural order and political stability. For Eliot, contemporary history had become, as James Joyce's Stephen declared in *Ulysses* (1922), "a nightmare from which he was trying to awake"—"an immense panorama of futility and anarchy," as Eliot put it in his renowned review of Joyce's modernist masterpiece. In his influential essay, "Tradition and the Individual Talent," (1919) Eliot stated:

> Yet if the only form of tradition, of handing down, consisted in following the ways of the immediate generation before us in a blind or timid adherence to its successes, "tradition" should positively be discouraged. We have seen many such simple currents soon lost in the sand; and novelty is better than repetition. Tradition is a matter of much wider significance. It cannot be inherited, and if you want it you must attain it by great labour.

Eliot's fecund notion of tradition is significant in that it promotes a historicist sensibility in artistic practice and cultural reflection. This historicist sensibility—regulated in Eliot's case by a reactionary politics—produced a powerful assault on existing literary canons (in which, for example, Romantic poets were displaced by the Metaphysical and Symbolist ones) and unrelenting attacks on modern Western civilization (such as the liberal ideas of democracy, equality, and freedom). Like Arnold's notion of culture, Eliot's idea of tradition was part of his intellectual arsenal, to be used in the battles raging in European cultures and societies.

Eliot found this tradition in the Church of England, to which he converted in 1927. Here was a tradition that left room for his Catholic cast of mind, Calvinistic heritage, puritanical temperament, and rebullient patriotism for the old American South (the place of his upbringing). Like Arnold, Eliot was obsessed with the idea of civilization and the horror barbarism (echoes of Joseph Conrad's Kurtz in *Heart of Darkness*) or, more pointedly, the notion of the decline and decay of European civilization. With the advent of World War II, Eliot's obsession became a reality. Again, unprecedented human carnage (50 million dead)—including an indescribable genocidal attack on Jewish people—throughout Europe, as well as around the globe, put the last nail in the coffin of the Age of Europe. After 1945, Europe consisted of a devastated and divided continent, crippled by a humiliating dependency on and deference to the USA and USSR.

The second historical coordinate of my genealogy is the emergence of the USA as *the* world power. The USA was unprepared for world power status. However, with the recovery of Stalin's Russia (after losing 20 million dead), the USA felt compelled to make its presence felt around the globe. Then, with the Marshall plan to strengthen Europe against Russian influence (and provide new markets for U.S. products), the 1948 Russian takeover of Czechoslovakia, the 1948 Berlin blockade, the 1950 beginning of the Korean War, and the 1952 establishment of NATO forces in Europe, it seemed clear that there was no escape from world power obligations.

The post-World War II era in the USA, or the first decades of what Henry Luce envisioned as "The American Century," was not only a period of incredible economic expansion but of active cultural ferment. In the classical Fordist formula, mass production required mass consumption. With unchallenged hegemony in the capitalist world, the USA took economic growth for granted. Next to exercising its crude, anticommunist, McCarthyist obsessions, buying commodities became the primary act of civic virtue for many American citizens at this time. The creation of a mass middle class—a prosperous working class with a bourgeois identity—was countered by the first major emergence of subcultures of American non-WASP intellectuals: the so-called New York intellectuals in criticism, the Abstract Expressionists in painting, the BeBop artists in jazz music. This emergence signaled a vital challenge to an American male WASP elite loyal to an older and eroding European culture.

The first significant blow was dealt when assimilated Jewish-Americans entered the higher echelons of the cultural apparatuses (academy, museums, galleries, mass media). Lionel Trilling is an emblematic figure. This Jewish entree into the anti-Semitic and patriarchal critical discourse of the exclusivistic institutions of American culture initiated the slow but sure undoing of the male WASP cultural hegemony and homogeneity. Lionel Trilling's project was to appropriate Matthew Arnold for his own political and cultural purposes—thereby unraveling the old male WASP consensus, while erecting a new post–World War II liberal academic consensus around cold war, anti-communist renditions of the values of complexity, difficulty, variousness, and modulation. In addition, the postwar boom laid the basis for intense professionalization and specialization in expanding institutions of higher education—especially in the natural sciences that were compelled to somehow respond to Russia's successful ventures in space. Humanistic scholars found themselves searching for new methodologies that could buttress self-images of rigor and scientific seriousness. For example, the close reading techniques of New Criticism (severed from their conservative, organicist, anti-industrialist ideological roots), the logical precision of reasoning in analytic philosophy, and the jargon of Parsonian structural-functionalism in sociology helped create such self-images. Yet towering cultural critics such as C. Wright Mills, W. E. B. Du Bois, Richard Hofstadter, Margaret Mead, and Dwight MacDonald bucked the tide. This suspicion of the academicization of knowledge is expressed in Trilling's well-known essay "On the Teaching of Modern Literature."

Trilling laments the fact that university instruction often quiets and domesticates radical and subversive works of art, turning them into objects "of merely habitual regard." This process of "the socialization of the antisocial, or the acculturation of the anticultural, or the legitimization of the subversive" leads Trilling to "question whether in our culture the study of literature is any longer a suitable means for developing and refining the intelligence." Trilling asks this question not in the spirit of denigrating and devaluing the academy but rather in the spirit of highlighting the possible failure of an Arnoldian conception of culture to contain what he perceives as the Philistine and anarchic alternatives becoming more and more available to students of the sixties—namely, mass culture and radical politics.

This threat is partly associated with the third historical coordinate of my genealogy—the decolonization of the Third World. It is crucial to recognize the importance of this world-historical process if one wants to grasp the significance of the end of the Age of Europe and the emergence of the USA as a world power. With the first defeat of a Western nation by a non-Western nation—in Japan's victory over Russia (1905), revolutions in Persia (1905), Turkey (1908), China (1912), Mexico (1911–12), and, much later, the independence of India (1947) and China (1948), and the triumph of Ghana (1957)—the actuality of a decolonized globe loomed large. Born of violent struggle, consciousness-raising, and the reconstruction of identities, decolonization simultaneously brings with it new perspectives on that long festering underside of the Age of Europe (of which colonial domination represents the *costs* of "progress," "order," and "culture"), as well as requiring new readings of the economic boom in the USA (wherein the black, brown, yellow, red, female, elderly, gay, lesbian, and white working class live the same *costs* as cheap labor at home as well as in U.S.-dominated Latin American and Pacific rim markets).

The impetuous ferocity and moral outrage that motors the decolonization process is best captured by Frantz Fanon in *The Wretched of the Earth* (1961). Fanon's strong words, though excessively Manichean, still describe the feelings and thoughts between the occupying British Army and colonized Irish in Northern Ireland, the occupying Israeli Army and subjugated Palestinians on the West Bank and Gaza Strip, the South African Army and oppressed black South Africans in the townships, the Japanese Police and Koreans living in Japan, the Russian Army and subordinated Armenians and others in the Southern and Eastern USSR. His words also partly invoke the sense many black Americans have toward police departments in urban centers. In other words, Fanon is articulating century-long heartfelt human responses to being degraded and despised, hated and hunted, oppressed and exploited, marginalized and dehumanized at the hands of powerful xenophobic European, American, Russian, and Japanese imperial countries.

During the late 1950s, 1960s, and early 1970s in the USA, these decolonized sensibilities fanned and fueled the Civil Rights and Black Power movements, as well as the student antiwar, feminist, gray, brown, gay, and lesbian movements. In this period we witnessed the shattering of male WASP cultural homogeneity and the collapse of the short-lived liberal consensus. The inclusion of African-Americans, Latino/a-Americans, Asian-Americans, Native Americans and American women into the culture of critical discourse yielded intense intellectual polemics and inescapable ideological polarization that focused principally on the exclusions, silences, and blindnesses of male WASP cultural homogeneity and its concomitant Arnoldian notions of the canon.

In addition, these critiques promoted three crucial processes that affected intellectual life in the country. First is the appropriation of the theories of postwar Europe—especially the work of the Frankfurt school (Marcuse, Adorno, Horkheimer), French/Italian Marxisms (Sartre, Althusser, Lefebvre, Gramsci), structuralisms (Lévi-Strauss, Todorov), and poststructuralisms (Deleuze, Derrida, Foucault). These diverse and disparate theories—all preoccupied with keeping alive radical projects after the end of the Age of Europe—tend to fuse versions of transgressive European modernisms with Marxist or post-Marxist left politics and unanimously shun the term "postmodernism." Second, there is the recovery and revisioning of American history in light of the struggles of white male workers, women, African-Americans, Native Americans, Latino/a-Americans, gays, and lesbians. Third is the impact of forms of popular culture such as television, film, music videos, and even sports, on highbrow literate culture. The black-based hip-hop culture of youth around the world is one grand example.

After 1973, with the crisis in the international world economy, America's slump in productivity, the challenge of OPEC nations to the North Atlantic monopoly of oil production, the increasing competition in high-tech sectors of the economy from Japan and West Germany, and the growing fragility of the international debt structure, the USA entered a period of waning self-confidence (compounded by Watergate) and a nearly contracting economy. As the standards of living for the middle classes declined, owing to runaway inflation, and the quality of living fell for most, due to escalating unemployment, underemployment and crime, religious and secular neoconservatism emerged with power and potency. This fusion of fervent neonationalism, traditional cultural values, and "free-market" policies served as the ground work for the Reagan-Bush era.

The ambiguous legacies of the European Age, American preeminence, and decolonization continue to haunt our postmodern moment as we come to terms with both the European, American, Japanese, Soviet, and Third World *crimes against* and *contributions to* humanity. The plight of Africans in the New World can be instructive in this regard.

By 1914 European maritime empires had dominion over more than half of the land and a third of the peoples in the world—almost 72 million square kilometers of territory and more than 560 million people under colonial rule. Needless to say, this European control included brutal enslavement, institutional terrorism, and cultural degradation of black diaspora people. The death of roughly 75 million Africans during the centuries-long transatlantic slave trade is but one reminder, among others, of the assault on black humanity. The black diaspora condition of New World servitude—in which they were viewed as mere commodities with production value, who had no proper legal status, social standing, or public worth—can be characterized as, following Orlando Patterson, natal alienation. This state of perpetual and inheritable domination that diaspora Africans had at birth produced the *modern black diaspora problematic of invisibility and namelessness.* White supremacist practices—enacted under the auspices of the prestigious cultural authorities of the churches, printed media, and scientific academics—promoted black inferiority and constituted the European background against which black diaspora struggles for identity, dignity (self-confidence, self-respect, self-esteem), and material resources took place.

An inescapable aspect of this struggle was that the black diaspora people's quest for validation and recognition occurred on the ideological, social, and cultural terrains of other nonblack peoples. White supremacist assaults on black intelligence, ability, beauty and character required persistent black efforts to hold self-doubt, self-contempt, and even self-hatred at bay. Selective appropriation, incorporation, and rearticulation of European ideologies, cultures, and institutions alongside an African heritage—a heritage more or less confined to linguistic innovation in rhetorical practices, stylizations of the body in forms of occupying an alien social space (hairstyles, ways of walking, standing, hand expressions, talking) and means of constituting and sustaining camaraderie and community (e.g., antiphonal, call-and-response styles, rhythmic repetition, risk-ridden syncopation in spectacular modes in musical and rhetorical expressions)—were some of the strategies employed.

The modern black diaspora problematic of invisibility and namelessness can be understood as the condition of *relative lack of Black Power to represent themselves to themselves and others as complex human beings, and thereby to contest the bombardment of negative, degrading stereotypes put forward by white supremacist ideologies.* The initial black response to being caught in this whirlwind of Europeanization was to resist the misrepresentation and caricature of the terms set by uncontested nonblack norms and models and fight for self-representation and recognition. Every modern black person, especially cultural disseminators, encounters this problematic of invisibility and namelessness. The initial black diaspora response was a mode of resistance that was *moralistic in content* and *communal in character.* That is, the fight for representation and recognition highlighted moral judgments regarding black "positive" images over and against white supremacist stereotypes. These images "re-presented" monolithic and homogeneous black communities, in a way that could displace past misrepresentations of these communities. Stuart Hall has talked about these responses as attempts to change "the relations of representation."

These courageous, yet limited, black efforts to combat racist cultural practices uncritically accepted nonblack conventions and standards in two ways. First, they proceeded in an *assimilationist manner* that set out to show that black people were really like white people—thereby eliding differences (in history, culture) between whites and blacks. Black specificity and particularity was thus banished in order to gain white acceptance and approval. Second, these black responses rested upon a *homogenizing impulse* that assumed that all black people were really alike—hence obliterating differences (class, gender, region, sexual orientation) between black peoples. I submit that there are elements of truth in both claims, yet the conclusions are unwarranted owing to the basic fact that nonblack paradigms set the terms of the replies.

The insight in the first claim is that blacks and whites are in some important sense alike—i.e., in their positive capacities for human sympathy, moral sacrifice, service to others, intelligence, and beauty or, negatively, in their capacity for cruelty. Yet the common humanity they share is jettisoned when the claim is cast in an assimilationist manner that subordinates black particularity to a false universalism; i.e., nonblack rubrics or prototypes. Similarly, the insight in the second claim is that all blacks are in some significant sense "in the same boat"—that is, subject to white supremacist abuse. Yet this common condition is stretched too far when viewed in a *homogenizing* way that overlooks how racist treatment vastly differs owing to class, gender, sexual orientation, nation, region, hue, and age.

The moralistic and communal aspects of the initial black diaspora responses to social and psychic erasure were not simply cast into simplistic binary oppositions of positive/negative, good/bad images that privileged the first term in light of a white norm so that black efforts remained inscribed within the very logic that dehumanized them. They were further complicated by the fact that these responses were also advanced principally by anxiety-ridden, middle-class black intellectuals (predominantly male and heterosexual), grappling with their sense of double-consciousness—namely, their own crisis of identity, agency, and audience—caught between a quest for white approval and acceptance and an endeavor to overcome the internalized association of blackness with inferiority. And I suggest that these complex anxieties of modern black diaspora intellectuals partly motivate the two major arguments that ground the assimilationist moralism and homogeneous communalism just outlined.

Kobena Mercer has talked about these two arguments as the *reflectionist* and the *social engineering* arguments. The reflectionist argument holds that the fight for black representation and recognition must reflect or mirror the real black community, not simply the negative and depressing representations of it. The social engineering argument claims that since any form of representation is constructed—i.e., selective in light of broader aims—black representation (especially given the difficulty of blacks gaining access to positions of power to produce any black imagery) should offer positive images of themselves in order to inspire achievement among young black people, thereby countering racist stereotypes. The hidden assumption of both arguments is that we have unmediated access to what the "real black community" is and what "positive images" are. In short, these arguments presuppose the very phenomena to be interrogated, and thereby foreclose the very issues that should serve as the subject matter to be investigated.

Any notions of "the real black community" and "positive images" are value-laden, socially loaded, and ideologically charged. To pursue this discussion is to call into question the possibility of such an uncontested consensus regarding them. Stuart Hall has rightly called this encounter "the end of innocence or the end of the innocent notion of the essential black subject . . . the recognition that 'black' is essentially a politically and culturally *constructed* category." This recognition—more and more pervasive among the postmodern black diaspora intelligentsia—is facilitated in part by the slow but sure dissolution of the European Age's maritime empires, and the unleashing of new political possibilities and cultural articulations among excolonialized peoples across the globe.

One crucial lesson of this decolonization process remains the manner in which most Third World authoritarian bureaucratic elites deploy essentialist rhetorics about "homogeneous national communities" and "positive images" in order to repress and regiment their diverse and heterogeneous populations. Yet in the diaspora, especially among First World countries, this critique has emerged not so much from the black male component of the left but rather from the black women's movement. The decisive push of postmodern black intellectuals toward a new cultural politics of difference has been made by the powerful critiques and constructive explorations of black diaspora women (e.g., Toni Morrison). The coffin used to bury the innocent notion of the essential black subject was nailed shut with the termination of the black male monopoly on the construction of the black subject. In this regard, the black diaspora womanist critique has had a greater impact than the critiques that highlight exclusively class, empire, age, sexual orientation, or nature.

This decisive push toward the end of black innocence—though prefigured in various degrees in the best moments of W. E. B. Du Bois, Anna Cooper, C. L. R. James, James Baldwin, Claudia Jones, the later Malcolm X, Frantz Fanon, Amiri Baraka, and others—forces black diaspora cultural workers to encounter what Hall has called the "politics of representation." The main aim now is not simply access to representation in order to produce positive images of homogeneous communities—though broader access remains a practical and political problem. Nor is the primary goal here that of contesting stereotypes—though contestation remains a significant though limited venture. Following the model of the black diaspora traditions of music, athletics and rhetoric, black cultural workers must constitute and sustain discursive and institutional networks that deconstruct earlier modern black strategies for identity-formation, demystify power relations that incorporate class, patriarchal and homophobic biases, and construct more multivalent and multidimensional responses that articulate the complexity and diversity of black practices in the modern and postmodern world.

Furthermore, black cultural workers must investigate and interrogate the other of blackness—whiteness. One cannot deconstruct the binary oppositional logic of images of blackness without extending it to the contrary condition of blackness/whiteness itself. However, a mere dismantling will not do—for the very notion of a deconstructive social theory is oxymoronic. Yet social theory is what is needed to examine and *explain* the historically specific ways in which "whiteness" is a politically constructed category parasitic on "blackness," and thereby to conceive of the profoundly hybrid character of what we mean by "race," "ethnicity," and "nationality." For instance, European immigrants arrived on American shores perceiving themselves as "Irish," "Sicilian," "Lithuanian," etc. They had to learn that they were "white" principally by adopting an American discourse of positively valued whiteness and negatively charged blackness. This process by which people define themselves physically, socially, sexually, and even politically in terms of whiteness or blackness has much bearing not only on constructed notions of race and ethnicity but also on how we understand the changing character of U.S. nationalities. And given the Americanization of the world, especially in the sphere of mass culture, such inquiries—encouraged by the new cultural politics of difference—raise critical issues of "hybridity," "exilic status," and "identity" on an international scale. Needless to say, these inquiries must traverse those of "male/female," "colonizer/colonized," "heterosexual/homosexual," et al., as well.

In light of this brief sketch of the emergence of our present crisis—and the turn toward history and difference in cultural work—four major historicist forms of theoretical activity provide resources for how we understand, analyze, and enact our representational practices: Heideggerian *destruction* of the Western metaphysical tradition, Derridean *deconstruction* of the Western philosophical tradition, Rortian *demythologization* of the Western intellectual tradition and Marxist, Foucaultian, feminist, antiracist or antihomophobic *demystification* of Western cultural and artistic conventions.

Despite his abominable association with the Nazis, Martin Heidegger's project is useful in that it discloses the suppression of temporality and historicity in the dominant metaphysical systems of the West from Plato to Rudolph Carnap. This is noteworthy in that it forces one to understand philosophy's representational discourses as thoroughly historical phenomena. Hence, they should be viewed with skepticism as they are often flights from the specific, concrete, practical, and particular. The major problem with Heidegger's project—as noted by his neo-Marxist student, Herbert Marcuse—is that he views history in terms of fate, heritage, and destiny. He dramatizes the past and present as if it were a Greek tragedy with no tools of social analyses to relate cultural work to institutions and structures or antecedent forms and styles.

Jacques Derrida's version of deconstruction is one of the most influential schools of thought among young academic critics. It is salutary in that it focuses on the political power of rhetorical operations—of tropes and metaphors in binary oppositions like white/black, good/bad, male/female, machine/nature, ruler/ruled, reality/appearance—showing how these operations sustain hierarchal world views by devaluing the second terms as something subsumed under the first. Most of the controversy about Derrida's project revolves around this austere epistemic doubt that unsettles binary oppositions while undermining any determinate meaning of a text; i.e., book, art object, performance, building. Yet, his views about skepticism are no more alarming than those of David Hume, Ludwig Wittgenstein, or Stanley Cavell. He simply revels in it for transgressive purposes, whereas others provide us with ways to dissolve, sidestep, or cope with skepticism. None, however, slides down the slippery, crypto-Nietzschean slope of sophomoric relativism as alleged by old-style humanists, be they Platonists, Kantians, or Arnoldians.

The major shortcoming of Derrida's deconstructive project is that it puts a premium on a sophisticated ironic consciousness that tends to preclude and foreclose analyses that guide action with purpose. And given Derrida's own status as an Algerian-born, Jewish leftist marginalized by a hostile French academic establishment (quite different from his reception by the youth in the American academic establishment), the sense of political impotence and hesitation regarding the efficacy of moral action is understandable—but not justifiable. His works and those of his followers too often become rather monotonous, Johnny-one-note rhetorical readings that disassemble texts with little attention to the effects and consequences these dismantlings have in relation to the operations of military, economic, and social powers.

Richard Rorty's neopragmatic project of demythologization is insightful in that it provides descriptive mappings of the transient metaphors—especially the ocular and spectacular ones—that regulate some of the fundamental dynamics in the construction of self-descriptions dominant in highbrow European and American philosophy. His perspective is instructive because it discloses the crucial role of narrative as the background for rational exchange and critical conversation. To put it crudely, Rorty shows why we should speak not of History, but histories; not of Reason, but historically constituted forms of rationality; not of Criticism or Art, but of socially constructed notions of criticism and art—all linked but not reducible to political purposes, material interests, and cultural prejudices.

Rorty's project nonetheless leaves one wanting owing to its distrust of social analytical explanation. Similar to the dazzling new historicism of Stephen Greenblatt, Louis Montrose, and Catherine Gallagher—inspired by the subtle symbolic-cum-textual anthropolgy of Clifford Geertz and the powerful discursive materialism of Michel Foucalt—Rorty gives us mappings and descriptions with no explanatory accounts for change and conflict. In this way, it gives us an aestheticized version of historicism in which the provisional and variable are celebrated at the expense of highlighting who gains, loses, or bears what costs.

Demystification is the most illuminating mode of theoretical inquiry for those who promote the new cultural politics of difference. Social structural analyses of empire, exterminism, class, race, gender, nature, age, sexual orientation, nation, and region are the springboards—though not landing grounds—for the most desirable forms of critical practice that take history (and "herstory") seriously. Demystification tries to keep track of the complex dynamics of institutional and other related power structures in order to disclose options and alternatives for transformative praxis; it also attempts to grasp the way in which representational strategies are creative responses to novel circumstances and conditions. In this way, the central role of human agency (always enacted under circumstances not of one's choosing)—be it the critic, artist, or constituency and audience—is accented.

I call demystificatory criticism "prophetic criticism"—the approach appropriate for the new cultural politics of difference—because while it begins with social structural analyses it also makes explicit its moral and political aims. It is partisan, partial, engaged, and crisis-centered, yet always keeps open a skeptical eye to avoid dogmatic traps, premature closures, formulaic formulations, or rigid conclusions. In addition to social structural analyses, moral and political judgments, and sheer critical consciousness, there indeed is evaluation. Yet the aim of this evaluation is neither to pit art objects against one another like racehorses nor to create eternal canons that dull, discourage, or even dwarf contemporary achievements. We listen to Ludwig van Beethoven, Charles Parker, Luciano Pavarotti, Laurie Anderson, Sarah Vaughan, Stevie Wonder, or Kathleen Battle; read William Shakespeare, Anton Chekhov, Ralph Ellison, Doris Lessing, Thomas Pynchon, Toni Morrison, or Gabriel García Márquez; see works of Pablo Picasso, Ingmar Bergman, Le Corbusier, Martin Puryear, Barbara Kruger, Spike Lee, Frank Gehry, or Howardena Pindell—not in order to undergird bureaucratic assents or enliven cocktail party conversations, but rather to be summoned by the styles they deploy for their profound insight, pleasures, and challenges. Yet all evaluation—including a delight in Eliot's poetry despite his reactionary politics, or a love of Zora Neale Hurston's novels despite her Republican party affiliations—is inseparable from, though not identical or reducible to, social structural analyses, moral and political judgments, and the workings of a curious critical consciousness.

The deadly traps of demystification—and any form of prophetic criticism—are those of reductionism, be it of the sociological, psychological, or historical sort. By reductionism I mean either one factor analyses (i.e., crude Marxisms, feminisms, racialisms, etc.) that yield a one-dimensional functionalism, or a hyper-subtle analytical perspective that loses touch with the specificity of an artwork's form and the context of its reception. Few cultural workers of whatever stripe can walk the tightrope between the Scylla of reductionism and the Charybdis of aestheticism—yet demystification (or prophetic) critics must.

The Existential Challenge

The existential challenge to the new cultural politics of difference can be stated simply: How does one acquire the resources to survive and the cultural capital to thrive as a critic or artist? By cultural capital (Pierre Bourdieu's term), I mean not only the high-quality skills required to engage in critical practices but, more important, the self-confidence, discipline, and perseverance necessary for success without an undue reliance on the mainstream for approval and acceptance. This challenge holds for all prophetic critics, yet it is especially difficult for those of color. The widespread modern European denial of the intelligence, ability, beauty, and character of people of color puts a tremendous burden on critics and artists of color to "prove" themselves in light of norms and models set by white elites whose own heritage devalued and dehumanized them. In short, in the court of criticism and art—or any matters regarding the life of the mind—people of color are guilty; i.e., not expected to meet standards of intellectual achievement until "proven" innocent; i.e., acceptable to "us."

This is more a structural dilemma than a matter of personal attitudes. The profoundly racist and sexist heritage of the European Age has bequeathed to us a set of deeply ingrained perceptions about people of color including, of course, the self-perceptions that people of color bring. It is not surprising that most intellectuals of color in the past exerted much of their energies and efforts to gain acceptance and approval by "white normative gazes." The new cultural politics of difference advises critics and artists of color to put aside this mode of mental bondage, thereby freeing themselves to both interrogate the ways in which they are bound by certain conventions and to learn from and build on these very norms and models. One hallmark of wisdom in the context of any struggle is to avoid knee-jerk rejection and uncritical acceptance.

Self-confidence, discipline, and perseverance are not ends in themselves. Rather, they are the necessary stuff of which enabling criticism and self-criticism are made. Notwithstanding inescapable jealousies, insecurities and anxieties, one telling characteristic of critics and artists of color linked to the new prophetic criticism should be their capacity for and promotion of relentless criticism and self-criticism—be it the normative paradigms of their white colleagues that tend to leave out considerations of empire, race, gender, and sexual orientation or the damaging dogmas about the homogeneous character of communities of color.

There are four basic options for people of color interested in representation—if they are to survive and thrive as serious practitioners of their craft. First, there is the Booker T. Temptation; namely, the individual preoccupation with the mainstream and its legitimizing power. Most critics and artists of color try to bite this bait. It is nearly unavoidable, yet few succeed in a substantive manner. It is no accident that the most creative and profound among them—especially those with staying power beyond mere flashes in the pan to satisfy faddish tokenism—are usually marginal to the mainstream. Even the pervasive professionalism of cultural practitioners of color in the past few decades has not produced towering figures who reside within the established white patronage system that bestows the rewards and prestige for chosen contributions to American society.

It certainly helps to have some trustworthy allies within this system, yet most of those who enter and remain tend to lose much of their creativity, diffuse their prophetic energy, and dilute their critiques. Still, it is unrealistic for creative people of color to think they can sidestep the white patronage system. And though there are indeed some white allies conscious of the tremendous need to rethink identity politics, it's naive to think that being comfortably nested within this very same system—even if one can be a patron to others—does not affect one's work, one's outlook, and, most important, one's soul.

The second option is the Talented Tenth Seduction; namely, a move toward arrogant group insularity. This alternative has a limited function—to preserve one's sanity and sense of self as one copes with the mainstream. Yet it is, at best, a transitional and transient activity. If it becomes a permanent option it is self-defeating in that it usually reinforces the very inferior complexes promoted by the subtly racist mainstream. Hence it tends to revel in a parochialism and encourage a narrow racialist and chauvinistic outlook.

The third strategy is the Go-It-Alone option. This is an extreme rejectionist perspective that shuns the mainstream and group insularity. Almost every critic and artist of color contemplates or enacts this option at some time in their pilgrimage. It is healthy in that it reflects the presence of independent, critical, and skeptical sensibilities toward perceived constraints on one's creativity. Yet it is, in the end, difficult if not impossible to sustain if one is to grow, develop, and mature intellectually; as some semblance of dialogue with a community is necessary for almost any creative practice.

The most desirable option for people of color who promote the new cultural politics of difference is to be a critical organic catalyst. By this I mean a person who stays attuned to the best of what the mainstream has to offer—its paradigms, viewpoints, and methods—yet maintains a grounding in affirming and enabling subcultures of criticism. Prophetic critics and artists of color should be exemplars of what it means to be intellectual freedom-fighters; that is, cultural workers who simultaneously position themselves within (or alongside) the mainstream while clearly aligned with groups who vow to keep alive potent traditions of critique and resistance. In this regard, one can take clues from the great musicians or preachers of color who are open to the best of what other traditions offer yet are rooted in nourishing subcultures that build on the grand achievements of a vital heritage. Openness to others—including the mainstream—does not entail wholesale co-optation; and group autonomy is not group insularity. Louis Armstrong, W. E. B. Du Bois, Ella Baker, Jose Carlos Mariatequi, M. M. Thomas, Wynton Marsalis, Martin Luther King, Jr., and Ronald Takaki have understood this well.

The new cultural politics of difference can thrive only if there are communities, groups, organizations, institutions, subcultures and networks of people of color who cultivate critical sensibilities and personal accountability—without inhibiting individual expressions, curiosities, and idiosyncrasies. This is especially needed given the escalating racial hostility, violence, and polarization in the USA. Yet this critical coming-together must not be a narrow closing-ranks. Rather it is a strengthening and nurturing endeavor that can forge more solid alliances and coalitions. In this way, prophetic criticism—with its stress on historical specificity and artistic complexity—directly address the intellectual challenge. The cultural capital of people of color—with its emphasis on self-confidence, discipline, perseverance, and subcultures of criticism—also tries to meet the existential requirement. Both are mutually reinforcing. Both are motivated by a deep commitment to individuality and democracy—the moral and political ideals that guide the creative response to the political challenge.

The Political Challenge

Adequate rejoinders to intellectual and existential challenges equip the practitioners of the new cultural politics of difference to meet the political ones. This challenge principally consists of forging solid and reliable alliances of people of color and white progressives guided by a moral and political vision of greater democracy and individual freedom in communities, states, and transactional enterprises; e.g., corporations, information and communications conglomerates.

Jesse Jackson's Rainbow Coalition is a gallant, yet flawed, effort in this regard—gallant due to the tremendous energy, vision, and courage of its leader and followers, yet flawed because of its failure to take seriously critical and democratic sensibilities within its own operations. In fact, Jackson's attempt to gain power at the national level is a symptom of the weakness of U.S. progressive politics and a sign that the capacity to generate extraparliamentary social motion or movements has waned. Yet given the present organizational weakness and intellectual timidity of Left politics in the USA, the major option is that of multiracial grass roots citizens' participation in credible projects in which people see that their efforts can make a difference. The salutary revolutionary developments in Eastern Europe are encouraging and inspiring in this regard. Ordinary people organized can change societies.

The most significant theme of the new cultural politics of difference is the agency, capacity, and ability of human beings who have been culturally degraded, politically oppressed, and economically exploited by bourgeois liberal and communist illiberal status quo. This theme neither romanticizes nor idealizes marginalized constraints on their life-chances for surviving and thriving. In this way, the new cultural politics of difference shuns narrow particularisms, parochialisms, and separatisms, just as it rejects false universalisms and homogeneous totalisms. Instead, the new cultural politics of difference affirms the perennial quest for the precious ideals of individuality and democracy by digging deep in the depths of human particularities and social specificities in order to construct new kinds of connections, affinities, and communities across empire, nation, region, race, gender, age, and sexual orientation.

The major impediments of the radical libertarian and democratic projects of the new cultural politics are threefold: the pervasive processes of objectification, rationalization, and commodification throughout the world. The first process—best highlighted in Georg Simmel's *The Philosophy of Money* (1900)—consists of transforming human beings into manipulable objects. It promotes the notion that people's actions have no impact on the world, that we are but spectators, not participants in making and remaking ourselves and the larger society. The second process—initially examined in the seminal works of Max Weber—expands bureaucratic hierarchies that impose impersonal rules and regulations in order to increase efficiency, be they defined in terms of better service or better surveillance. This process leads to disenchantment with past mythologies of deadening, flat, banal ways of life. The third and most important process—best examined in the works of Karl Marx, Georg Lukacs, and Walter Benjamin—augments market forces in the form of oligopolies and monopolies that centralize resources and powers and promote cultures of consumption that view people as mere spectatorial consumers and passive citizens.

These processes cannot be eliminated, but their pernicious effects can be substantially alleviated. The audacious attempt to lessen their impact—to preserve people's agency, increase the scope of their freedom and expand the operations of democracy—is the fundamental aim of the new cultural politics of difference. This is why the crucial questions become: What is the moral content of one's cultural identity? And what are the political consequences of this moral content and cultural identity?

In the recent past, the dominant cultural identities have been circumscribed by immoral patriarchal, imperial, jingoistic, and xenophobic constraints. The political consequences have been principally a public sphere regulated by and for well-to-do white males in the name of freedom and democracy. The new cultural criticism exposes and explodes the exclusions, blindnesses, and silences of this past, calling from it radical libertarian and democratic projects that will create a better present and future. The new cultural politics of difference is neither an ahistorical Jacobin program that discards tradition and ushers in new self-righteous authoritarianisms nor a guilt-ridden leveling anti-imperialist liberalism that celebrates token pluralism for smooth inclusion. Rather, it acknowledges the uphill struggle of fundamentally transforming highly objectified, rationalized, and commodified societies and cultures in the name of individuality and democracy. This means locating the structural causes of unnecessary forms of social misery (without reducing all such human suffering to historical causes), depicting the plight and predicaments of demoralized and depoliticized citizens caught in market-driven cycles of therapeutic release—drugs, alcoholism, consumerism—and projecting alternative visions, analyses, and actions that proceed from particularities and arrive at moral and political connectedness. This connectedness does not signal a homogeneous unity or monolithic totality but rather a contingent, fragile coalition-building in an effort to pursue common radical libertarian democratic goals that overlap.

In a world in which most of the resources, wealth, and power are centered in huge corporations and supportive political elites, the new cultural politics of difference may appear to be solely visionary, utopian, and fanciful. The recent cutbacks of social service programs, business take backs at the negotiation tables of workers and management, speedups at the workplace, and buildups of military budgets reinforce this perception. And surely the growing disintegration and decomposition of civil society—of shattered families, neighborhoods, and schools—add to this perception. Can a civilization that evolves more and more around market activity, more and more around the buying and selling of commodities, expand the scope of freedom and democracy? Can we simply bear witness to its slow decay and doom—a painful denouement prefigured already in many poor black and brown communities and rapidly embracing all of us? These haunting questions remain unanswered yet the challenge they pose must not remain unmet. The new cultural politics of difference tries to confront these enormous and urgent challenges. It will require all the imagination, intelligence, courage, sacrifice, care, and laughter we can muster.

The time has come for critics and artists of the new cultural politics of difference to cast their nets widely, flex their muscles broadly, and thereby refuse to limit their visions, analyses, and praxis to their particular terrains. The aim is to dare to recast, redefine, and revise the very notions of "modernity," "mainstream," "margins," "difference," "otherness." We have now reached a new stage in the perennial struggle for freedom and dignity. And while much of the "First World" intelligentsia adopts retrospective and conservative outlooks that defend the crisis-ridden present, we promote a prospective and prophetic vision with a sense of possibility and potential, especially for those who bear the social costs of the present. We look to the past for strength, not solace; we look at the present and see people perishing, not profits mounting; we look toward the future and vow to make it different and better.

To put it boldly, the new kind of critic and artist associated with the new cultural politics of difference consists of an energetic breed of New World *bricoleurs* with improvisational and flexible sensibilities that sidestep mere opportunism and mindless eclecticism; persons from all countries, cultures, genders, sexual orientations, ages, and regions with protean identities who avoid ethnic chauvinism and faceless universalism; intellectual and political freedom fighters with partisan passion, international perspective, and, thank God, a sense of humor that combats the ever-present absurdity that forever threatens our democratic and libertarian projects and dampens the fire that fuels our will to struggle. Yet we will struggle and stay, as those brothers and sisters on the block say, "out there"—with intellectual rigor, existential dignity, moral vision, political courage, and soulful style.

Cornel West is professor of Religion and director of Afro-American Studies at Princeton University.

Originally published in Out There: Marginalization and Contemporary Cultures, *(eds.) Russell Ferguson et al., © 1990 The New Museum of Contemporary Art and Massachusetts Institute of Technology. Reprinted with permission of the publisher.*

The Role of the University

The articles in Part 3 speak to the role of the university and of educational institutions generally in educating young Americans in the practice of democratic public life. **Benjamin R. Barber** outlines the broad features of the university as a civic institution. Barber considers two models of the university frequently invoked by education reformers. One—the "purist model"—calls for a refurbished ivory tower. The other—the "vocational" model—demands uncritical servitude to society's economic needs. Barber proposes a third model according to which the university not only *has* a civic mission, but *is* a civic mission. On this model, "learning is a social activity that can take place only within a discursive community bringing together reflection and experience." Universities in a democratic society should be forums of dialogue and communication.

The next four selections deal more specifically with curricular modifications. **Ralph Ketcham** draws on Jefferson to raise anew the question of how self-government can be achieved. Like Jefferson, we must adapt the ancient ideal of liberal education to our time and circumstances. In that spirit, Ketcham sketches a vision of liberal education that is "profound, integrated, and radical." Liberal education so conceived can prepare students for the public office of citizen. There is an insoluble linkage between self-government, liberal education, and citizenship.

Daryl Smith considers the politics of difference (cf. West) in light of institutional structures and campus organization. What we must seek, she says, is a multicultural campus. To obtain this we will have to rethink our educational philosophies. She raises questions such as: What if diversity were made part of mission statements? Does diversity conflict with equality? Should conflict be avoided or confronted? How should hiring policies be modified? Review processes? Does diversity mean assimilation? How much interaction occurs on campus? What kind of intellectual climate is most congruent with a diverse student body? What kind of leadership does a multicultural campus require? How must the curriculum be revised? Diversity, she concludes, "will provide the greatest of resources for the revitalization of higher education."

According to **J. Donald Moon**, democracy is based upon belief that we can manage our collective lives through political action and our belief in the equality of citizens. Neither can be achieved without civic education. Moon proposes three objectives for a liberal arts curriculum: a breadth of learning, a common intellectual culture that can serve as a conduit through which expert knowledge informs public discourse, and cultivation of practical judgment through the integration of different areas of knowledge. Democracy strives "to create a moral community in which the norms determining our common life arise from a process of public discourse."

Richard Dagger attempts to clear away the confusion that bedevils our attempts at educational reforms by positing two goals for education: autonomy and civic virtue. Properly understood, these goals are most likely to produce an educated democratic citizenry.

Elizabeth K. Minnich takes the view that the goal of civic education is not primarily to pass on knowledge, but rather to develop civic virtues understood in the old sense of "virtue"; that is, as expressions of excellence. Central among the civic virtues are judgment and public talk, two concepts discussed by other authors (e.g., Mathews and Moon). Judgment, Minnich holds, is the ability to bridge theory and practice. Public talk is the process that enables us to reach judgment. She argues that "a curriculum for civic education will grow out of a series of conversations that should themselves exemplify the process of civic interaction we seek to instill in our students." This, in turn, will require a special pedagogy. Those who would teach the civic arts must be educated against the dominant tradition, which separates theory from practice.

Johnnella E. Butler spells out the implications of a politics of cultural diversity. She urges a "scholarly conversation" to move us beyond the narrowness of the debate about Ethnic Studies and Women's Studies. By incorporating the categories of these disciplines—race, class, gender, ethnicity—into our scholarship, we can understand better what African-Americans, Latino-Americans, Asian-Americans, and Native Americans can bring to the public table. This, in turn, will produce a more literate citizenry and give deeper meaning to our self-understanding as a pluralistic society.

Finally, **Henry Giroux** looks beyond the university to educational institutions in general. He recommends a pedagogy that responds to the need for inclusivity adumbrated in the essays at the end of Part 2. He takes up cudgels against neoconservative voices that have dominated the recent debate about the purpose of education (the "new elitists," he calls them) and proposes a philosophy that "aims at providing educators with a moral and political vision which extends rather than limits the promise and possibilities of principled democratic society." He views schools as "public cultures" and educating students as "an introduction into how culture is organized, a demonstration of who is authorized to speak about particular forms of culture, and what culture is considered acceptable and what isn't," thus complementing the thesis put forth by Cornel West.

"Learning is a social activity that can take place only within a discursive community bringing together reflection and experience."

The Civic Mission of the University

by Benjamin R. Barber

The modern American university is embroiled in controversy, fueled by deep uncertainty over its pedagogical purposes and its civic role in a "free" society. At times the college establishment seems to know neither what a free society is nor what the educational requisites of freedom might look like. Nonetheless, both administrators and their critics have kept busy, for like zealots, (classically defined as people who redouble their efforts when they have forgotten their aims), they have covered their confusion by embellishing their hyperbole. They wring hands and rue the social crises of higher education—apathy, cynicism, careerism, prejudice, selfishness, sexism, opportunism, complacency, and substance abuse—but they hesitate when faced with hard decisions, and prefer to follow rather than challenge the national mood.

Students, reflecting the climate in which they are being educated, are, well, a mess. Minority students at Dartmouth receive anonymous hate letters from their peers, and feminists at Dartmouth are sent notes enclosed in condoms reading, "You disgust me." Students at the University of Utah are voting members of the "Who Cares?" party in student government, embracing their promises to pay their way by "panhandling, and running strip bars, raffles, and prostitution." Youthful high jinks, perhaps: after all, a decade earlier, students at Wisconsin had elected the "Pail and Shovel" party into office (its platform: stealing, wasting as much money as possible); and panty raids of one kind or another have been campus staples for a century. Yet one can only feel uneasy when these newer signs of distress are read in conjunction with the wave of racism, overt sexual discrimination, and homophobia that is sweeping America's campuses; or when they are correlated with national patterns of student political apathy (less than one-fifth of the 18-to 24-year-old population voted in the 1986 congressional election, less than one-half of the 37 percent of the general population that voted); or, more pointedly, when they are seen to induce paralysis among school administrators who have necessarily abjured the infantalizing tactics of "in loco parentis" without, however, having a clue about what might take its place.

The privatization and commercialization of schooling continues apace. At the college level, we still honor teaching in the abstract, but we mainly reward research. To be sure, the two should be congruent, and administrators are fond of saying that only great scholars—superb researchers toiling on the frontiers of their discipline—can be good teachers. But good teachers need to spend at least a few hours a week in the classroom. No matter how gifted, the educator cannot practice the teaching craft in front of a computer, in the laboratory, or at the library.

The reality is, as Jacques Barzun recently pointed out, that research and scholarship have not only become ever more narrow and specialized and thus remote from teaching, but they have taken the very culture which is their putative subject and held it hostage to their reflexive scholastic concerns. "Since William James, Russell, and Whitehead," Barzun reminds us, "philosophy, like history, has been confiscated by scholarship, and locked away from the contamination of cultural use." And, we might add, from the contamination of educational use. The new scholasticism that is academic specialization has in fact turned the study of culture into the study of the study of culture—self-conscious preoccupation with method, technique, and scholarship displacing a broad humanistic concern for culture itself. We no longer simply read books; we study what it means to read books; we do not interpret theories but develop theories of interpretation. We are awash in what W. Jackson Bate of Harvard calls "self-trivialization," pursuing an intellectual quest that takes us farther and farther from students and the world in which they are supposedly being educated to live.

Two Universities

There are two positive models of the university being purveyed today to address the current crisis in education. Mirror images of each other, one calls for a refurbished ivory tower, while the other calls for an uncritical servitude to the larger society's aims and purposes (read whims and fashions). Neither is satisfactory. We may call the first the purist model and the second the vocational model. The first is favored by academic purists and antiquarian humanists and is an embellishment on the ancient Lyceum or the medieval university. In the name of the abstract pursuit of speculative knowledge, it calls for insulating the university from the wider society. Learning for learning's own sake: not for career, not for life, not for democracy, not for money; for neither power nor happiness, neither career nor quality of life, but for its own pure sake alone. To the purist, knowledge is radically divorced from time and culture, from power and interest; above all it eschews utility. It aspires to reconstruct Aristotle's Lyceum in downtown Newark—catering, however, to the residents of New Athens rather than of New Haven or Newark.

In the Lyceum, knowledge is mined from the great intellectual veins running through the canyon of the canon. What the canon teaches is that there is a knowledge that is not conditioned by culture and interest, that is not some other century's fashion or some other culture's dominant paradigm, but which—transcending time and space—has earned the status of, if not universal truth, at least universal wisdom. This claim to universality uproots the canon from the contexts that might once have created it. (That Eton in the nineteenth century had one science master, one math master, one modern languages master, and twenty-seven classics masters teaching Latin and Greek and the cultures they mediated is seen as a product of the canon, rather than a force conditioning its modern incarnation.) On the other hand, belief in the independent and objective veracity of the canon does not prevent purists from seeing all other knowledge, all deviations from the canon (such as feminist studies or comparative religion), as the subjective effects of contemporary cultural contexts that are transient, contingent, and subjective; that is to say, the product of liberal pedagogical conspiracies and political interest.

The vocational model abjures tradition no less decisively than the purist model abjures relevance. Indeed, it is wildly alive to the demands of the larger society it believes education must serve. Where the purist rejects even the victories of modernity (equality, social justice, universal education) as so many diseases, the advocate of education as vocational training accepts even the ravages of modernity as so many virtues—or at least as the necessary price of progress. The vocationalist wishes to see the university go prone before modernity's new gods. Service to the market, training for its professions, research in the name of its products are the hallmarks of the new full-service university, which wants nothing so much as to be counted as a peer among the nation's great corporations that serve prosperity and material happiness. Forging dubious alliances with research companies, All-American

U. plies corporations for program funding and stalks the public sector in search of public "needs" it can profitably satisfy. In each of these cases, it asks society to show the way, and it compliantly follows.

If this requires that teaching be subsumed to research and research itself reduced to product-oriented engineering, so be it. If it means taking bribes, such as advertising, that privatize and commercialize education in ways wholly inconsistent with learning, that is the price of survival. If it requires that education take on the aspect of vocational training, and that the university becomes a kindergarten for the corporate society where the young are socialized, bullied, and otherwise blackmailed into usefulness, then the curriculum must be recast in the language of opportunism, careerism, professionalism, and, in a word, commerce. Where the philosopher once said all of life is a preparation for death, the educational careerist now thinks all of life is a preparation for business—or perhaps, more bluntly, that life is business.

A Dialectic of Life and Mind

The first of our two models is aristocratic, humanistic, and poignantly nostalgic—not merely Luddite in C. P. Snow's sense, but profoundly antimodern: it wishes to educate the few well and perceives in the democratic ideal an insuperable obstacle to excellence.

The vocationalist knows these predilections for sequestration to be dangerous and probably impossible. For him, education and its institutional tools are for better or worse embedded in the real world. His pedagogical tasks are socialization not insulation, integration not isolation. Education must follow where society leads: support it, ape it, reinforce it, chase it, undergird it, affirm it, preserve it. Whatever society wants and needs, the university tries to supply. Indeed, society defines the university rather than the other way round. Society says what, the scholar as researcher shows how; society says Yes or No, the teacher helps the pupil pronounce the words; society says I need doctors, I will pay lawyers, students nurture medical skills and acquire legal credentials. Education as vocationalism in service to society becomes a matter of socialization rather than scrutiny, of spelling out consequences rather than probing premises, of answering society's questions rather than questioning society's answers. Where once the student was taught that the unexamined life was not worth living, he is now taught that the profitably lived life is not worth examining.

Neither purist nor vocationalist recognize that education is a dialectic of life and mind, of body and spirit, in which the two are inextricably bound together. Neither acknowledges how awkward this makes it for a liberal arts university at once to serve and challenge society, to simultaneously "transmit" fundamental values such as autonomy and free thinking, and create a climate where students are not conditioned by what is transmitted (transmission tends toward indoctrination), and where thinking is truly critical, independent, and subversive (which is what freedom means). For such a university must at once stand apart from society in order to give students room to breathe and grow free from a too insistent reality; and at the same time it must stand within the real world and its limiting conditions in order to prepare students to live real lives in a society that, if they do not mold it freely to their aspirations, will mold them to its conventions. To live eventually as effective, responsible, critical, and autonomous members of communities of discourse and activity, students must be both protected from a too precipitous engagement in them and acclimatized by responsible and critical participation in them.

If the young were born literate there would be no need to teach them literature; if they were born citizens, there would be no need to teach them civic responsibility. But of course educators know that the young are born neither wise, nor literate, nor responsible—nor, despite the great rhetoric to the contrary, are they born free. They are born at best with the potential for wisdom, literacy, and responsibility, with an aptitude for freedom which is, however, matched by an aptitude for security and thus for tyranny.

The Civic Mission

Thomas Jefferson regarded habituated belief as an enemy not only of freedom but of usable conviction, and argued that "every constitution and every law naturally expires at the end of 19 years." Canons, like constitutions, are also for the living, and if they do not expire every 19 years they surely grow tired and stale and heteronomous as time passes. Which is not to say they must be discarded: only that they must be reassessed, relegitimized, and thus reembraced by the current generation. A canon is no use if it is not ours, and it becomes ours only when we reinvent it—an act impossible without active examination, criticism, and subversion. That is why teachers cannot teach the canon properly without subverting it. Their task is not to transmit the canon but to permit their students to reinvent it. Paradoxically, only those "truths" founded on abstract reason which students can make their own, founded on their own reason, are likely to be preserved. Waving the *Republic* at their young will do nothing for restoring literacy or extending the truths of the old.

What I wish to urge is a far more dialectical model of education: one that refuses to prostrate itself, its back to the future, before the ancient gods of the canon, but is equally reluctant to throw itself uncritically, its back to the past, into the future as envisioned by the new gods of the marketplace. This argument suggests not that the university *has* a civic mission, but that the university *is* a civic mission, is civility itself, defined as the rules and conventions that permit a community to facilitate conversation and the kinds of discourse upon which all knowledge depends. On this model, learning is a social activity that can take place only within a discursive community bringing together reflection and experience. On this model, knowledge is an evolving communal construction whose legitimacy rests directly on the character of the social process. On this model, education is everywhere and always an ineluctably communal enterprise.

I mean to suggest much more than that democracy and education are parallel activities; or that civic training and the cultivation of knowledge and judgment possess a parallel structure. I am arguing that they are the same thing: that what distinguishes truth, inasmuch as we can have it all, from untruth, is not conformity to society's historical traditions or the standards of independent reason or the dictates of some learned canon, but conformity to communicative processes that are genuinely democratic and that occur only in free communities.

The conditions of truth and the conditions of democracy are one and the same: as there is freedom, as the community is open and inclusive and the exchange of ideas thorough and spirited, so there is both more democracy and more learning, more freedom and more knowledge (which becomes, here, ideas conditionally agreed upon). And just as no argument will be privileged over other arguments simply because of how or from whom it originates, so no individual will be privileged over other individuals simply because of who he is (white or male or straight) and where he comes from (old money, good Protestant stock, the United States of America).

Once this is understood, we can move beyond the old instrumental arguments on behalf of democracy that rest the case for citizen training inside the university on the prudential need to shore up democracy outside the university. These arguments are powerful—neither education nor research can prosper in an unfree society, and schooling is the only way we are likely to be able to produce citizens who will uphold freedom—but they are prudential. The prudent Jefferson is known for his linkage of education and democracy: if, Jefferson writes in his *Notes on Virginia*, the people are the "ultimate guardians of their own liberty," then we had best "render them safe" via a prudent and thorough education. "The only sure reliance for the preservation of our liberty," he writes to James Madison in 1787, is to "educate and inform the whole mass of the people."

However, my argument here goes well beyond Jefferson's instrumental formula making education "the guarantor of liberty." It suggests that liberty is the guarantor of education; that we not only have to educate every person to make him free, but we have to free every person to make him educable. Educated women and men make good citizens of free communities; but without a free learning community you cannot educate women and men.

The Sense of Community

Walt Whitman, who refused to wall off democracy from life, or life from poetry, or poetry from democracy, mocks those who try to cut the fabric of democracy to the sorry measure of their own tiny imaginations (he must have had the first political scientist in mind!):

> Did you too, O friend, suppose democracy was only for elections, for politics, and for a party name? I say democracy is only of use there that it may pass on and come to its flower and fruits in manners, in the highest forms of interaction between men, and their beliefs—in religion, literature, colleges and schools— democracy in all public and private life. . . .

The point where democracy and education intersect is the point we call community. For if democracy is a mode of associated living, then it is also true, Dewey has written, that "in the first place, the school must itself be a community of life. . . ." Dewey is framing a careful philosophical argument rather than just a provocative metaphor. He is insisting that the "realization of the meaning of linguistic signs . . . involves a context of work and play in association with others." He is saying that in the absence of community there is no learning; that language itself is social, the product as well as the premise of sociability and conversation.

We should comprehend him, for underlying the pathologies of our society and our schools—beneath the corruptions associated with alcohol and drugs, complacency and indifference, discrimination and bigotry, and violence and fractiousness—is a sickness of community: its corruption, its rupturing, its fragmentation, its breakdown; finally, its vanishing and its absence. We can no more learn alone than we can live alone, and if little learning is taking place in American schools and colleges it may be because there is too much solitude and too little community among the learners (and the teachers, too). Schools that were once workshops of intimacy have become as alienating as welfare hotels and as lonely as suburban malls. They lack neither facilities nor resources, neither gifted teachers nor able students; but they are for the most part devoid of any sense of community. And without community, neither the almighty canon nor the almighty dollar can do much to inspire learning or promote freedom.

Dewey's conception of education is often deemed "progressive," yet in fact it harks back to classical and neoclassical models of *paideia* and *bildung*. *Paideia* was the term the Greeks used to encapsulate the norms and values of public life around which citizenship and learning were organized. To be an educated Athenian was to be a free and participating citizen. These were not two distinctive roles, two parallel forms of training; they were a single identity revolving around common norms each individual made his own. Imagine

Socrates recommending a canon to his pupils, or telling an Athenian youth that what he learned in the Lyceum was not meant to apply to life beyond the bleached stones where the two of them sat in the sun conversing. The German Enlightenment term *bildung* possessed the same unifying cultural thrust; it brought together under the rubric of life, learning, and self-reflective experience the same ideals of the fully developed citizen of a civil cosmopolis. The education of Emile (Rousseau) or the education of the young Werther (Goethe) was a lifetime task of which schooling represented only a phase. Emile did not imagine his pupil could separate the cultivation of his civility from the reading of books; Goethe never conceived that Werther could or should wall off his life from his learning.

The trouble with the purist's canon is that it renders knowledge a product stripped of the process by which it is endowed with its quickening vitality and its moral legitimacy. The canon does not produce the cultural education the Germans called *bildung; bildung* produces the canon, which consequently needs to be no less flexible and mutable than the life processes that make it. The trouble with the vocationalist's servitude to society is that it fails to distinguish society or society's fixed conventions from the free society and the unique educational prerequisites that condition freedom. A free society does not produce *bildung,* which is always critical of it; *bildung* produces a free society, keeping it from ossifying and perishing—helping it to overcome its most difficult contradiction: the institutionalization and petrification of the spirit of freedom that animates it.

Common Living

We can address these troubles, both those of the purists and those of the vocationalists, by insisting on the centrality of community to both education and democracy, both convention and freedom. Where in the quest to preserve the canon is a concern for the communal conditions of learning upon which its revival (and thus its preservation) depend? In the rush to serve the society that beckons from beyond the school yard, what has happened to the schoolyard's own precious community, whose delicate ties alone permit the young to learn the art of civility and to create a common language in the face of private differences, so that they might conduct a conversation about common knowledge and shared belief?

It is not really a matter of making the liberal arts university into a community; for it already is a community, however corrupt and frangible it has become or however little it is seen as such by its privatized inhabitants (students, faculty, and administrators alike). It is a matter of recognizing the communal character of learning, and giving to community the attention and the resources it requires. Learning communities, like all free communities, function only when their members conceive of themselves as empowered to participate fully in the common activities that define the community—in this case, learning and the pursuit of knowledge in the name of common living. Learning entails communication, communication is a function of community. The equation is simple enough: no community, no communication; no communication, no learning; no learning, no education; no education, no citizens; no citizens, no freedom; no freedom—then no culture, no democracy, no schools, no civilization. Cultures rooted in freedom do not come in fragments and pieces: you get it all, or you get nothing.

The sociopathologies that currently afflict American universities (renewed racism, substance and alcohol abuse, alienation, suicide) are then anything but contingent features of higher education, mere symptoms that can be isolated and treated one by one like so many cuts on an otherwise healthy body. They speak rather to a disease of the whole, a systemic affliction of education's integral body, which is nothing less than the community of teachers and students in which education subsists.

If we wish to treat the symptoms, I suggest we try to treat the disease: the corporal weakness of community itself. I will not try here to specify what it might mean to reform our universities and colleges focusing on the needs of community rather than the demands of a canon or the needs of a hungry society. But when I think about how crucial teaching is to all education and thus to democracy, I am put in mind of what a remarkable stanza that brings Walt Whitman's "A Song of Occupations" to its conclusion. Whitman writes:

> When the psalm sings instead of
>   the singer,
> When the script preaches instead
>   of the preacher,
> When a university course
>   convinces like a slumbering woman
>   and child convince. . .
> I intend to reach them my hand
>   and make as much of them as I
>   do of men and women.

Whitman always reminds us of the obvious; perhaps because it is the obvious that we always forget. Canons don't teach, teachers teach. Poems cannot enchant, only poets can do that. History will not preserve us from the errors of the past, but historians just may, if they are teachers.

Education is finally a matter of teachers teaching students; and where teachers teach and students learn, there we will discover community. Or, to put it the other way around, only where there is a genuine community will there be genuine teachers and students and anything resembling genuine learning.

Does the university have a civic mission? Of course, for it is a civic mission: the cultivation of free community; the creation of a democracy of words (knowledge) and a democracy of deeds (the democratic state). Perhaps it is time to stop complaining about the needs of society and worrying about the fate of the canon and despairing over the inadequacies of students, which after all only mirror our own. Perhaps the time is finally here to start thinking about what it means to say that community is the beginning and the end of education: its indispensable condition, its ultimate object. And time then, if we truly believe this, to do something about it in words and in deeds.

Benjamin Barber holds the Walt Whitman Chair in Political Science at Rutgers University and is author of many books, including Liberating Feminism; Strong Democracy: Participatory Politics for a New Age; *and, most recently,* The Conquest of Politics. *He collaborated with Patrick Watson on the ten-part television series,* The Struggle for Democracy, *as well as the book that accompanied the series.*

From the Kettering Review, *Fall 1989. Reprinted with permission of the author.*

"The liberal arts explore the past in ways that
project profoundly, integratively, and radically into
the future."

The Liberal Arts and
Civic Education

by Ralph Ketcham

Jefferson opened up for Americans, and for many others around the
world, the pregnant, beguiling questions of whether humans can make good
use of the life of freedom, and whether self-government can result in good
government. In his own education, career, and writings, he showed how
human capabilities and aspirations could be fashioned into a life of remarkable scope, depth, and achievement. Like Leonardo and Goethe, Jefferson
gives us some glimpse of the potential inherent in human genius and purpose-
fulness. But he had the additional good fortune to be able to bring his talents
and intentions to bear on a formative moment in the life of a fledgling nation.
He had an opportunity to attend to the perennial question facing any democracy: Can the people of any nation or community—finally all the people—be
so educated, circumstanced, and experienced that they can govern themselves wisely, if given the opportunity? Jefferson regarded this as a question
of uncertain answer, but he took it with profound seriousness, and devoted
his life to seeing if the affairs of a nation could be so ordered that the answer
might be "yes." And since the question is *still* before us and *still* of uncertain
answer, Jefferson's concerns and aspirations—if not, after two centuries, his
specific answers—are of lively significance to us.

We must ask, as Jefferson did, whether the United States, as a new kind of nation, has a shining future, whether its form of democratic government is suited to human nature and to current exigencies, and whether the nation's educational philosophy and system are properly attuned to play their vital role in nourishing its public life. To pursue this inquiry, we must, as Jefferson did in planning his own university, look first at the ancient idea of liberal education to see what its nature and uses might be as the twentieth century draws to a close. Then, again following the example of the author of the first plan for public education in Virginia, we must look more specifically at the dimension of liberal education that prepares the citizens and leaders of a self-governing society for their public roles. Finally, we must assess the implications and potential of this preparation for the definition and attainment of that cherished but elusive goal, making self-government *good* government.

Profound, Integrated, and Radical

When Jefferson explained his plan for the University of Virginia to the legislature, he proposed a blend of what we would call practical or professional education, and more general or liberal education. He proposed studies in natural science, law, and medicine suited to the training of professionals, but also, and foundational to them, studies in ancient and modern languages, mathematics, government, history, political economy, philosophy, English language and literature, and fine arts. Jefferson, like educators in the Western world for more than 2,000 years, supposed that such broad learning was a necessary basis for any well-educated human being. He also supposed, conventionally, that such studies rested on a core of readings, some ancient and some modern, that embodied and inculcated the basic values and aspirations of the civilization of which his state and nation were a part. Among his goals at the new university were "to develop the reasoning faculties of our youth, enlarge their minds, cultivate their morals, and instill in them the precepts of virtue and order"; and "to form them to habits of reflection and correct action, rendering them examples of virtue to others, and of happiness within themselves."[1]

In 1989, this language has both a quaintly unfamiliar cast and the tired familiarity of the statements of objectives at the beginning of American college catalogues. It carries the familiar acknowledgment that institutions of higher learning seek to nourish the habits, understandings, and aspirations essential to a full and satisfying and estimable human life—they accept responsibility to be more than vocational training schools. But Jefferson's sentences are also replete with phrases that provoke uneasiness, perhaps even recoil, in modern educators: "cultivate morals," "precepts of virtue and order," and "correct action." Common reactions to such words are "What business do schools have 'cultivating morals'?" or "Whose 'precepts of virtue' do we presume to teach our diverse students?" or "Should college studies be pointed toward generalized 'action,' to say nothing of supposing any particular pattern is 'correct' for all students?" In posing these questions, of course, we do no more than acknowledge the considerable shift in "climate of opinion" that has occurred in the two centuries between Jefferson's day and our own. We should note, though, that Jefferson—like nearly all profound civic educators—had ideas of morality and virtue and order and correctness which, he thought, not only possessed intrinsic validity (he termed them "natural law" or "moral sense") but had to be at the center of any proper education.

What might we do, then, to recapture for our day the full Jeffersonian sense of the noble uses humankind can make of the life of freedom we so cherish? I would suggest, to begin with, nothing less than the reinvigoration of the idea of liberal education suited to the needs of the approaching twenty-first century. To do this, we must recognize our common foundations and again devise an education of depth, scope, and coherence that will give students a sense of the fullness of life to which they might aspire.

Perhaps the best way to grasp the essence of liberal education is to think of it not so much as a certain substance or content, but as possessing three characteristics: it must be *profound,* it must be *integrated*, and it must be *radical*.

What does it mean to be profound? Educationally, at least, it means to read and be exposed to the good, deep stuff that challenges and then enriches and enlarges the most important concerns one has about oneself and the world one lives in. Its essence is found in the great works of art and literature and history and philosophy the world around. If one asks "Why read the works of Shakespeare or Thucydides or Melville or Confucius or Kawabata or Virginia Woolf or Rousseau or Burke or Dostoyevski or Joyce Carol Oates or Toni Morrison?" the answer in each case is the same: *they are profound.* They probe the human psyche, revealing its depths and torments and potential in ways that compel understandings to be stretched and deepened. Big questions have been opened and explored. The mind thus touched can never again be quite as content with triviality. The "canon" of such works, of course, is not fixed, since it is continually being added to by rediscovery and creation, but the standard remains the same: humanity has been enriched. Hamlet and Prince Genji and Captain Ahab and Alyosha Karamazov and Morrison's Sethe belong to us all because they stand for something in the deepening of our own lives and souls—enlarge our freedom not only by opening doors but also by revealing exciting or poignant or terrifying ways we might go through them. Are we not then liberated in the most profound sense?

The requirement that liberal education be *integrated* is of heightened concern in our age of specialization and of reductionist studies because of the inherent tendency to examine the trees closely—all right up to a point, but in the end incomplete and unsatisfying. One prominent executive made the point in remarking that in his world of specialized scholars and sophisticated think tanks and elaborate bureaucracies, there were far too few "experts in the situation as a whole." This deficiency is apparent enough in the realm of scholarly inquiry and public policy, but in a way it is even more poignantly harmful to young minds seeking meaning in the world they live in. We must first recognize that no matter how important and challenging and brilliantly taught any specialized courses might be (and thus worthy in their own right), random assemblages of them will seldom amount to more than that. Study after study of the reaction of students to college underclass "distribution requirements" come to the same conclusion: the effect is simply incoherent and chaotic. Students find such requirements a waste of time and learn implicitly that things don't add up. One student's program at a prestigious university without a core curriculum included courses in "Arctic archeology," "anger," "counseling," and "the unsolved problems of biology"—all splendid courses by themselves, the student thought, but taken together they lacked both coherence and comprehensiveness.

There are, to be sure, beguiling justifications. The faculty gets to teach whatever idiosyncratic courses suit its fancy (and are relieved of the burden of planning and teaching survey and foundational courses), while students have the "freedom" to choose courses as they please. Things are open-ended, diverse, creative, with everyone "free" to pursue individual interests. But a serious flaw is apparent: there is neither pattern nor effective guidance to help students "get it together." No systematic, required courses give students foundations, big pictures into which they might then fit specialized pieces. Large, integrative works are likely to be neglected as attention focuses on the results of "the latest research." Connections between things are likely to receive less emphasis than the examination of parts. Even less likely is the explanation of pattern and purpose and cosmology, not with the idea of imposing orthodoxy, of course, but simply to give students the repeated experience of confronting and considering such integrations—surely an important part of the desire by humans to know about the world they live in. It may be that the whole is greater than the sum of the parts, and students need to have instruction acknowledging that. The enlightening, stretching experience one has in confronting such integrative minds as Max Weber's or Arnold Toynbee's or Joseph Campbell's needs to be an incessant part of higher education. It is clear, at any rate, that the sort of broad understanding of the world Jefferson got from reading Cicero and Montesquieu and Gibbon must still, in a way suited to the twenty-first century, be part of the intention of liberal education. Institutions of higher learning and their faculties have that inescapable responsibility.

Finally, liberal education must be *radical*, in that it opens up to students something of the range of potential and alternative humankind has attempted and explored and envisioned for itself through time and across space. Only thus can one be free of the confines of one's own (small, narrow, stultifying) world and begin to imagine and pursue a brighter, more beckoning one, however practically difficult its realization might be (awareness of such obstacles, of course, is part of intelligent radicalism). Such radicalness as much searches the present as the past, as much the distant as the close at hand, and as much humankind's inward as outward journeys in pursuit of aspirations that might liberate and ennoble life. In advising a young nephew about religious and philosophic studies Jefferson urged him first to "divest yourself of all bias in favor of novelty and singularity of opinion. . . . Fix reason firmly in her seat, and call to the tribunal every fact, every opinion. . . . Neither believe nor reject anything, because other persons, or descriptions of persons, have rejected or believed it. Your own reason is the only oracle given you by heaven, and you are answerable, not for the rightness, but uprightness of the decision."[2] Unless students experience the exhilaration that goes with such honest inquiry, with such openness to "novelty and singularity of opinion," they risk forever being confined within their biases, limitations, and shortsightedness.

Peter Kropotkin wrote in his "Letters to the Young" that they should "ask what kind of world do you want to live in? What do you need to know? What are you good at and want to work at to build that world? Demand that your teachers teach you that." The young, that is, must, if they are to be truly liberated, have had visions set before them, and paths pointed out toward their realization of fuller, better ways to live. Thus, to read the likes of Plato and Thoreau and Marx and Margaret Fuller and M. L. King, Jr. and Gandhi and Emma Goldman—great envisioners of ideals that can challenge orthodoxies and open minds to alternatives—is also an essential part of true liberal education. Recall that the words "theory" and "theater" both derive from the Greek *thea*, which means *the act of seeing*. In the company of Aristotle and Shakespeare, of Hannah Arendt and James Baldwin, students must be led to "the act of seeing" dimensions and depths previously unknown to them.

There is a danger, of course, that the very eloquence and zeal of some of these great minds could be used to justify dogmatic, oppressive, or totalitarian political regimes. (See, for example, the trenchant observations of E. M. Cioran and Hans Christoph Buch in the Fall 1986 issue of the *Southern Humanities Review.*) Confucius, Rousseau, Burke, Plato, and Marx have been used (or abused?) in that way, and even Dostoyevski, Toynbee, and Gandhi have appeared dangerous to the most open, tolerant, and pluralistic conceptions of free and democratic polities, such as that in Karl Popper's *The Open Society and Its Enemies.* To be profound, integrated, and radical tends to be in tension with the openness (emptiness?), the procedural emphasis (unsubstantial?), and the inclusiveness (uncritical?) that are central to such theorists of freedom and democracy as J. S. Mill and John Dewey. Surely, though, this tension results from the extreme, opposite tendencies in each outlook. The most extreme, rigid idealism of Plato and Confucius is totalitarian, just as extreme procedural emphasis in democracy is vacuous. Neither, however, is compatible with the rich humaneness of the deep, central core of the liberal tradition. Totalitarianism of all varieties is properly understood as *illiberal.* In the broad overlapping of the profound, the integrated, and the radical aspects of a liberal education with the essentials of free, self-governing societies there is deep resonance and compatibility one with the other. One can go from Rousseau and Hegel to Marx and Lenin and even Hitler, but one does not *have* to nor does the outlook of D. H. Lawrence lead necessarily, as Bertrand Russell asserted, "straight to Auschwitz." Indeed, the case can be made that such journeys soon depart from the starting points *properly understood* —proper understandings likely to receive powerful support from a study of the full range of the liberal arts at their best. In fact, a deep sensitivity to the values of the liberal arts is a useful corrective of both tendencies toward dogmatism and fanaticism and to mere procedural or conflict-of-interest models of democracy—as Jefferson would have understood and his plan for the University of Virginia sought to combat.

Liberal education means, then, to bring students to a liberating sense of the nature of the world they live in and of their own potential as human beings. It would thus seem self-evident that a liberal education would have to be profound, integrating, and radical: to be shallow, fragmented, and conventional is to miss the nature of the world and of our human potential, to have trivial answers to the big questions, "Who am I? and Why am I here?" Before we can be anything more specific—in vocation, in life-style, even in nationality—we must be fully liberated human beings. Indeed, we might say that any rich understanding of job, life-style, or nationality must rest on the qualities that infuse genuine liberal education.

Our Public Office

This idea of liberal education has a special meaning in the public life of a self-governing society. It means the sort of education required by *all* people in such a society, whatever their particular skills or walks of life, in order for them to perform properly in their *public office as citizens.* Jefferson put it simply in his first proposal, in 1779, for a system of universal primary education suited to the nation's new independent status: all citizens thus "would be qualified to understand their rights, to maintain them, and to exercise with intelligence their parts in self-government." Such education, he explained to John Adams after each had served as President of the United States, "would raise the mass of the people to the high ground of moral respectability necessary to their own safety, and to orderly government. . . . Worth and genius would thus be sought out from every condition of life, and completely prepared by education for defeating the competition of wealth and birth for public trusts." To skeptics who thought this too high an idealism, Jefferson replied, "if we think [the people] not enlightened enough to exercise their control [over government] with a wholesome discretion, the remedy is not to take it from them, but to inform their discretion by education."[3]

Horace Mann picked up Jefferson's argument in the 1840s when he pointed out to the people of Massachusetts that "one of the highest and most valuable objects, to which the influence of a school can be made conducive, consists in training our children in self-government. A republican form of government, without intelligence in the people," Mann continued, "must be, on a vast scale, what a madhouse, without superintendent, or keepers, would be, on a small one. . . . The very terms, *Public School,* and *Common School,* bear upon their face, that they are schools which the children of the entire community may attend. Every man . . . is taxed for their support . . . on the same principle that he would be taxed to defend the nation against foreign invasion . . . because the general prevalence of ignorance, superstition, and vice, will breed Goth and Vandal at home, more fatal to the public well-being, than any Goth or Vandal from abroad."[4]

Mann's theory of public education was thus an idea guided fundamentally by its *public purpose.* He advocated in Massachusetts a system of education funded by the state (thus public in one sense), and he intended that these schools be open to every child (thus public in yet another sense), but even more he was intent on the stake the public had in them to prepare young people to be good citizens.

This insistence on the public purpose of American education has remained strong. Advocates of the "Americanization" of immigrants, and especially of their children, had in mind mainly the need to train for self-governing citizenship those whose backgrounds made that taxing role unfamiliar. Even proponents of the new, comprehensive universities, though intent on scientific, technical, and vocational studies, also argued that the nation's public life needed the infusions of knowledge and practical proposals such studies afforded. John Dewey made the connection explicit in explaining an updated philosophy of *Democracy and Education* (1917). Assuming as Jefferson and Horace Mann had, that democracy required a properly educated citizenry, Dewey simply brought new pedagogical and psychological insights to bear on the nature of that education. To Dewey, the classrooms themselves, especially at the elementary level, had to be little "laboratories of democracy" where students acted out the processes of discussion ("learning by doing") and public awareness that were the foundations of effective self-government. More recently, though, the emphasis on specialization, technical studies, and vocation that undermined liberal education generally has taken its particular toll on civic education. A social science group requirement often reflected the general education offerings on grounds that it better reflected the diverse researches of the faculty, which in any case no longer had interest or belief in the "common core of studies" idea.

In fact, university preoccupation with the public policy dimensions of the social sciences reveals dramatically how off target such work is from the Jeffersonian ideal of "informing the discretion" of citizens-to-be. In the first place, the direction of instruction is reversed: instead of beginning with the perspective and attitude of the potential citizen which might then confront public questions, study tends to begin, investigatively, with a social science analysis of various "public policy" problems. Resting on the sophisticated, quantitative research of university faculty and policy studies institutes, the problems receive systematic analysis in graduate seminars and upper-division courses in the various social science majors. Then, in a "trickle-down" theory, the methodology, data, and conclusions of such investigations become the basis for introductory courses in the lower division, in community colleges, and in high schools. One popular "policy studies" major at a large university, for example, announces that its students will "learn to collect social science data, analyze public policies from the perspective of several social science disciplines, use basic computer and statistical techniques, and communicate analyses."[5] One must examine public problems—health care, tax rates, pollution of the environment, crime, etc.—so that one knows the facts. Students utilize investigations "in the literature," do surveys of their own, and assemble the data according to the approved modes of analysis. The world is thus pictured as a vast and complicated series of "problems" that require first and foremost to be researched and analyzed—exactly the tasks for which graduates of university social science departments are best trained and suited. Furthermore, as the facts are accumulated, including, in policy analysis, the "input" of the various "actors" and of concerned special interest groups, the usual assumption is that conclusion or policies will arise from the carefully manipulated aggregation of the data; the whole is simply the sum of the parts.

Though the process of arriving at policy positions is not generally seen as consciously competitive, it is usually undertaken within the "conflict-of-interest" assumption that in an open and pluralistic society—policy is best understood as the result of diverse and competing interests. Harking back to Madison's tenth *Federalist Paper,* "conflict-of-interest" theory sees tyranny prevented and policy properly hammered out as a multitude of interests (the more the better) clash and interact. The process is presumed fair, and policy best determined, if access is open to all, if all then engage in vigorous self-advocacy, and if the decisions are made, after compromise, by majority vote. Justice, or the public good, is thus defined simply as the result of this open and democratic process; or at least it is presumed that one cannot do any better than that in a free society. Explicitly rejected, or perhaps simply ignored, is any notion that the public good might be defined, in Madison's terms, as the rationally determined "permanent and aggregate interests of the community."

Whatever the overall merit and demerit of this outlook, it implies, or at least seems to entail, a problematic lack of completeness in facing the full scope of political judgment and participation in a free and democratic society. It is a politics and a citizenship without a center, a purpose, a guiding perspective. It is thus susceptible to use or abuse depending on what purpose or perspective, stated or implied, enlists its methods and skills. To cite an extreme illustration, Adolf Eichmann presumably had high skills of statistical analysis, policy implementation, and communication of results, but we would not regard him as an exemplary public servant. Why not? Precisely because he lacked a humane purpose and perspective.

In speaking of the whole, merely behavioral and quantitative emphasis in contemporary social science, Leo Strauss once remarked that "it would be false to call the new political science diabolic; it has no attributes peculiar to fallen angels . . . nor is it Neronian. Nevertheless one may say that it fiddles while Rome burns. It is excused by two facts: it does not know that it fiddles and it does not know that Rome burns."[6] That is, behavioral and quantitative social scientists, intent on the minute and sophisticated examination of various parts of the body politic, often fail to realize how much their researches draw them into arcane, abstract trivia; they fiddle. On the other hand, their studies often neglect the larger problems of the world, the wider public and moral and humane concerns that give shape and quality to human life. Thus, at least as far as one might gather from the sophisticated explanation of their work in scholarly journals, they disclaim interest in whether or not Rome is burning. Though Strauss' judgment is not entirely fair, he does properly make an important point: modern social science, however effective in gathering and analyzing data, insufficiently attends to the need political decision makers have for guidance from larger, more public-spirited perspectives and purposes. And insofar as social sciences foregoes interest in such matters, it simply is incomplete training for those taking part in government. The point, of course, is analogous to the incompleteness in one's education when attention to vocational training excludes the liberal arts.

If we return then, to the concern of Jefferson and Horace Mann for "training our children in self-government," what can we say about education for citizenship in 1989? I would suggest, following the distinguished philosopher Joseph Tussman,[7] that we begin by regarding the citizen in a democracy as an officeholder in government. That is, in discussing, voting, and acting in a self-governing society, the citizen is part, actually one of the ultimate parts, of the government itself. Thus, the role differs only in degree from that of any elected or appointed official, or even from that of a monarch in a society ruled by one person. The essential obligation this entails, as we expect (though don't always receive) from all officeholders, is a perspective and habit that puts the public interest, the good of the country as a whole, above private, selfish, dynastic, class, or any other partisan interest. In training young people for the "office of citizen," which in the United States all enter at age eighteen, then, we must start and end with nourishing the essential, public-spirited stance expected of any public official.

Our sometimes cynical age is inclined, at this point, to ask for a definition of "public spirit," or "the public interest," or even to question whether such an idea can have an objective meaning. In the conflict-of-interest model, the public interest is often defined simply as the result of the self-interested forces at work in the political arena. Hence, in a free society it receives its definition from the interplay of a multitude of special interests. It neither assumes nor requires that any "public interest" objectively understood either exist or be sought directly by anybody. This view is beguiling because it allows, even encourages, individuals and groups to pursue their own interests, and because it relieves everyone—citizens as well as higher officials— from having to think about the common good. Indeed, such thought is often held to be delusive nonsense at best (I've heard it described in college classrooms as "bullshit"), and the sure path to totalitarian bigotry—the closed society—at worst.

Is this the stage we have reached in the late twentieth century, or is there some way to think meaningfully about "public spirit" in our day? I would suggest that the idea is a vital part of the American political tradition, and alive and well in a multitude of common sense perceptions. At the Constitutional Convention, Franklin extolled the commitment to freedom and self-government that had caused thousands of ordinary people to fight in the revolutionary armies. He saw also, in the quest for a new life that drew other thousands (eventually millions) from the oppression of the Old World to the opportunities of the New, a unique potential for a willing acceptance of the obligations of citizenship in the adopted country. He insisted, as well, that land and wealth qualifications for suffrage ought to be eliminated because such possessions bore no correlation to the *qualitative* requirements of good citizenship. In reasoning that would become the theme of Jefferson's life and thought Franklin believed that the essential qualification for the office of citizen was a public-spiritedness that arose not from wealth or status or class or sex or race, but from an intention, a willingness, eventually a habit, to seek the common good.

This capacity requires initially a proper perspective. The public interest can be said to begin with an interest in the public, the taking seriously of the existence of a political community of which one is a part and the possibility of participating usefully in its common affairs. The foundation of this perspective is evident in a simple illustration: a committee is appointed to honor a respected and much beloved colleague about to retire. All agree on the idea of an honoring celebration, but have various incomplete, and perhaps incompatible notions of what to do. Since the *intention* is shared, though, a constructive discussion can and often does lead to an integrated plan better than any of the scattered ideas people had on their own. We might say the committee had an interest in the public; a sense of the objective need to contribute to the larger purpose. On the other hand, if some member of the committee offers self-interested arguments (say a restaurant owner who wants to make money by catering the celebration), it is perceived readily as an alien, inappropriate perspective, one that is *not* interested in the general good. The difference between self-interested and disinterested perspective is clear, as is the varying capacity of individuals to attain such perspective. Also apparent is the possibility of a result greater than the sum of the parts arising from the public intentions of the members, and the dysfunctional effect of a merely selfish orientation. In admittedly more complex and ambiguous ways, these same distinctions in perspective, and the varying potential for common achievement, are present in discussions of all public issues and reveal the central need in training for the office of citizen: to encourage an interest in the public as an objective reality and as an approach both within human potential and capable of yielding unpredictable benefits.

Such an idea of citizenship, of course, has an ancient and honored lineage. It was central to Aristotle's argument that good government depended on the public virtue of those who ruled (all the citizens in a constitutional polity) and to the Renaissance "civic republican" model requiring an independent, reasonable, and responsible citizenry. It was also central to Jefferson, Horace Mann, John Dewey, and other American proponents of democratic citizenship. All attended primarily to the "quality of the parts," the nourishment of the vital "public spirit" as well as practical skills of those who would take part in self-government. In our day, despite the preoccupation of generations of social scientists with research skills and policy analysis and the useful application of them to American public life, the need for "public spirit," proper perspective, remains as strong as ever.

An important part of such education for "the office of citizen" is some study of the development of responsible freedom and self-government, most notably in Western civilization. Attention to what Walter Lippmann has called "the tradition of civility," the attitudes and practices essential to the process of democracy over the centuries, the growth of free government in Anglo-America, and the ideas undergirding the American Constitution would help students understand the rich connotations of democratic citizenship. In any case, it is clear that constructive participation in free and democratic government must be grounded in some understanding of the evolution, principles, and practices of such government. These define, we might say, the liberal core of the public-spiritedness basic to all civic education.

Lest this approach seem unduly utopian about the capacity of human beings to achieve a public-spirited posture, let us remember first the possibly even greater utopianism of supposing that everything is all right in democratic societies when *no one* is expected or even encouraged to achieve such a perspective; when it is supposed sufficient to simply open up the political process to all people, groups, and interests, and then analyze various policies. Such a dynamic *might* work well, or at least be the best we can do in a free and pluralistic society, but in our interdependent world, one suspects this is less and less likely to suffice. Problems of global ecology and world peace may in our day require the forethought, reasoned approach, and concern for the good of the whole central to the "office of the citizen" and may *not* be amenable to a "sum-of-the-parts" approach. Instead, that is, of being naively optimistic about human nature, the encouragement of the human potential for a vision beyond the narrowly selfish may, as the twenty-first century approaches, be the only practical thing left for us—or at least more practical than the very dubious optimism of supposing everything will be all right if we simply pursue our own special interests in free and open political arenas.

The highest wisdom, in matters of government, then, is to recognize the realistic way democracy prevents tyranny by encouraging a pluralism that disperses power, but to see as well, the critical need to cultivate human capacities for justice, good will, reason, and public spirit in order that, in Faulkner's phrase, we might not only survive, but prevail. It is only mildly comforting, after all, to have a polity that, by setting interest against interest, prevents the worst results. Indeed, it is not even always the case that this happens; compromises fall between stools, or conflicting pathologies combine into potent, evil conspiracies. At least as important, if we are to do more than merely survive, is to draw forth, encourage, cultivate that part of our humanity which allowed Jefferson to suppose in the Declaration of Independence that "just" government "derived from the consent of the governed." There simply is no escaping the equations which link just government, effective public education, and the qualities nourished by the liberal arts.

But what is good government? Can it be defined in anything like objective terms? Or is it merely "the interest of the stronger," or perhaps an idea that is simply defined differently at different times for different societies? Every ancient tradition known to humankind, of course, would insist on the reality and pursuit of good government as supremely important. Mythologies typically include stories of wise and heroic leaders presiding over good government. The peoples of East Asia have for millenia seen their civilizations as centering around a unified, powerful, and moral state. Their traditional Confucian outlook regards good government by learned, wise, and public-spirited officials as the very essence of the good life for everyone in the society. Plato spent a lifetime inquiring after the ideal state, and Aristotle made a distinction between *good* and *bad* governments, the essential point, whatever the number who governed or the processes. The distinction was always between government on behalf of the good of the whole on the one hand, and government by a brutal tyrant or selfish oligarchy or mindless democracy on the other. That is, good rule arose fundamentally not from process or form of government, but from intention or purpose or quality of result.

Aristotle paid such attention to the good and bad versions of the various forms of government because he took government itself so seriously. It existed, he said in his famous aphorism, "for the sake of the good life, not for the sake of life only." The state existed not for mere security or commerce or prevention of crime, but "for the sake of a perfect and self-sufficing life, . . . for the will to live together in friendship, . . . for the sake of noble actions, and not of mere companionship."[8] As for Ronald Reagan, so for Aristotle there was great danger from bad government, but he would never have supposed the answer was to diminish or minimize government; that would to the Greek thinker have been timid and futile and cowardly. Government was simply too much a part of human nature, human society, and human potential to be downgraded and trivialized.

Though the ideas of theorists of contract government, of utilitarians, and especially of social Darwinist laissez-faire ideologues, as well as the existence in Anglo-America at times of minimalist states, have sometimes obscured any deep sense of the importance of good government (often equated with little government), in the twentieth century we should be even more aware than Aristotle was of its critical importance. Some nations have been fortunate to have been, on the whole, fairly well governed—Canada, the Netherlands, Britain, New Zealand, Scandinavia, the United States, and, at least relatively, perhaps nations such as Venezuela, Thailand, and the Ivory Coast. On the other hand, consider the horrors visited on the people of some nations in the twentieth century by bad governments: Germany, USSR, Iran, Argentina, Cambodia, China, and Uganda, among others, come to mind. It is also possible for fortunes to change as regimes change—contrast Stalin with Gorbachev; Mao's Great Cultural Revolution with Deng's opening to the West, or Argentina today with its situation 10 or 40 years ago. The point is that the way human society is governed is of enormous, often transcending importance to the quality of life lived by its people.

If one asks, though, properly and insistently, more precisely what are the hallmarks of good government—how can we tell it from bad—we can easily set some down. For Americans the preamble to the Constitution may furnish a ready framework for such an inquiry. It stated, after all, the purposes which the new Constitution was to serve. The process of government, detailed in the body of the Constitution, that is, was merely instrumental to the purposes, the qualities to be nourished by the government, enunciated in the preamble.

What, for example, are the connotations of the words "more perfect Union"? The phrase has to do not only with the structure and processes of government, the formal union, but more profoundly with the quality of the bonds. Were suspicion, insecurity, and alienation common in the attitudes of, and relationships among, the people and parts of the Union? Or, on the other hand, were trust, good will, and common purpose characteristic of the bonds? It is clear, at any rate, that the existence of attitudes of trust and good will make for better government than do attitudes of suspicion and alienation. We know the difference, that is, between the good and bad qualities.

The general meaning of justice, raised above its cynical definition as "the interest of the stronger" as Plato shows it can be, also seems clear. Surely it signifies fairness, equity, compassion, and "minding one's own business" diligently and responsibly, rather than corruption, inequality, arbitrary privilege, and greed. We can affirm readily the relative justice or lack of it, and the aspects of life where it exists more or less, in various polities past and present. Is the treatment of accused persons more equitable in Great Britain or in Chile? Are the needs of hungry people dealt with more justly in the People's Republic of China or in Ethiopia? Are elections fairer in Canada or in Mexico? The answers to these questions surely help us define good government and see its greater reality in some places than in others.

The meaning of "domestic tranquility" is equally clear. A society possessing it would be orderly, obedient to law, safe, peaceful, and characterized by a certain quietude and unaggressiveness. On the other hand it would not be chaotic, lawless, violent, and its people filled with fear and discord and hostility. A good government, then, would accentuate the first qualities and diminish the latter.

To "provide for the common defence," especially in a dangerous world of sovereign (and anarchic) nations, is also an undeniable task of good government. The devastations of invasion, war, and colonialism—the effects of inadequate common defense—are obvious, as are the blessings of a society's control over its own destiny. That is, a government that possesses the wisdom, diplomatic skill, military effectiveness, internal vigor, and willing support of the people (what Jefferson meant in 1801 when he declared that the United States had "the strongest government on earth")[9] needed to assure national integrity is surely better than one that leaves the nation vulnerable to violent and predatory neighbors.

Promoting the "general welfare" is perhaps the broadest, most positive of the injunctions laid on government—and, since it provokes less agreement on specifics, it is also the most controversial. It seems, in fact, to open countless disputes over "the welfare system," allocation of resources, industrial policy, and so on—and these are not matters on which a free and diverse people are likely to reach easy policy agreement. Indeed, some are so problematic that many observers argue government ought to reduce its initiatives and responsibilities regarding "the general welfare." (Such diminishment may, in fact, at times, be the best way to "promote the general welfare," but this ought to be a reflective choice of government itself, not a dogma.) Again, though, general guidelines that distinguish better from worse are discernible. Are not growth, prosperity, and beauty in a society better than stagnation, poverty, and ugliness? And is it not also clear that, with thoughtful, well-informed, and public-spirited attention, our governments (local, state, and national) might move the society we all live in toward the better, rather than the worst, of those directions? Any government worthy of the name, in fact, must accept the responsibility Athenian citizens were sworn to: "to transmit this city, not less but greater, better and more beautiful than it was transmitted to us"—that is, to promote its general welfare.

Finally, the preamble of the Constitution enjoins that the union "secure the blessings of liberty"—a charge soon to be clarified by the addition of a bill of rights. The freedoms and rights there set forth—freedom of religion and expression, freedom from unreasonable search and seizure, the right to trial by jury, and so on—define the more formal "blessings of liberty" that a good government must protect. These liberties, moreover, no matter how morally obligatory or theoretically "unalienable" they might be, are made real in any society only when accepted and given effect by government. When courts and their officers prevent invasions of religious liberty, when government disciplines itself in assuring the rights of the accused, and when the enforcement of law makes our streets safe, then, and only then, are we really free to worship as we please, to prevent our unlawful imprisonment, to walk the streets at will, and so on. Only, too, in a free society can creativity, enterprise, pluralism, and diversity truly flourish. Government cannot itself accomplish those things, but its proper conduct and encouragement can make them more possible. Oppositely, bad governments can impose repression, brutality, and conformity. The press gangs, the storm troopers, the secret police, the lynch mobs, the concentration camps of history leave little doubt about what the blessings of liberty are—or about the critical impact good or bad government can have on our lives.

If we were to make composite lists, then, of all the qualities of good government—trust, fairness, prosperity, protection of rights, and so on—and then all the qualities of bad ones—corruption, fear, poverty, brutality, and so on—we get a graphic sense both of what good government is and of how important it is in our lives. Our tending to forget this has been heightened, probably, by what Walter Lippmann called the "brief spell of exceptionally fine weather" that prevailed so far as government was concerned in the Western world and especially in the United States between 1814 and 1914. During that century, governments faced relatively little of the harsh need, Lippmann argues, to "tax, conscript, command, prohibit, . . . to assert a public interest against private inclination." Thus, the notion grew "that in a free and progressive society it is a good thing that the government should be weak. . . . It had been possible to dream ... that in the rivalry of the diverse interests all would somehow come out for the best. . . . The public interest could be equated with what was revealed in election returns, in sales reports, balance sheets, circulation figures, and statistics of expansion. . . . The public good could be thought of as being immanent in the aggregate of private transactions."[10] In the United States, this has remained a potent view (does it sound like Ronald Reagan?) that both guides and oversimplifies our response to government 75 years after the "fair weather," except for brief intervals, has largely passed (and maybe it was largely a delusion even then). In any case, Americans face large problems of reunderstanding the place of government in their society, and of recapturing a sense of what good government really means.

We must recall at this point why Jefferson was a conditional democrat; he endorsed democracy only insofar as he saw prospects that it might result in the ideals proclaimed in the preamble and in other statements of "public right." He spent a lifetime seeking to frame governments properly in order to assure their fidelity to the people and to increase the likelihood that the people would be thoughtful, responsible, public-spirited citizens (members of the body politic). This meant that government would respect and protect the rights of the people (a Lockean dictum), but just as critically, that the people, as governors, would take thought collectively to pursue the good society as a whole (an Aristotelian dictum). This dual commitment, perhaps conferred upon us by the accident of the time of our nation's founding, is nonetheless the continuing wager of our long experiment in democracy: that self-government can be good government. Jefferson, at least, would have had little use for the first did it not result in the second—and I suppose, if the wager were put that way to us, two centuries later, neither would we.

And it is only an understanding tying together the liberal arts, public education, and good government that can help us win the wager. Leaders will need a thorough and sophisticated education in arts, letters, science, philosophy, and public right in order to fulfill the demanding tasks before them. They have much to do to enhance and promote "the good society." To properly choose and support such leaders, and to be able to judge them, and replace them if necessary, the people will need to be properly educated for *their* public task. Implicitly, the more the principles of the liberal arts permeate in some fashion all levels of education, and the more often larger portions of the population have access to the higher forms of liberal studies, the more cultivation there will be of public virtue. And only its widespread existence in a society, among all officers from citizens to senators and presidents, can result in a good movement that may fulfill the human potential for an ennobled common life.

Public philosophy in our day must come the same full circle it did as Jefferson sought educational reform in Virginia and founded its university. The circumstances, of course, are different, and recognition of the need to include the full range of our diverse people in the equation of government must now be more intense, but we can recognize all the central propositions as relevant for our day. Genuine human fulfillment requires a liberal, liberating education that opens up the profound insights, the integrating perspectives, and the radical alternatives that allow human life to transcend the limitations of ignorance, self-concern, and struggle for survival. However much we attend to the important needs of special and vocational studies, we must as well, if our humanity is to be fulfilled, place those studies in a wider, liberating, human context. Jefferson knew that, and so do we, if we stop to think about it. Then we also know that in a self-governing society, the public spirit necessary to fulfill the universal office of citizen means largely to possess this sense of a wider context and project it into every public deliberation from neighborhood conversations and primary school classrooms to city council meetings and national election campaigns. Public education, that is, must be thought of in the large sense of nourishing the sensibility in every person, and especially in every young person apprenticed to, and eventually filling, the office of citizen, of what the general good might be. Finally, it is equally clear that such public-spiritedness reveals to us both the importance of our common purposes as a political community and the potential we have to govern ourselves wisely and well. Especially in the interdependent world of the looming third millenium, we cannot afford the luxury of thinking that government itself is unimportant, or that in a democratic society we can safely leave it to others.

When the same Dumas Malone, with whose biography of Jefferson we started, was asked what most distinguished the Founders from our present generation of political leaders, he said that "they knew more about the past, and had thought more about the future." The liberal arts attend precisely to both qualities: they explore the past in ways that project profoundly, integratively, and radically into the future. Effective *public* education applies the lessons of such a perspective to the office of citizen held by all members of a self-governing polity. And the end result of such exploration and application can be the "good government from reflection and choice" that Publius held up as the only outcome that could prevent the advent of the democratic age from being "considered as the general misfortune of mankind."[11] The power of the linkages here noted measures our large responsibilities as educators and gives us a glimpse of the judgment that history may make upon us. Will we, as teachers and as Americans, be seen as good and faithful stewards of our public trust, or will we be seen as having ignored or betrayed that trust by having failed to educate liberally, to encourage civic responsibility, and to govern well? At the center of this calling is the simple, yet awesome, task Jefferson undertook near the beginning of his public career: to see that all citizens "be qualified to understand their rights, to maintain them, and to exercise with intelligence their parts in self-government."

Ralph Ketcham, professor of History and Political Science at Syracuse University, is the author of Individualism and American Life.

Originally published in Southern Humanities Review, *23 (Fall 1989): 321–340. Reprinted with permission of the author.*

Notes

1. Report of the Commissioners for The University of Virginia, August 4, 1818; in Merrill D. Peterson, ed., *The Portable Thomas Jefferson* (New York: Viking Press, 1975), pp. 333–339.

2. Jefferson to Peter Carr, August 10, 1787; in Peterson, *The Portable Thomas Jefferson*, pp. 425–427.

3. Jefferson "autobiography," 1821, in Adrienne Koch and William Peden, eds., *The Life and Selected Writings of Thomas Jefferson* (New York: Modern Library, 1944), p. 52; Jefferson to John Adams, October 28, 1813, in Lester J. Cappon, ed., *The Adams-Jefferson Letters: The Complete Correspondence Between Thomas Jefferson and Abigail and John Adams* (Chapel Hill, NC: University of North Carolina Press, 1959), II, 387–391; Jefferson to W. C. Jarvis, September 28, 1820, in Edward Dumbauld, ed., *Thomas Jefferson: Political Writings, Representative Selections* (New York: Liberal Arts Press,1955), p. 93.

4. Mann, ninth and twelfth Annual Reports, 1845 and 1848; reprinted in S. Alexander Rippa, ed., *Educational Ideas in America: A Documentary History* (New York: D. McKay Company, 1969), pp. 195–202.

5. "The Policy Studies Major," Syracuse University, 1988.

6. Leo Strauss, "Epilogue," in H. J. Storing, ed., *Essays on the Scientific Study of Politics* by Walter Berns and Others (New York: Holt, Rinehart and Winston, 1962), p. 327.

7. Joseph Tussman, *Obligation and the Body Politic* (New York: New York, Oxford University Press, 1960).

8. Aristotle, *Politics*, Book III, Chapter 9.

9. First Inaugural Address, March 4, 1801; Koch and Peden, eds., *The Life and Selected Writings of Thomas Jefferson*, p. 323.

10. Walter Lippmann, *Essays in the Public Philosophy* (Boston: Little Brown Publishers, 1955), pp. 15–16.

11. *The Federalist, No. 1;* Clinton L. Rossiter, ed., *The Federalist Papers*. Alexander Hamilton, James Madison, John Jay. With an Introduction, Table of Contents, and Index of Ideas by Clinton Rossiter (New York: New American Library, 1961), p. 33.

"The current literature suggests that campus climates are more chilly than welcoming, more alienating than involving, more hostile than encouraging. Indeed, in higher education, the condition of diversity is all too often a condition of alienation."

Embracing Diversity as a Central Campus Goal

by Daryl G. Smith

Historically, by focusing so much on the entering characteristics of students, we have reflected an assumption that our institutions are perfect and that the burden of failure rests on student incompetence. Our task now is to shift our focus from the problems students bring to an institution to the ways in which the institution must itself change.

Such a reframing of the issue has an important impact on the answers we find at every level—from how we evaluate students to where we look for solutions. For example, when retention is referred to as the "student dropout rate," it implies a problem with the student. Alternatively, when it is "institutional graduation rate," the focus is on the institution. Jaramillo correctly points out that "as long as we condone the use of metaphors which conjure up a scenario of individual initiative and responsibility for educational failure, change will not occur."[1]

The need to reframe our conception of the relation between the campus and its students becomes especially urgent when we consider the goals of the emerging multicultural campus. As I have read the literatures about the college experience in general—and that of women, adult learners, those with learning and physical handicaps, and people of color in particular—one theme has emerged over and over again: alienation. The current literature suggests that campus climates are more chilly than welcoming, more alienating than involving, more hostile than encouraging. Indeed, in higher education, the condition of diversity is all too often a condition of alienation.

Students, who are seen as different, experience powerful and alienating instances of racism, discrimination, and stereotyping; campus attitudes and behaviors that isolate them; campuses that have socially, physically, or programmatically made them think that they do not belong, are not welcome, or are not expected to succeed. Members of visible minorities whose numbers are small in the institution are often invisible as individuals but highly visible as group members. While individual failures are perceived as failures for the entire group, individual successes are often overlooked.

If we are to have truly multicultural campuses, we must shift our framework from one that focuses solely on assisting or accommodating those who are different so they can survive in an alien world, to creating a campus world which is not alien and which promotes success. The reward of this effort will be an improved capacity to educate in a pluralistic society for a pluralistic world.

An important source of alienation comes from the perception that the institution is not supportive of diversity, does not value it, and does not consider it part of its mission. Indeed, there are many subtle or not so subtle messages implying that dealing with diversity is seen as a problem.

Suppose, instead, that an institution were to link diversity to its essential educational mission. By reframing the mission in this way, the institution is focused on a rationale for change motivated by its need to be successful—not just because it "has to." The climate on our campuses will not substantially change unless we see that creating a multicultural campus is not a diversion from, but central to, the purpose of education. As we focus on providing support for those who are different, we must simultaneously educate everyone for living in a multicultural society. Indeed, those who have had experience in multicultural contexts provide an important resource for accomplishing these goals, while most others will require assistance.

Of the many obstacles to our ability to effect this change, the most fundamental is the perception that diversity conflicts with quality. Yet a fundamental characteristic of the most successful programs and institutions is that performance and quality are assumed and are not compromised. The consistency of diversity and excellence is taken for granted in the mathematics workshop developed by the Berkeley mathematician Uri Treisman and the records of Howard University and the ten public universities selected for a national study of successful institutions, including Brooklyn College and Temple University.[2] These are not places where students who are different feel that although they were admitted, they are expected to fail. High standards designed to weed students out are different from high standards in an institution where students are expected to succeed and are given the support to do so. These institutions hold themselves accountable for excellence, and place great care on deciding how standards will be evaluated.

Many other institutions, however, continue to use inappropriate measures to assess quality. Using scores on certain standardized tests which underpredict student performance, having to attend certain graduate schools, or being required to publish in certain journals on certain topics are examples of quality indicators that seriously undervalue the excellence of many nontraditional groups. The same could be said of some campus discussions about core materials to be included in the curriculum. The unfamiliarity of most campus faculty with certain works by women or people of color does not necessarily render these works of less quality than "classic" works. Rather, it suggests that most traditional disciplines have been very narrow. If we continue to define quality in limited ways, most persons on the margin will be excluded or devalued. The fundamental predisposition of higher education has been to maintain homogeneity and to adapt only when necessary. A critical example of this may be occurring in discussions of whether some institutions have set limits on access for Asian-Americans because they might become overrepresented in the student body. The credibility of higher education's commitment to quality and diversity is weakened when institutions limit the access of Asian-Americans in the name of diversity and that of African-Americans and Latino students or faculty in the name of quality. The net result of both is to perpetuate homogeneity. We, as faculty, play a critical role in analyzing our discussions and debates to see if the implicit values pit quality against diversity or support the status quo.

Few societies, and relatively few institutions, have created successful and diverse communities. Few of us even know what that would mean. It is essential, therefore, that the process by which these communities are developed have the benefit of participation from people of diverse experience. Without diversity in the faculty and administrative leadership of our institutions, the ability to make thoughtful decisions, establish priorities, and deal with issues will be severely hampered. Our failure to develop that leadership over the last 20 years will place many of our institutions in significant jeopardy as our educational goals shift toward a more multicultural perspective and as our student bodies become more diverse. Higher education will be looking to replace half a million faculty members in the next decades. How will we function as multicultural communities unless we are multicultural at all levels?

Despite all the lip service paid to affirmative action, many campus programs have focused on meeting legal guidelines and validating statistically that "qualified persons" were not available. If we are serious this time about the intent of affirmative action, it is important that the question be framed so as not to put all the emphasis on the difficulties in "the pipeline." We must pursue carefully developed and activist search processes that put us in touch with talent. We must craft job descriptions to relate to campus needs and new developments in the disciplines and not simply fall prey to what has been or what once was viewed as essential in the discipline. We must scrutinize hidden assumptions about where we can find talent. If we can only look to places that have excluded, then, indeed the pipeline will be nearly empty. Historically African-American colleges are the point of origin of a large percentage of minority faculty teaching in our colleges and universities. To ignore them as a resource because they lack the prestige of some other institutions is to invalidate the search process. Indeed, it is in the early part of searches—the development of job descriptions, curricular evaluations, and screening of résumés—that our processes are set up to fail. We have been more than ready to rely on symbolic indicators of excellence than to evaluate excellence in terms of the individuals involved.

We must also look to support and develop the talent on the campus and reevaluate the criteria used to determine success. In areas of faculty evaluation and reappointment, many of our traditional measures of excellence (specific methodologies, specialized subject areas, specific graduate programs, certain journals) have served to exclude. This is a critical area and one in which a fundamental reevaluation of traditional criteria of excellence must take place if we are to avoid setting excellence in conflict with diversity. Before blind reviews emerged as the norm in the peer review process, we know that gender was in and of itself a factor in selection. But the blind review process does not mean the elimination of bias which comes from a narrow focus on certain research questions or from setting limited choices for methodology. Our disciplines are changing, and many of those who have facilitated these changes have had to function at the margin of their disciplines. Their research has often not been published in mainstream journals; their research questions have not always been deemed acceptable in the field. As a result, such work has not been given sufficient consideration by review processes which put more weight on *where* one is published than on the substantive merits of *what* is published. One of the challenges we face is that many faculty are not in good positions to judge the merit of such work because their own background is so limited.

Moreover, the issues of alienation, "burnout," and lack of retention are issues for faculty and staff just as they are for students. In listening to the stories of minority faculty and staff, one cannot help but be moved by the burden such people face as they attempt to be role models and model scholar/teachers and serve on every committee dealing remotely with multicultural issues on campus while simultaneously experiencing explicit or subtle forms of harassment, isolation, and racism. The result is a revolving door, an extravagant waste of human resources and a major obstacle to change.

As campuses across the country focus on issues of multiculturalism, concern grows that being able to attract people may favor wealthier institutions with more resources. My own perception is, however, that campuses truly engaged in creating supportive campus climates for faculty, staff, and students will be seen as more desirable than those that expect to buy faculty and staff without making fundamental changes.

Early notions of a diverse community assumed an assimilation model. Most campuses have moved beyond that approach and many now talk about a diverse community based on mutual respect and celebration of differences. However, all institutions, even the most complex, inevitably make decisions which involve fundamental perspectives about community, learning, teaching, and resource allocation. With diversity comes differences in perceptions about what these decisions should be and who and how they should be made. Inevitably, then, conflict will emerge at the institutional, group and individual level. The question cannot be how to avoid conflict. Campuses will need to be able to face conflict, work through it, and, most importantly, learn from it.

Institutions must decide on those structures, priorities, and values that must be shared and those in which diversity and pluralism can function and thrive. The process of finding the balance between fragmentation and homogeneity is an important one, and one which must benefit from multicultural perspectives. The process of working through conflict must be seen as an important part of creating thriving social and intellectual multicultural communities. Our institutions will need to develop positive mechanisms for dealing with, and learning from, the issues which arise out of the conflict. Individuals will need to expect that personal efforts will not always be appreciated and that some behaviors and attitudes will be called into question. This process has the potential to be a significant source of learning at all levels.

One of the important measures of the quality of life on campus is the level and quality of interaction within and among groups. Yet, all too often, campuses focus on the apparent self-selection or voluntary isolation of students of color into their own respective groups. In contrast, the evidence is that many of the students from underrepresented groups have much more contact with majority students and their culture and value that interaction more than many majority students. This is yet another example of targeting those on the margin in contrast to looking carefully at the ethos of the institution.

The issue that needs addressing here focuses on the quality of interaction among all individuals and groups, the degree to which majority populations reach out to others, and the ways in which the campus fosters interaction. What is the quality of professional and social interaction among faculty? How much interaction occurs on campus, in residence halls, in classes, and among faculty colleagues? To what degree are people learning from one another and in dialogue with one another? Do people seem genuinely interested in learning from difference? Does the classroom climate foster learning from one another and about different perspectives and skills? What efforts are being made to develop skills in multicultural communication? Are programs on campus designed to help foster an appreciation of diversity? Are policies and procedures in place which make the environment safe for dissent and respectful of difference? How swift and clear is the institutional and faculty response to racism, sexism, and homophobia on campus?

The burden for responding to these questions rests with institutional leadership. All too often we have relied on underrepresented groups to push for change. All faculty must take responsibility for creating a climate in which students, faculty, and staff feel supported, expected to succeed, respected, and valued as individuals and as group members.

While one might look to campus programs and functions like student affairs to evaluate and address the climate of the campus, the academic and intellectual life of the campus and the role of the faculty remain the critical factors in how the campus is perceived by individuals and groups. On some campuses, the dialogue about the curriculum is framed in terms of the need to offer additional courses about women and people of color so that *they* will feel comfortable. If campuses recognize the importance of educating students (and the rest of us) to live in a multicultural society, then the curriculum must play a key role and must go beyond simply adding a few courses *for* students of color or *for* women. What we need is a curriculum capable of educating all students about and for the pluralism of the society and world of which they are a part.

Curricular transformation involves rethinking the fundamental assumptions about knowledge and about the ways we teach. Looking at race, class, and gender invites reconceptualization. Looking at American or world cultures from the perspectives of groups which have been at the margin provides important new perspectives. Knowledge of American history and culture requires an ability to deal factually and conceptually with diversity. Even the study of Western civilization encompasses greater diversity than would be apparent from most courses on the subject. With respect to subjects like math and science, which appear to be "neutral," fundamental questions remain to be raised about the topics of inquiry, methods, and how these subjects have been taught, and how diverse groups of students can best learn them.

Educating in a multicultural context involves not only what we teach but also how we teach and the climate in which our classrooms function. Often, faculty discussions in this area focus on content and cognitive issues without recognition of the important role of the classroom climate. While many students have succeeded, for many it has been in spite of pedagogy rather than because of it. In my view, the competitive approach to learning emphasized in many fields does not provide an adequate climate for learning for most students. The common practice of grading on the curve necessarily pits one student against another and makes performance subject to the abilities of others in a given class. Each faculty member will need to evaluate and understand the kinds of classroom approaches and environments which inhibit and block success or prompt people to avoid certain fields altogether. Faculty will also need to be adept at working with the variety of approaches to learning that students bring to class.

How faculty treat students and how we model a response to differences in background and perspective are critical to setting a climate on campus in which everyone is a learner as well as teacher. Treating students with respect and dignity is essential. I wish I could say that this has been assumed.

The task of reeducating ourselves is often a daunting one, certainly not comfortable and not always easy. Yet to engage the question of educating for a multicultural society requires familiarity with sources, methods, and literatures that were not part of the training of many faculty. In addition, perspectives are being introduced which fundamentally alter the nature and content of the curriculum and of research. Higher education and the disciplines have dealt with this many times before. For example, when the personal computer first arrived, most of us understood that we would need to learn to use it, and we did. We did not want the institution, the field, or ourselves to be seen as out of date with respect to new technology. Moreover, our institutions found a way to assist us. We cannot afford to be out of date with respect to the knowledge that is now emerging and its implications for teaching, learning, and research. Many more resources are available today to faculty interested in looking at their fields from new disciplinary or interdisciplinary perspectives, and increasing numbers of institutions providing support to faculty to engage in that process.

Faculty activism, leadership, involvement, and development will be essential if our campuses are to succeed in efforts to prepare ourselves and future generations for a much more complex set of challenges. This sort of change will take time and commitment. Pragmatically, though, as long as we keep adding and changing because we "have to," we will resent the time and resources expended. If there is a single lesson to be learned, it is that we cannot simply add and stir. We must shift our own frame of reference to see that we each have a great deal to gain from this effort—greater success as teachers, greater participation in the forefront of research as scholars, greater comfort on our campuses for everyone. Truly, diversity will provide the greatest of resources for the revitalization of higher education.

Daryl G. Smith is associate professor of Higher Education and Psychology at The Claremont Graduate School. She is author of The Challenge of Diversity: Involvement or Alienation in the Academy?

Originally published in Academe *76 (Nov/Dec 1990): 29–33. Reprinted with permission of the author.*

Notes

1. Jaramillo, Mari Luci, "Institutional Responsibility in the Provision of Educational Experiences to the Hispanic American Female Student," *The Broken Web: The Educational Experience of Hispanic American Women,* edited by T. McKenna and F. I. Ortiz (Encino, CA: Floricanto Press, 1989).

2. Richardson, Richard C. Jr., Howard Simmons, Alfredo de los Santos, "Graduating Minority Students," *Change* 19(3):20–22.

"The retreat to subjectivism and relativism is ultimately corrosive of democracy itself. It deprives public discourse of seriousness because it means that there can be no expectation of agreement reflecting a rational consensus on issues of public life."

Civic Education, Liberal Education, and Democracy

by J. Donald Moon

Democracy is premised upon twin commitments: to the possibility that through political action we can direct our collective lives, and to the equality of citizens. The first is an old vision of political life, one which conceives of politics not as a struggle over position, power, and wealth, but as a form of human freedom. In the *Laws* Plato complained "that no human being ever legislates anything, but that chances and accidents of every sort, occurring in all kinds of ways, legislate everything for us."[1] Plato envisioned a form of political activity which would not leave our collective fates to chance, but would enable us to self-consciously direct our affairs in accordance with the aspirations and commitments we have deliberately accepted. At least as an ideal, the political sphere can be a realm of human freedom, one in which we use our energies and wit not simply to adapt to our fate, but consciously to shape it.

If democrats share Plato's vision of politics in the service of human freedom, we reject his view that it must therefore be the preserve of an elite. For us the insight necessary to discern the proper direction of public life, to call to account those charged with responsibility for our common affairs, and to recognize those qualities of character and judgment required in our leaders, is not a result of specialized, technical training, but is available to ordinary men and women. Not every citizen will actively participate in governance, and many will prefer to lend their support to others whose skills and ambitions enable them effectively to advance their viewpoint. But every citizen is entitled to an equal voice, at least in choosing representatives, and each has the opportunity both in normal life and in political activity to develop the practical judgment necessary for deliberation on public affairs.

Democrats have long recognized the importance of civic education in providing citizens with the qualities necessary for political involvement. Like Plato, they have seen that the schools will necessarily play a crucial role in preparing people for citizenship. Indeed, one of the reasons why democrats have always valued universal, public education is that it can provide a common experience to all citizens. At least ideally, the public school is a place where young citizens gather for a common purpose, and on an equal footing. From this perspective, however, the place of civic education in the university is a good deal more problematic.

Civic education in the college liberal arts curriculum raises a troubling issue for democrats because it may threaten their commitment to equality. In spite of the large numbers of individuals who go on to higher education in America, the vast majority of the citizens of our country do not enter college, let alone complete bachelor degrees. Those who do constitute an elite, a relatively small group who will, over time, come to exercise a disproportionate influence over our public life, and who will enjoy a significant share of the other values our society makes available to its members. These facts must already be of concern to democrats. Do we not compound the problem by proposing and designing a special program or set of programs in civic education for this elite, a program which may—simply because of its exclusivity—serve to mark off this group farther from the rest of the citizenry, and so lead us even farther from the democratic ideal?

I would not wish to deny this danger, but I will argue that it is more than counterbalanced by the special contribution that liberally educated men and women can make as citizens to democratic discourse. To the extent that the ideals of liberal education are realized, there will be a large group of individuals who have the skills necessary to harness specialized knowledge to the purposes of democracy. To understand the role of liberally educated citizens in a democracy, we must consider the ways in which the growing importance of technical experts in public life may undermine democratic values, the objectives of liberal education, and the nature of democratic discourse. On the basis of these considerations, we can decide what forms of civic education in the university will contribute to democractic equality, rather than to the privileges of an elite.

Technical Expertise and Democracy

It is a commonplace that the problems we face—in the environment, in managing the economy, in controlling the development of technology, in international affairs—involve great technical complexities. And the tremendous growth in the scale of government has made the control of the governmental apparatus itself one of the central problems of politics. To address these problems, democracies call into existence, or press into political service, individuals with special training to formulate and implement policies. In many cases, these individuals staff the administration, controlling the day-to-day implementation of policy, and contribute in key ways to the formulation of new initiatives. In other cases, experts from outside of government are recruited, and they play a key role in defining the terms of public discourse and the alternative courses of action the polity confronts.[2]

That experts must play a central role in our public life is not a matter to be seriously questioned. But it does pose difficult issues for democrats, since it calls into question the ideal of the citizenry deciding the direction of public life. As Weber argued some 60 years ago, because citizens and even full-time elected officials are in the position of dilletantes vis-à-vis the "specialized officials" who staff government departments and have both the technical knowledge required for their offices, and knowledge of the facts and administrative processes vital to intelligent decision making, there is a danger that much of the effective power of decision will fall into the hands of these officials. One of the great dangers of our time, Weber argued, is the growth of a new kind of despotism, one which is based on knowledge and the conscious application of rationality to human affairs, which "is busy fabricating the shell of bondage which men will perhaps be forced to inhabit someday, as powerless as the fellahin of ancient Egypt."[3]

Weber's nightmare is not, it should be noted, a modern version of Plato's dream, a vision of a state based on knowledge, and ruled by a genuine elite. For unlike Plato's philosopher-kings, the experts who would rule today are not men and women with a synoptic view of political affairs and the understanding of what must be done to direct society as a whole to its proper ends. The organization of knowledge today involves a high degree of specialization, and the kind of mastery that qualifies one as an expert is necessarily purchased at the price of a certain narrowness. Outside of one's own specific field, the "expert" is as much a dilettante as anyone else. Domination based on knowledge, then, results not merely in the subversion of democracy, but also in the ossification of politics as different areas of public life come to be effectively controlled by unaccountable experts, without any coordination of their activities in terms of a unified vision.

Specialization and, with it, a certain fragmentation of culture are unalterable features of our world. Recognizing this, some commentators have called for the replacement of democratic politics with some kind of "technocracy," where specialists are empowered to make the increasingly technical decisions regarding public policy, free from the interference of others. Sometimes, this vision is combined with a view of "democracy," in which the "people" are called upon periodically to offer ritualistic legitimations of elite rule through elections. But these "elections" have more the character of plebiscites, occasions for ordinary citizens to affirm their commitment to the regime, rather than an institution through which public discourse comes to be focused, leading to decisions about the shape and direction of public life.

The Objectives of Liberal Education

It is in this context that the liberal arts colleges and universities have an important role to play in sustaining the possibility of democracy. One of the special tasks of liberal education is the reproduction of a common intellectual culture that provides a space within which expert knowledge can be made available to nonspecialists (who will include, of course, people with different areas of expertise), and can therefore inform public discourse. This responsibility is reflected in the goals of a liberal education, which include breadth of learning, the integration of different areas of knowledge, and the cultivation of practical judgment.

The goals of breadth and integration have been approached in different ways at different times and in different institutions, though the most common means include the development of "core" curricula and "generalization" requirements which obligate students to take courses outside of their areas of concentration. Behind the commitment to liberal learning is the belief that the narrow specialist is impoverished as a human being and that even specialists must be able to locate their discipline in relation to other areas of study. Thus, the liberal arts curriculum is designed to enable students to develop a critical awareness of the modes of inquiry characteristic: of different disciplines, and to provide them with an exposure to their central ideas and methods. Ideally, students should develop the skills necessary to understand complex arguments from different domains, to critically assess them, and to restate these arguments in other terms. By creating bridges among discourses based on different assumptions or motivated by different concerns, liberal arts institutions can help sustain a common intellectual culture, facilitating communication among specialists and providing an opening for all citizens to participate in public life.

The cultivation of practical judgment, the third objective of liberal education mentioned above, has come increasingly to be seen as problematic in the academy today. Naturally, it is paid a certain symbolic respect, for most will agree that liberal education is not merely an intellectual achievement, but also involves reflection on the ways our knowledge can and should be used. But we have, it appears, become doubtful of the legitimacy, or possibility, of civic education in particular, and moral education in general. One reason for this is skepticism regarding the cognitive status of moral and political judgments. This skepticism is widely shared among our students, who are quick to dismiss or relativize "value" judgments as "matters of opinion," or even taste. As they become more sophisticated, their reasons for their skepticism may deepen, but it is seldom challenged. Indeed, the better the education, the more likely it is to be reenforced, as more and more of their deepest assumptions are identified and held up to critical scrutiny. To the extent that liberal education undermines the "naturalness" of traditions, it casts into doubt the very possibility of finding a standpoint from which considered judgments can be made, and so encourages a retreat into subjectivism.

It is often thought (especially, I think, by our students) that democracy itself requires such skepticism regarding practical matters. For isn't it easier to practice the democratic virtues of tolerance, compromise, and respect for others (including their opinions) if we abandon the view that there are right or wrong answers to the questions we face? Don't these virtues themselves rest on skepticism, for why should we tolerate error? And how can we respect it? Sometimes students will even argue that efforts to criticize or challenge a value position are "undemocratic." They feel that it is only because moral and political judgments are matters of "opinion" and that everyone's opinions should be counted equally. If it were possible to provide rational grounds for practical knowledge, then it would be one more subject of "expertise," and moral experts, not common citizens, would be the proper rulers. Thus, the very effort to provide rational arguments for practical judgments seems to threaten what they view as an essential presupposition of democracy.

The Nature of Democratic Discourse

This retreat to subjectivism and relativism, however, is ultimately corrosive of democracy itself. In the first place, it undermines the possibility of public discourse. It deprives discourse of seriousness because it means that there can be no expectation of agreement reflecting a rational consensus on issues of public life. Discourse, then, is reduced to the display of opposed positions, rather than the consideration of reasons that are intended to convince, not merely sway, an audience. Moreover, this view breeds a certain cynicism, encouraging the development of manipulative attitudes toward others. For it supports a view of public life as inherently governed by the play of power and the calculation of interest—of politics reduced to who gets what, when, and how.[4]

The apparent connection between democracy and skepticism rests on a number of errors. One of the most common is the confusion of "value pluralism" with skepticism. Democracy—or, at least, the liberal democracy of the West—rests on a commitment to value pluralism, the belief that there is a diversity of goods, a variety of ways of life that is of genuine worth, enabling people to live full and satisfying lives. These ways of life achieve different ends and require different commitments; it may sometimes be possible to combine them, but there are irresolvable conflicts among them. Sometimes these conflicts are a result of scarcity, as when one must juggle the conflicting demands and commitments of work and family life, or choose to pursue certain forms of excellence over others. But sometimes these conflicts go deeper, as between a religious life of humility and service to others, and a commitment to a form of secular accomplishment that requires a high degree of self-assertion.[5] There can be good reasons for a particular individual to choose one over another, but there is no general way of reconciling or ranking the values and ends when they conflict. As Berlin has argued, there is no "final solution" which can transform the diversity of goods into a harmonious order.[6]

It is against the background of value pluralism that we can understand one of the most important aspects of public discourse in a democratic society, for it is through public discourse that men and women come to formulate and accept the principles that will govern their collective lives. In nondemocratic systems, some elite is entrusted with the task of prescribing the rules governing the conduct of members of the society. When they obey these rules, they necessarily subject themselves to the decisions of the elite. Even if they obey willingly, in an important sense they are unfree, because the authority they obey is external to them. The democratic ideal, however, is the creation of a moral community, a community in which the norms determining our common life arise from a process of public discourse in which individuals come to see the point and need for certain rules, and so accept them as binding upon themselves. To the extent that this ideal is realized, social relationships can be based on *moral* norms, in the sense of norms which all parties to the relationship freely acknowledge because each recognizes them as binding. As such relationships come to displace patterns of interaction based on unreflecting acceptance of tradition, or the capacity of certain groups or classes to impose their will on others through force and manipulation, the democratic concept of a free society is realized.

The democratic ideal, then, envisions the active constitution of a moral community in a context of value pluralism. Given this vision, we can see why tolerance and mutual respect are important democratic values. Further, we can understand why democratic societies are characterized by a commitment to a distinction between the "public" and the "private" realms, and to something like "neutrality" as a principle governing the public sphere. Discourse among individuals who hold different values, but who seek agreement on the norms governing their relationships, obviously rests on tolerance and mutual respect, on a willingness to consider the needs and aspirations of others. And while discourse may sometimes require a direct engagement with, and dispute about, the character of the ends which the parties pursue, very often it will lead to an effort to "bracket" such disagreements. In these cases, participants in the discourse will try to demarcate those areas of social life where individuals may freely pursue their own aspirations and those where a common set of norms must be observed. And if agreement is to be forthcoming on such norms, it will be necessary that they accord fair consideration to the conflicting values at stake. Neutrality will be an important principle precisely because it articulates the idea that the norms governing our common life must not unduly disadvantage any group in the community in their efforts to promote the ends they have accepted.[7]

The bases for the values of tolerance, mutual respect, and the limitations on the scope of political authority, then, are not to be found in any kind of skepticism, but in the ways in which public or moral (or, more generally, practical) discourse is "constructive." The point of such discourse is to enable men and women to "construct" a moral world, so to speak, by discovering those principles of association to which all can subscribe. And the constructive nature of practical discourse also demonstrates why it is not a form of discourse that can be closed to people who do not possess "special" qualifications. Rather, it must be open to all who have the capacity to hold values which give point to their lives, and who are able to act on principles in their relationships with others—that is, to all who have the qualities necessary for moral action and responsibility, or normal adults.

Liberal Education and Democratic Discourse

If participation in public discourse does not require special qualifications, there is nevertheless a distinct contribution that liberally educated men and women can make to it. With their skills in bridging different areas of discourse, and with the breadth of education they have received, liberally educated individuals can play a critical role in, as it were, "translating" the specialized knowledge bearing on political issues into an idiom accessible to all participants in public life. There are a number of different ways in which they can play this role, involving varying levels of public engagement. At the most passive level, they constitute a fairly large audience for books, journals, radio and television programs, and public lectures which provide information for nonspecialists on a vast range of topics, thereby contributing to a fund of socially available knowledge and a common intellectual culture. At a more active level, many liberal arts graduates (including those who have gone on to advanced or professional study) are among the producers of this knowledge. But their most direct contribution to public discourse comes in the context of particular issues, when they can use their skills to discover the sorts of technical considerations relevant to an issue, find experts to address it, and assist in the presentation of knowledge so that it can be understood by all citizens.

There are any number of examples of this sort of activity. An obvious one occurred a couple of years ago in a Connecticut community, when a group of citizens became involved in the planning for a garbage-to-energy plant to replace the town's landfill. The problem involved many technical issues, and much of the group's work consisted in discovering relevant information and finding qualified authorities who could assist them in understanding it, and then conveying what they had found to the public generally, as well as to concerned officials. In the end, they were successful in blocking the town's original proposal, since they were able to convince a significant group of people that the risk that plan posed for underground water supplies was too great. This judgment, it should be stressed, is not a technical judgment; it is not a judgment which experts or a college-educated elite have any special authority to make. But it is a judgment that citizens cannot make without information and analysis that must be provided by experts. And liberally educated persons can play an important role in facilitating the public acquisition of such information and analysis.

The Content of Civic Education

An important aspect of civic education consists of the traditional liberal arts objectives of breadth and integration of knowledge. Not surprisingly, civic education also requires the cultivation of practical judgment—the third objective of liberal education I alluded to above. In certain respects, the cultivation of practical judgment is as much a part of a traditional understanding of liberal education as it is a part of civic education. The study of norms and values is the subject of such traditional disciplines as ethics and political theory, and exposure to these concerns should be part of the general education of all students. In particular, we might expect liberal arts graduates to be familiar with some of the most important traditions of moral and political thought, to have seriously confronted questions such as moral relativism and the grounding of moral judgments, the critical analysis of norms and values, the problem of applying general principles to specific cases, and to the place of ethical commitments in various branches of scholarship. It would be hard to defend a conception of liberal education today that did not include some attention to the ways in which knowledge might be used in practical life, and the consequences of this for the creation of knowledge itself.

To a large extent, then, liberal education *is* civic education. But if liberally educated citizens are to play the distinctive role in democracratic discourse I have described, their education in the social sciences should include specific attention to the ways in which specialized knowledge can enter into public life. It is not enough simply to be able to translate from one mode of discourse into another, so that ordinary citizens can understand enough to make intelligent judgments. We must also help our students see that there are different ways in which specialized knowledge—especially the kinds of knowledge offered by the social sciences—can be "used" in public affairs. One of the difficulties in attaining this objective is that the academy is deeply divided on this question.

The dominant position, represented by students of "policy analysis," conceives of the "application" of knowledge in essentially instrumental terms. In this view, "knowledge" in the sense relevant for practical judgment consists of an understanding of the causal relationships which bear upon those situations which concern us. In the example above, the specialized knowledge of the geologist concerned the probable consequences for the purity of groundwater of the building of a waste treatment plant in a particular location, given the geological formations found there. If we[8] want to achieve a particular result—say, the preservation of the purity of groundwater—then the geologist can tell us which locations of waste-treatment facilities will minimize contamination.

This instrumentalist view of the application of knowledge to practical questions is a powerful one in our culture, tied as it is to the success of the natural sciences in providing the understanding necessary for exerting control over various natural processes. For many years, the conception of knowledge on which it is based—the understanding of causal relationships—represented the ideal for the social sciences. Our hope was to develop powerful social theories that could be used to predict and explain social phenomena by setting out the laws which governed them. In this way, public policy informed by these theories could be used to solve or control problems such as unemployment, juvenile delinquency, political instability, and war.

This generalization of a particular conception of knowledge to the social sciences, however, raises special difficulties. For the social sciences are, in an important sense, forms of civic discourse. Because their subject is human action, and because the social scientists who construct social theories are also social actors, the social sciences are themselves ways in which we represent ourselves, ways in which we understand our own lives and activities. With an exclusively instrumentalist understanding of knowledge, however, we come to conceive of ourselves and our activities as "objects," whose behavior is determined by specific causal factors that can be manipulated in order to alter "undesirable" behavior and avoid certain outcomes. This vision of social knowledge, then, supports a particular conception of politics, one that focuses on the manipulation of causal factors to realize particular objectives. While it does not rule out democracy and public discourse, it constrains them in important ways. The task of democratic politics is to determine what objectives we should realize, what trade-offs to make among the various values we hold. While this task can be informed by expert knowledge of the costs of various proposals, a process in which liberal arts graduates can play an important role, it represents democratic decisions as essentially the expression of preference, or arbitrary will. And as this vision of public life comes to be widely diffused and a consensus grows on the kinds of problems we can hope to solve at acceptable cost, the scope for public deliberation decreases and the place of specialists and technically trained experts increases.

Critics of the instrumentalist model, recognizing its implications for democratic discourse, have often sought to reject it entirely. Social phenomena, they argue, are unlike natural events: they are in part constituted by the concepts and beliefs, by the "self-understandings" of social actors. Actions, for example, have the character they have because they express the beliefs and purposes of the actors. One cannot, for example, be said to vote or obey an order unless one had certain understandings of what one was doing—unless one saw oneself as making a choice among alternatives, or as subject to some authority. To represent social activities as if they were merely natural-events objects governed by causal laws, is a deep mistake, for it is to reify the self-understandings that make up a particular form of life, to treat them as if they were necessary, unalterable constituents of the world, when in fact they are rooted in particular forms of social life. Social knowledge, on this account, does not consist of an understanding of the causal laws determining the behavior of certain variables. Rather, it is more akin to interpretations of the meanings of the practices and self-understandings of a particular group at a particular time. And the way in which knowledge can enter into public discourse is not so much by informing its participants as to the possible trade-offs among different objectives, but by enlightening them as to the significance of their practices. The relationship of knowledge to practice is not, then, a manipulative or instrumental one, but one that is, at least potentially, self-transformative. For as citizens come to understand themselves better, they may decide deliberately to alter certain of their practices and the concepts and beliefs which they had previously held in an un-self-conscious manner. The entire framework of policy analysis, then, is rejected by these critics in favor of a model of deliberative enlightenment.

Civic education in our colleges and universities should reject the exclusive reliance on either of these extreme models, in favor of some (albeit tension-filled) acceptance of both. The critics of policy analysis are correct in noting that social phenomena are not "objects" in the way that an instrumentalist vision of social science conceives of them, and in pointing to the critical role of actors' self-understandings in constituting the social world. This has now come to be widely appreciated among social scientists, and some of the best works of social science are essentially interpretative in nature, works that articulate and clarify the meanings of social practices. By enabling us to understand ourselves better, social science can contribute to reasoned public judgment. And because such social science is ultimately rooted in, and must return to, the language of social actors, it is itself a form of public discourse.

On the other hand, the policy analysts are correct in conceiving of social processes as, in some sense, "objectified." Not everything that *happens* in social life is something that someone (or some group) *does*. We cannot, at least not in general, understand depressions or revolutions or suicide rates or illiteracy simply in terms of the intentions or the self-understandings of social actors. Many of the phenomena which most concern us, and which we must control if we are to determine the direction of our public lives, are the unintended and unanticipated outcomes of actions directed at entirely different (and usually rather modest) ends. The analysis of the causal processes which produce them, and the communication of these analyses to a larger public, is essential if we are to realize the democratic ideal.[9]

Liberal education has a vital role to play in enabling young men and women to make an important contribution to democracy. But it can only play this role if the importance of civic education in the process of liberal learning is recognized, particularly the centrality of what I have called the cultivation of practical judgment. This will require not only the study of the traditional concerns of ethics and political theory, but also specific attention to the social sciences, and the ways in which social knowledge can enter practical life. We should enable students to see the need for an instrumentalist understanding of knowledge, and equip them with the skills to communicate that understanding to a larger public. But we must also avoid the common error of assuming that this is the only way in which knowledge can enter public discourse, and design programs in which social inquiry is itself seen as a form of public discourse. There are deep obstacles to the realization of democracy's commitments to politics as a form of human freedom and to equality. A stronger program of civic education in our universities may go some way to realizing both of these commitments.

J. Donald Moon is professor of Government, Wesleyan University, Middletown, Connecticut.

Originally prepared for the Hastings Center's Foundations of Civic Education Project, Nov. 1988. Reprinted with permission of the author.

Notes

I would like to thank J. Peter Euben, Bruce Jennings, and Nancy Schwartz for helpful comments on an earlier draft of this essay.

1. *Laws* 709a, Pangle trans.

2. For the argument of this section (and much of this essay) I am indebted to the work of Habermas, particularly his "Technical Progress and the Social Life-World" and "The Scientization of Politics and Public Opinion," in *Towards a Rational Society* (Boston: Beacon Press, 1970).

3. Max Weber, "Parliament and Government in a Reconstructed Germany," in his *Economy and Society,* Vol. 2, G. Roth and C. Wittich, eds. (Berkeley: University of California Press, 1978), p. 1402

4. The phrase is Harold Lasswell's.

5. See Charles Taylor, "The Diversity of Goods," in his *Philosophical Papers,* vol 2 (Cambridge: Cambridge University Press, 1985), pp. 230–47.

6. Isaiah Berlin, "Two Concepts of Liberty," in his *Four Essays on Liberty* (Oxford: Oxford University Press, 1969), pp. 167–72.

7. I do not mean to suggest that the concept of neutrality is without difficulties, nor that it can be fully achieved. Like most of the topics covered in this essay, a full discussion would require a considerable digression.

8. In using the term "we" here and subsequently, I ignore (or beg the question) of just how its identity is determined, and what conditions would justify its use. That is obviously an important topic in the theory and practice of democracy.

9. For a somewhat fuller discussion of the connection between these two models of social science and political practice, see my "Interpretation, Theory, and Human Emancipation," in Elinor Ostrom, ed., *Strategies of Political Inquiry* (Beverly Hills, CA: Sage Publications, 1982).

"Autonomy requires people to look inward so that
they may govern themselves, while civic virtue
demands that they look outward and do what they
can to promote the common good."

Education, Autonomy, and Civic Virtue

by Richard Dagger

Almost everyone agrees that we face an educational crisis in the United States today. There is less agreement, however, on the exact nature of the crisis and the proper response to it. This lack of agreement is itself significant, for the failure to agree on what we want our schools to do is largely responsible for the problems we now face. In the absence of such an agreement, we simply expect our schools to meet the demands of everyone vocal enough to make himself or herself heard. The result, according to John Chubb and Terry Moe, the authors of a recent and controversial book on American's schools, is that public schools "must make everyone happy by being all things to all people—just as politicians do."[1]

If this is so, then what is to be done? Logically, there are only two alternatives to the present condition. The first is to try to find or forge a consensus on the proper purpose of education, then direct our schools to pursue that purpose. The second, abandoning hope of achieving this consensus, is to allow schools to define their own purposes by encouraging competition between a variety of schools pursuing a variety of goals. This is the point of the so-called *choice* approach, advocated most recently by Chubb and Moe. As they see it, "schools have no immutable or transcendent purpose. What they are supposed to be doing depends on who controls them and what these controllers want them to do."[2] The solution, then, is to free individual schools to pursue whatever goals they deem appropriate, thereby freeing parents and students to choose the schools most congenial to their inclinations. Schools should have to compete for customers in the marketplace, in other words, and successful schools, like successful magazines, will find "their niche—a specialized segment of the market to which they can appeal and attract support."[3]

There may be much to recommend this approach to education. It is only in its most extreme form, however, that educational "choice" escapes the need to arrive at some sort of agreement about the purpose of education. In Chubb and Moe's proposal, for instance, schools will have to meet certain standards—for teacher certification, graduation requirements, and nondiscrimination, among others—if they are to qualify for the public funds that follow students to the schools they and their parents choose. In their scheme, apparently, a Nazi may not receive public funds for teaching the importance of racial purity in a school open only to Aryans, not even if the Nazi can find a specialized segment of the market from which to attract support. At some point, then, some public decision will have to be reached about what schools must and must not do. Even "voucher" proposals encounter this problem, for without some standards to determine what counts as an honest-to-goodness school, anyone who teaches anything could have a claim on the public funds supporting the vouchers. The only way to escape this difficulty is to adopt an extreme libertarian position and call for either anarchy or Robert Nozick's "minimal state," in which there will be neither public funding, nor public schools, nor any requirement that anyone see to the education of children.

If we do not want to follow the market mentality all the way to anarchy or the minimal state, we shall have to face up to the task of forging an agreement on the purposes of education—or, more narrowly, of what we want our schools to do. This, to be sure, is no easy task in a society as diverse as ours; but neither is it an impossible one. There are educational goals, albeit quite general ones, on which we can and should agree. This is evident in the distinction we now draw implicitly between various specialized schools —business schools, dance schools, schools of broadcasting, and so on—and schools *simpliciter*. The purpose of the latter is not to prepare people for a specific career or activity, but in some way to prepare them for life. There is a difference, in other words, between *training*, which is the business of the specialized school, and *education*, which is the business of the school as such.

These distinctions suggest that the task of reaching a consensus on the goals of our schools is not hopeless. Unfortunately, they do not take us very far toward accomplishing that task. One may doubt, for instance, that there is any great insight in the observation that the business of the school is to educate. Even if we add that the purpose of education is in some way to prepare people for life, we still have to reach agreement on what "preparing people for life" entails. Given the variety of views in this country about how life should be lived, it is not easy to see how this can be done. My suggestion, however, is that we ought to think of preparation for life in terms of autonomy and civic virtue.

It is often alleged that autonomy and civic virtue are competing, or even incompatible, goods. Any steps we take to promote autonomy will come at the expense of civic virtue, according to this view, and vice versa. To ask schools to promote both, then, is to ask the impossible. In this essay I argue that autonomy and civic virtue, properly understood, are not incompatible, but complementary goals. I further suggest that autonomy and civic virtue provide better goals for our schools and our children than the competitive model so often favored by civic and business leaders.

Autonomy and Civic Virtue: Complementary Goals

Autonomy and civic virtue are often taken to be incompatible with one another because one has to do with individual liberty, the other with collective responsibility. Autonomy requires people to look inward so that they may govern them*selves*, while civic virtue demands that they look outward and do what they can to promote the common good. The two concepts also seem to be at home in different traditions of political thought, or different forms of political discourse. Autonomy has been the concern of liberals, on this view, while civic virtue has occupied the attention of classical republicans and communitarians. Thus "autonomy" seems to be a key term in the "rights-talk" of liberal theorists, and "civic virtue" a key term in a different vocabulary that centers on virtue.

Autonomy and civic virtue are different from one another, of course; if they were identical, we presumably would have no need for one of the two concepts. But this hardly proves them to be incompatible goods. The connection between autonomy and liberalism, on the one hand, and civic virtue and republican or communitarian views, on the other, is not as strict or necessary as it may seem. Some liberal writers, such as John Stuart Mill and T. H. Green, seem to want to encourage civic virtue, even if they do not use the term. There are also writers of a republican bent, such as Rousseau, who are clearly concerned with what we now call autonomy. I do not believe, then, that we must consign autonomy and civic virtue to distinct and incommensurable political traditions or "discourses" as necessarily incompatible terms. On the contrary, I believe that the two concepts exercise considerable appeal today precisely because they indicate what is of value in these two, not altogether distinct, traditions of political thought. Rather than regard autonomy as a purely individualist notion and civic virtue as a collectivist or communitarian ideal, in other words, we should look to their union as part of what Charles Taylor has called *holist individualism*—"a trend of thought that is fully aware of the (ontological) social embedding of human agents, but at the same time prizes liberty and individual differences very highly."[4] With that in mind, let us now take a closer look at the concepts in question.

Autonomy as Self-Mastery

Because autonomy is something we may predicate of a number of things —nation-states, corporations, and sewer districts, among them—it is necessary to be clear that my concern here is with the autonomy of the individual person. This is particularly important in view of the tendency of some writers on education to use "autonomy" in the sense of a school's independence, or freedom from interference. There is nothing wrong with this usage, but it must not be confused with *personal autonomy*.

The starting point is much the same, however. Whether we are referring to persons, schools, or nation-states, the literal meaning of "autonomy" is still self-rule, self-legislation, or self-government. The difficulty, of course, lies in determining what is involved in self-rule. But we may begin by noting that autonomy assumes a *self* that is *capable* of leading a self-governed life.

At the conceptual core of autonomy is the notion of a self as a distinct person capable of making choices. Someone who cannot distinguish himself or herself from others cannot possibly lead a self-governed life, for such a person cannot conceive of himself or herself as a person with a distinct identity; nor can someone who suffers from some form of multiple or divided personalities. Autonomy implies, then, some fairly strong sense of selfhood —a sense that we do not expect infants to possess, but that we usually hope children will develop as they mature. An amnesiac cannot be autonomous, therefore, because amnesia deprives the victim of the memories that largely constitute his or her sense of self. This point is especially important because autonomy is associated with freedom, and in some ways the amnesiac seems to be the freest person of all—free to assume, that is, whatever identity she finds most desirable. Yet the person who suffers from amnesia is generally anxious to *discover* who she is, not to *create* herself out of her sense of what or who she wants to be. The problem is that she has no identity to help her decide what or who *she* wants to be. In some circumstances, perhaps, we might be inclined to regard amnesia as a form of liberation; but we should never consider it a step toward autonomy.

If autonomy requires a fairly strong sense of self, it also requires that the self be capable of making choices. A person is self-legislating, *autonomous* rather than *heteronomous*, to the extent that she chooses the principles by which she lives. But if she truly *chooses* the principles that guide her conduct, the autonomous person must *be aware* of the alternatives from which she can choose. Someone who does the right thing instinctively, without reflection, in the manner of Melville's Billy Budd, may be a good and decent person, but not an autonomous one. Autonomy requires awareness: awareness of the choices open to us in life, and awareness also of our capacity to choose. If we can lead self-governed lives, then, it is because we are able to think of ourselves as something more than objects at the mercy of forces over which we have no control, like so many leaves tossed about by the wind.

Because these forces may be internal as well as external, autonomy is sometimes regarded as *self-mastery*. This raises interesting and difficult problems, for it may be taken to mean that the self is not a single thing—or even that a person consists of more than one self. Sometimes people speak of a "lower" or "base" self, which leads us into temptation, and to which they oppose a "higher" or "true" self that struggles to keep us on the straight and narrow path. The autonomous person, on this view, is the one who achieves self-mastery by suppressing the impulses of the lower self in order to follow the inclinations of the higher.

To think in this way, however, is to misconceive autonomy. It misconceives autonomy because it leads to self-denial, perhaps even self-destruction. On this view, in other words, self-mastery is much like the relationship between master and slave, with the higher self, usually conceived to be reason or soul, called upon to exercise strict control over the lower, usually understood as appetite or flesh. But appetite or flesh, with all its insistent impulses, is natural to human beings, so the attempt to rise above and master it—and thus to divorce the "true" self from that "lower" self rooted in nature—is necessarily a form of self-denial. If we accomplish this denial, what is left? Pure reason or soul, all form and no content.

What is the alternative? Do we want to say that the person who acts on every fleeting impulse is autonomous? No, for there is a point to the distinction between autonomy and heteronomy; but it is a point that can be captured in a conception of autonomy that does not require a divided, contentious self. If the model of a heteronomous person is a creature of impulse, incapable of deferring gratification or exercising any control over his or her appetites, the model of the autonomous person is one who knows these appetites and inclinations (among other things) well enough to bring them into harmony, and thus to achieve integrity through their integration. This comes closer to self-realization than to self-denial. If it involves self-mastery, it is the craftsman's mastery of a craft—the mastery of an orchestra conductor, for instance, or of the football quarterback who directs his teammates toward their goal—and not the mastery of the slave owner. If autonomy is self-mastery, in short, it is mastery *of* self, not mastery *over* self.

Civic Virtue and Citizenship

Unlike personal autonomy, which relates to the abstract notion of the self, civic virtue refers to a particular role that a person may occupy—the role of *citizen*. Someone exhibits civic virtue, that is, when he or she does what a citizen is supposed to do. In this respect, civic virtue is like the other virtues, which typically relate to the performance of some role or the exercise of a certain skill.

Our concept of virtue derives from the Greek *arete*, or excellence, by way of the Latin *virtus*, which carried from its association with *vir* (man) the additional connotations of strength and boldness. To be virtuous, then, was to exhibit excellence in a particular skill or craft, or to perform admirably in a particular role or occupation. It was also possible to display a more general form of virtue by manifesting, to a high degree, the qualities of a good person. This was (and is) possible, however, only when there was (and is) some fairly clear notion of what a person is supposed to be. Personhood, in other words, must be conceived as a role that one may play, complete with criteria for determining when one is playing the role properly. In this sense, a virtuous person is like a virtuoso musician, someone who does with great skill what a musician is supposed to do.

This suggests that there is a conceptual connection between the ideas of virtue and of good. Just as it would be absurd to say that Jones is a virtuoso pianist, but not a good one, so it would be absurd to say that Smith is a virtuous person, but not a good one. Such a connection does not hold between the ideas of autonomy and of good. We may think that autonomy itself is good, but we need not contradict ourselves when we say that Adams is an autonomous person, but not, all things considered, a good one.

As a role-related concept, then, virtue refers to the disposition to act in accordance with the standards and expectations that define the role or roles a person performs. The more specific the role, the more specific the virtues associated with it will be. A steady hand may be among the virtues of a carpenter and a surgeon, for instance, but not of an accountant or poet. There are some character traits or dispositions that seem useful to almost everyone, however, and these are what we sometimes think of as "the virtues" —including the classical virtues of wisdom, courage, temperance, and justice, or a sense of proportion. These are virtues—along with honesty, loyalty, compassion, and others—not so much because they work to the advantage of the person who possesses them, but because they work to the advantage of the people with whom he or she associates. Virtues are valuable because they promote the good of the community or society, not because they directly promote the good of the individual person. This may be why chastity, which no longer seems so vital to the welfare of society, may be less widely regarded as a virtue than once it was.

To be virtuous, then, is to perform well a socially necessary or important role. This does not mean that the virtuous person must always go along with the prevailing views or attitudes. On the contrary, Socrates and John Stuart Mill have persuaded many people to believe that questioning and opposing the prevailing views are among the highest forms of virtue. In making this case, however, they rely on the claim that the social gadfly and the unorthodox thinker are really promoting the long-run interests of society—and thereby performing a social role of exceptional value.

Even if it might be shown that some virtues have no social value at all, it is clear that *civic virtue* will not be among them. Civic virtue simply is the disposition to do what is best for one's community, and to do it even—or especially—when one's private interest seems to point in a different direction. Understood in this way, civic virtue was a key concept of the classical republicans, and it survives today in the exhortations to do one's civic duty that regularly appear at election time. The fear of corruption and conflicts of interest also betray its traces. There are signs of a revival of a more straightforward appeal to civic virtue in the writings of various republican or communitarian theorists, of course, and even some who identify themselves with liberalism are showing an open interest in civic virtue of some sort. So there is reason to believe that a brief examination of the classical republicans' conception of civic virtue is worthwhile.

There appear to be three basic elements in civic virtue as the classical republican writers understood it. The first is the fear of *corruption*. Corruption is the opposite of virtue, for it consists in shirking one's duty as a citizen. This could take the passive form of neglecting one's civic duties in favor of one's personal pleasures, such as indolence or the pursuit of luxury; or it could take the active form of advancing one's personal interests at the expense of the common good. This was most likely to happen when ambition and avarice, the desire for power and wealth, would tempt a citizen to overthrow the rule of law and install a tyranny in its place.

The second key ingredient in the classical republicans' conception of civic virtue is fear of *dependence*. They regarded the citizen, following Aristotle, as someone who rules and is ruled in turn. The person who is completely dependent on another may be ruled, but is in no position to rule. The rule of law is essential, therefore, as a means of avoiding personal dependence. In a government of laws, not of men, the citizen is subject to the laws, not to the demands and whims of rulers who act without restraint. The republicans also typically defended private property as a way of guaranteeing that the citizen would not be dependent on others for his livelihood. Some, notably James Harrington and Rousseau, went further, suggesting that private property should be maintained, but distributed in such a way as to prevent anyone from being so wealthy as to render other citizens dependent. As Rousseau put the point in the *Social Contract*,[5] everyone should have something, but no one too much.

The fear of dependence indicates, finally, the importance of *independence*, or *liberty*, in the republicans' conception of civic virtue. The virtuous citizen must be free, but not simply free to go his own way. This may be a form of freedom, but it is not a form of citizenship as they understood it. The citizen is free, they held, when he participates in the government of his community. As part of the community, the citizen will recognize that the government of common affairs is more or less directly *self*-government. If it requires the occasional sacrifice of one's personal interests, so be it; for this is necessary not only in the name of civic duty, but also in order to enjoy the rights and liberties of the citizen of a self-governing polity.

This, then, is what civic virtue was—and what it still is, according to those theorists who want to revive the republican spirit in contemporary politics. The question we must now consider is whether the revival of civic virtue is compatible with the desire for personal autonomy. I believe that it is. More than that, I believe that the three elements of the classical republicans' conception of civic virtue can help us to see how the two may effectively complement one another.

Personal Autonomy and Civic Virtue

The autonomous person chooses the principles by which he or she will live, which implies some degree of critical reflection on the principles available. With civic virtue, however, the emphasis is not on choice, but on acting, perhaps without reflection, to promote the common good. The unquestioning soldier who makes the "ultimate sacrifice" for his or her country provides a good example. It is easy enough to see, then, how autonomy and civic virtue can seem to be at odds with one another, for it is certainly possible for someone to exhibit civic virtue without being autonomous, just as it is possible for an autonomous person to put his or her well-being above the interests of anyone or anything else.

But this is to say that personal autonomy and civic virtue are different from one another, not that they are incompatible. It is also possible that their differences are complementary. To be precise, it is possible that autonomy and civic virtue, properly understood, are related concepts that can and should complement one another. Another look at the three principal elements of the classical republicans' conception of civic virtue should begin to make this clear.

First, the republicans' fear of corruption is largely a fear of human weakness. Indolence and love of luxury, ambition and avarice—these vices constantly beckon people to forsake their civic duties and disregard the claims of the common good. The threat of corruption is graver at some times than others, they believed, but it is always a threat. To stave it off, it is necessary to establish mixed government and the rule of law, perhaps even to rotate public offices among the citizenry and to prevent the concentration of wealth and property in the hands of a few. But these devices will never extirpate the threat, for it springs from selfish and ultimately self-defeating desires implanted in human nature. To hold them in check while directing people's attention and devotion to the common good is, therefore, to achieve a form of *self-mastery*. In this respect, civic virtue and autonomy have something in common.

This is true with regard to the second feature of civic virtue, as well. In this case, the republicans' distinction between dependence and independence has a direct counterpart in the distinction between heteronomy and autonomy. The connection is probably clearest in the works of Rousseau, a republican writer who inspired the philosopher most often identified with the distinction between autonomy and heteronomy—Immanuel Kant. Rousseau proclaims that the only way to overcome "dependence on men"—and thus to promote freedom—is to rely on the impartial rule of law and the general will. The general will,[6] moreover, is not some disembodied force that resides in the community as a whole. Instead, it is the will that every citizen has *as a citizen*—the will to act in the public interest because that is the one interest all citizens share *as citizens*. If the rule of law frees people from their dependence on others, then, they will be free to make laws in accordance with the general will that each one shares. This, as Rousseau puts it in the *Social Contract*,[7] is "moral liberty," that is, living in accordance with laws that one makes for oneself. Another name for this is autonomy.

The connection between autonomy and civic virtue is perhaps most obvious with regard to the third element of civic virtue—the idea that liberty is participation in government, and, therefore, self-government. Since autonomy means "self-government," one might say that the concept of civic virtue entails a commitment to autonomy, in some sense of the word. Again, this commitment is probably clearest in Rousseau's writings. For Rousseau, in fact, it seems not only that civic virtue entails self-government, but that autonomy is possible only when civic virtue prevails. For unless the *general will of the citizen* takes precedence over the *particular will of the man*, in Rousseau's terms, no one can experience moral liberty.[8]

From the perspective of the classical republican conception of civic virtue, in short, autonomy and civic virtue are far from incompatible ideals. The same result emerges from a further analysis of the concept of autonomy. To begin with, autonomy "has to be worked for," which leads Robert Young[9] and other philosophers to regard it as *"a character ideal or virtue."* More to the point, autonomy is not something that one can achieve solely through individual effort. It has to be worked for, certainly, but it also has to be cultivated or developed. An infant may have the ability to lead a self-governed life within her, like a seed, but this ability must be nourished and developed by others before she can ever hope to be autonomous. Recognizing this, the autonomous person should also recognize a duty of some sort to those whose help has made and continues to make it possible for her to lead a reasonably self-governed life. In a country or community in which this help sometimes takes the form of more or less impersonal public assistance or cooperation, the corresponding duty is a civic duty. Thus the autonomous person has a reason to exhibit civic virtue, at least when the community, as a whole, plays a significant part in fostering personal autonomy.

How might a community do this? There are many ways, including the rule of law, provision for the common defense, and protection from diseases and disasters. One of the most important and most common is education—the topic with which I began this paper, and to which I now return.

Education for Autonomy and Civic Virtue

With education, as with autonomy and civic virtue, it is useful to begin with etymology. Our word "education" derives from the Latin *educere*, which means to lead or draw out, and from which we retain "educe." Originally, then, education involved drawing out or developing the potential within a person—or, for that matter, within other animals. This could consist of the activity of leading out a specific ability, such as the ability to perform some skill or craft, but in the last two centuries education has been distinguished from training, with the understanding that education, *as such* is concerned with cultivating the whole person, thereby developing those human attributes that make a worthwhile life possible.[10]

Such a conception of education is obviously congenial to the view that autonomy is the ability or capacity to lead a self-governed life. Like other capacities and abilities, autonomy begins as a potential that must be *realized*, in both senses of the word, before a person can become autonomous. But this can only happen if the potential is drawn out through education of some sort. It is not surprising, then, to find some educators and philosophers insisting that the purpose of education—or at least one of its most important purposes—is the promotion of autonomy.

Much the same can be said of the relationship between civic virtue and education. Like the other virtues, civic virtue is a character trait or disposition that is not likely to thrive without encouragement and cultivation. This cultivation can occur in a number of ways, but there is a widespread expectation, in this country and others, that schools are responsible for much of the *civic education* a person receives. In the last decade, in fact, the need for civic education began to attract, once again, the attention of political theorists.

So it is not uncommon for educators and others to regard either personal autonomy or civic virtue as capacities or dispositions that schools ought to develop. There have even been some hints at the combination of the two. In 1918, for instance, the National Education Association's Commission on the Reorganization of Secondary Education issued a report, *Cardinal Principles of Secondary Education*, which called for a focus on the goals of "specialization"—"whereby individuals may become effective in the various vocations and other fields of human endeavor"—and "unification"—"the attainment of those common ideas, common ideals, and common modes of thought, feeling, and action that make for cooperation, social cohesion, and social solidarity"[11] "Specialization" does not correspond exactly with autonomy, of course, but the similarities are close enough to suggest that the attempt to establish autonomy and civic virtue as the aims of education is not far-fetched.

One can also explain or justify much of what takes place in our public schools—or much of what is supposed to take place there—in terms of autonomy and civic virtue. In broad terms, the curriculum begins in the primary school by stressing basic skills, then goes on to offer more options and individual choice in secondary school, then even more for those who go on to colleges and universities. The basic skills enable children to "function" in the world, to begin with, and anyone who fails to acquire these skills is almost certain to remain too dependent on others to have a chance to become autonomous. By enhancing the capacity for self-expression, moreover, these skills help the child to overcome frustration and strengthen self-esteem. This is true of the ability to work with numbers, and express oneself through them, as it is of reading and writing. And as the word "basic" suggests, these skills also provide a base from which students can go on to understand better what options are open to them and what their choices entail.

Although the term itself is seldom used, the attempt to foster civic virtue, or (good) citizenship, is also incorporated in the curriculum. Indeed, civic virtue receives more explicit attention than autonomy, since state laws typically require students to study American history and government, to pass tests on the state and national constitutions, and to take courses in social studies and "civics." Even time devoted to the basic skills of reading, writing, and arithmetic contributes to civic virtue, furthermore. Those who lack these skills are likely to remain dependent on others—dependent for information and political guidance as well as dependent for a livelihood and other forms of assistance—and thus to fall far short of the republican ideal of citizenship. By helping students acquire and develop these skills, then, the school promotes independence in the sense appropriate to both autonomy and civic virtue.

The desire to promote personal autonomy and civic virtue may also figure in the "hidden curriculum." In addition to the explicit curriculum, that is, schools also teach by example, especially the example of the organization and conduct of the school and classroom. Student governments are supposed to help students learn the value of democracy, for instance, and the conduct of teachers is supposed to exemplify some of the virtues—such as "empathy, trust, benevolence, and fairness"—that make cooperation in general and democracy in particular possible.[12] Teachers who encourage students to raise questions and to think for themselves presumably help to develop the autonomy of their charges.

There is, however, another side to the story here. Because of the emphasis within schools on order and organization—typically hierarchical organization—the implicit curriculum often discourages autonomy and teaches only a passive conception of citizenship. According to Richard Battistoni:[13]

> The presence of a hidden curriculum in high schools is severely disruptive to the political education of future democrats. Not only does the "authoritarian atmosphere" of order and discipline promote attitudes of passivity, unhealthy dependency, submission, competition, and inequality that may be transferred to the polity, but it also prevents the actual teaching of values essential to democratic political behavior.

Where autonomy and civic virtue are concerned, then, there seems to be considerable room for improvement. This is true of the explicit as well as the implicit or hidden curriculum. But there is also reason to believe that school administrators and teachers recognize the promotion of something like personal autonomy and civic virtue to be among their chief responsibilities. That they already do this supports my claim that fostering autonomy and civic virtue can and should be the acknowledged aims of our schools—and gives us good reason to try to improve our schools in these respects.

Conclusion

Now I want to conclude by indicating why I believe my approach is superior to what seems, judging from the statements of civic and business leaders, to be its chief rival—the view that the purpose of education is to prepare our children, and thus our country, for economic competition. There are three reasons why I think it is better to take autonomy and civic virtue as our goals. The first is that an education for autonomy and civic virtue will give as much time and attention to the basic skills as the competitive model, thus promising to accomplish what the competitive model wants to accomplish. Second, the approach I have defended is more comprehensive and accommodating than the competitive model. It can help to prepare children for competition, but it will also give them a wider vision, thereby offering an opportunity for growth to those who decide, upon reflection, that the competitive life is not the life they want to lead. It should also prove valuable in helping students to become adaptable—a trait that is supposed to be increasingly important in a world of "career burnout" and rapid change.

Finally, the competitive model points in two undesirable directions. On the one hand, it encourages us to think of children as resources to be marshaled in the struggle to maintain our national economic strength. On the other, it leads children to see themselves as isolated individuals locked in competition with one another—competition for jobs, money, and status. Thus the competitive model points either in a collectivist or an intensely individualist direction. In the first case, it devalues the individual, who becomes a mere resource; in the second, it affords little hope of maintaining social bonds and loyalties. In the first case, it denies autonomy; in the second, civic virtue. Neither of these is acceptable.

With autonomy and civic virtue, however, we have the basis for an education grounded in holist individualism. Such an education proceeds from the view that no one is a self-created person, yet almost everyone has the capacity to exercise a considerable degree of control over his or her life.

This capacity ought to be developed, furthermore, for it is a vital part of a worthwhile life; and a society that encourages the development of this capacity deserves the support of those it helps in this way. Autonomy and civic virtue are not, on this view, incompatible goods, but two sides of the same conception of the relationship between individuals and the political order. This conception is already implicit in much of our thinking about education in this country. The task now is to make it explicit—and to act on it.

Richard Dagger is associate professor of Political Science at Arizona State University.

This is a revised version of a paper delivered at the 1990 Annual Meeting of the American Political Science Association. Reprinted with permission of the author.

Notes

1. *Politics, Markets, and America's Schools,* The Brookings Institution, p. 54.

2. *Ibid.,* (p. 30).

3. *Ibid.,* (p. 55).

4. "Crosspurposes," Nancy L. Rosenblum, ed., *Liberalism and the Moral Life,* p. 163).

5. Rousseau, *Social Contract,* Book I, Chapter 9.

6. Rousseau, Book II, *Emile*

7. *Social Contract,* Book I, Chapter 8.

8. *Ibid.,* Book I, Chapter 6.

9. *Personal Autonomy,* p. 9.

10. R. S. Peters, "Further Thoughts on the Concept of Education," in Peters, ed., *The Philosophy of Education.*

11. Richard Battistoni, *Public Schools and the Education of Democratic Citizens,* p. 81).

12. Amy Gutmann, *Democratic Education,* p. 61.

13. Richard Battistoni, *Public Schools and the Education of Democratic Citizens,* p. 121.

"The public is not at its best a marketplace, or a battlefield, or a negotiating arena in which thing-like opinions and interests are exchanged, fought over, or traded."

Some Reflections on Civic Education and the Curriculum

by Elizabeth K. Minnich

Others have sufficiently addressed the question of why there is now a great need to develop a stronger sense of citizenship in our young people. And others have suggested a variety of curricular and extracurricular means toward that end. My purpose here is to reflect on the meaning of civic education in a college curriculum, in part by considering some possible means for its achievement.

To begin, I would like to consider *judgment* and *public talk*, two of the activities central to civic life that are simultaneously means and ends. The goal of civic education is not only or even primarily to pass on knowledge; it is to develop civic virtues in the old sense of virtue, i.e., as expressions of excellence of kind. Central among the civic virtues is judgment. We can, then, focus on (although not limit ourselves to) consideration of judgment: What is it, how can it be taught not just theoretically but practically—and how can it be developed?

Judgment

Judgment is the ability to bring principles to particulars without reducing those particulars to simple instances. That is, judgment is neither deduction nor induction—it does not translate principles into rules, nor does it turn particulars into instances, into abstract cases illustrative of principle.

We have judges in courts of law precisely because we know that the application of rules to individuals without the mediation of judgment is dangerous.

For example, if we have a law against stealing which we are to apply to all instances of stealing directly, we will soon find ourselves prosecuting children in the same way we prosecute adults and treating first offenders the same way we treat repeat offenders. The role of the judge—of the person we entrust with the responsibility of exercising judgment—is to apply the law to each individual case such that neither is violated, such that both are taken into account.

Judgment is an act, almost a leap, of mind in which an irreducibly concrete, individual, particular person or situation is recognized as fully as possible in its own right—and then is brought together with (not subsumed under) a principle. Or a principle, comprehended in its own terms, is brought to a particular and so understood in relation to the particular as well as in relation to other principles.

In different language, a person of whom we say easily "She has good political judgment" is one who recognizes in a new situation what makes it familiar so that she can bring experience to bear; *and yet* she is also one who recognizes equally the claim of that which is indeed new. One who simply applies rules (learned from experience or from books) to all new situations does not have good judgment; one who is so impressed by the uniqueness of new situations that no past learning (no rules, no generalizations, no principles) seems apt also has poor judgment.

A good judgment can be explained, but it cannot be proved; there is no rational necessity behind it. We tend to call good political judgment also "intuition," "sixth sense," "street smarts," indicating that it emerges from something other than (or better, *more* than) knowledge to which others have equal access. When someone explains to us why he made the judgment he made, we can see it, recognize it, learn from it—but next time judgment is called for, we cannot simply apply what we saw and learned. From this notion of judgment, a lot can be said about other virtues that prepare us for it, such as imagination, memory, the "enlarged mentality" (Kant), the ability to think consistently and coherently, and, of course, courage.

Judgment, then, can be said to be the ability we have to bridge theory and practice. If we would like to open the space for students to exercise and, hence, develop such an ability, it would seem that they need practice as well as theory in their civic education.

Public Talk

Arriving at judgment in this sense requires a process of public talk that is both a means and an end. I will suggest that a curriculum for civic education grow out of a series of "conversations" that should themselves exemplify the process of civic interaction we seek to instill in our students. The conversations themselves, then, model a different perspective on public talk than tends to be the norm. The conversations start with the assumption that it is not opinions already held, or facts and information already available, that are critical. They start with the assumption that, while we all have opinions and can have pertinent facts, good talk does not consist of a trading of, or negotiation between, such preexistent stances and evidence.

The public is not at its best a marketplace, or a battlefield, or a negotiating arena in which "thing-like" opinions and interests are exchanged, fought over, or traded. At its best, the public is where we find—through conversation with others—a deeper level of understanding of our own opinions and a level of understanding of ourselves and others. Such understanding would allow us to work together. That "working together" may mean that we have found a deeper level of common concern and, hence, can agree, although we initially thought we disagreed. It can also mean that we have come to clearer understanding of how we differ, but that we have done so in a way that reaffirms our shared commitment to a vision of the public and of political process that is not only tolerant of, but can be responsive to us all, even as we differ. One can stand "losing" on a particular issue if, in working for it, one has felt well treated and reaffirmed in one's faith in the democratic process—in large part because the deepest value is preserving that process.

Where public talk is not considered merely a means to an end but as itself a central aspect of—even an end for—public life, disagreements become not so much problems to be solved as invitations to further engagement. It could even be said that too much agreement is more of a threat to public talk, to public life, than disagreement. And, of course, "disagreement" should not be heard only in the narrow sense, as meaning "irreconcilable opposition on the most fundamental level." "Disagreement" as we experience it in public often means simply that we start from different assumptions; that we have until this moment had different information; that we use key words in slightly different ways; that we care most about different (but not necessarily incompatible) values or goals. Such "disagreement" is very often simply the experience of human difference—and without such differences, conversation would hardly be worth having. It is what makes public life interesting: "inter-est" is that which "is between us."

Civic Virtues and Political Science

The obvious opening on campuses for teaching civic education is individual courses because they are most easily changed. However, there are advantages and disadvantages to beginning at that level. The difficulties that often arise derive from situations suggested by the following observations:

- Course planning tends to start in departments with discussion that centers on the discipline, e.g., of what classes are needed to fill in a good program in Political Science.

- Such needs tend to be determined by the faculty in the department (sometimes in conversation with a dean or provost) and to express the training and interests of the faculty members, to reflect their sense of what it takes to "cover" the field.

- "Coverage of the field" tends to refer not to the subject matter (e.g., politics) but to the discipline (e.g., Political Science) and to be informed by the question of what a professional academic needs to have studied to be credible (or to prepare to study in graduate school to become credible) to other professionals in the academic community. The model that faculty members have in mind is not someone who is skilled in the *praxis* of politics; the model is someone who is prepared to hold his or her own among other political scientists.

- What is offered in a department, then, tends to reflect the present faculty members' understanding of how to prepare undergraduates to go on to graduate school to become academic professionals in a discipline.

- Such methods as studio courses, practicums, and internships differ in being designed to develop techniques and skills that are professionally useful outside of the academy. These courses still have a very hard time receiving full academic credit at most liberal arts institutions. The academy perpetuates the old notion that knowing and doing, theory and practice, should be distinguished such that the former is covered by "education," the latter by (mere) "training." Hence, the "good" schools, the prestigious departments, are peopled not by professionals who understand the practice that is relevant to their field (as politics is to Political Science, writing to Literature, painting and sculpture to Art History) but by those who know the theory respected by their academic colleagues. (The degree of emphasis on theory over practice differs between disciplines, of course.)

Thus, to educate undergraduates for citizenship, to offer education and training in the civic arts, requires a different orientation from that which is usual in academia. The basis for analysis of what needs to be offered to students should become not primarily academic or professional certification but also practice *(praxis)* in the world.

Changing the Question

To prepare for a different orientation, perhaps it would be helpful to plan and hold some conversations about what is most important for a good education in the civic arts. That possibility suggests a few other considerations that may need to be taken into account.

When the question moves from one of planning courses to fit into a discipline or department to "what makes for a good citizen?" those to be involved ought not to be restricted to any one department, nor to academia itself. Citizenship education is interdisciplinary because it focuses on a subject, not on any one academic field. That is—like American Studies, Women's Studies, and Urban Studies —"Civic Studies" begins with an effort to comprehend the subject that is at issue without immediate reference to an existent body of theory or set of methods or body of accepted important works. The disciplines become tools of understanding to be brought to bear on, and tested for adequacy against, the subject: What do the academic disciplines offer that is appropriate to this subject, what is useful, what illuminating? Furthermore, sources of knowledge and experience that are not represented within academically defined disciplines need also to be considered. It could be said that such fields are predisciplinary at the same time as they are multidisciplinary and interdisciplinary. They are subjects not yet turned into defined academic territory. At some point civic education may indeed become a discipline itself, one that is more than an amalgam of preexistent academic materials; but today it is not. That may be to our advantage; it is certainly our challenge.

But we should also reach beyond the academy. Do academics know what makes a good citizen? Are they the best or the primary people to work on the subject that needs to be comprehended? Perhaps some do, and are; but their academic credentials are not what indicates their qualification to design such programs. The first question is still before us: What makes a good citizen? And with that question, the related one: Who can help us think about that question?

More Civic Conversations

I can envision a series of conversations between community activists, local elected officials, journalists who cover politics, and some political thinkers (some of whom are academics). Participants would represent various groups of citizens and political persuasions; the point is not what particular positions people hold but what they bring to the question of what allows people to be active, responsible, and effective in the polity.

Such conversations would need to be facilitated, and they would benefit from at least two official listeners whose task it is to hear what is said, to reformulate and return it to the group for clarification and, finally, to write up what is learned.

The results of those conversations, prepared for general sharing by the listeners, could then be discussed with people selected for their wisdom about the public life, whether they be academics or not. That is, the conversation starts with those who know the area from their experience, and then engages with those who have thought about such experiences. Again, facilitators and listeners are essential.

The next step would be to bring the results of both sets of conversations to those who could teach or have taught courses on civic education on campuses, along with those whose support for such courses is essential (e.g., academic officers). The focus of this third set of conversations would be formulation of material directly helpful to teachers.

The final result of this series of conversations would not be creation of "ideal" courses that anyone could teach anywhere. It would consist of an analysis of what needs to be taught along with some initial thoughts about possible models. The report prepared by the listeners would take up the results from the conversations about civic practice and consider them theoretically and practically. At each stage of conceptualization, the effort needs to be to avoid the split between theory and practice that is all too familiar not only within liberal arts educational systems but, deeply, within the dominant tradition that informs those systems.

Faculty members who already have taught or want to teach courses designed to develop the civic virtues will be important throughout the process. Such "teachers" are simultaneously practitioners, from whom anyone wishing to design a good civic education needs to learn, and students, with whom those who wish to see such education must work. Despite academic traditions, practices, and systems that work against their developing courses in civic education, individuals can and have transcended those limitations. Conversations directed toward developing materials to support faculty members interested in working in this area depend heavily on such special individual teachers.

Theory and Practice

Throughout, it is critical to find out not just what people say but what they mean, to pull out the theory that is implicit in their practices and beliefs, to explore the practice that is implied by their theory and their ways of constructing knowledge.

It is also essential to practice and prepare for good pedagogy in any programs that may finally develop. People always learn better when they are, or are becoming, aware of the predispositions they bring with them into the learning situation. And in looking for the mutual implications of theory and practice in the thinking of activists and academics, we are ourselves practicing good pedagogy—pedagogy appropriate to the political realm in which equals engage with each other in discussion and action that always have both theoretical and practical meaning, implications, consequences.

The conversations in which I would look for understanding of civic life are not, then, like survey research projects or opinion sampling or any other method that starts from individual positions as if they were givens. The conversations are designed to start the process of reflecting on opinions, experiences, implicit or acknowledged theories in the company of others—in public talk— so that the process is itself true to the civic experience at its best. Theory, pedagogy, and practice are then held together throughout, are enacted together.

Within the dominant tradition, we are familiar with the distinction between "theoretical wisdom" and "practical wisdom" and believe that they can be developed and held separately from each other. That separateness, as it were, of two sorts of wisdom seems also to be borne out by experience: one can be a superb political theorist and be entirely ineffective in public life; one can be effective in public life and know nothing of political theory. There are physicians who are superb at medical research and yet are not good diagnosticians; there are physicians who are superb diagnosticians and yet are not sophisticated medical scientists. There do, indeed, seem to be two ways of knowing. Our challenge is to understand both in such a way that we can bring them into fruitful conversation with each other.

To teach the civic arts, teachers are needed who genuinely offer both theoretical and practical wisdom. Special preparation for teachers of the civic arts is needed. Teachers (who tend to have theoretical wisdom, not practical) are needed who can and will work with those who do have practical wisdom.

Education and "Real Life"

Good civic education will provide for public experience as well as theory. Because practice, with experience, tends in our curricula to fall into something like "skill enhancement" categories—and so to fall out of the liberal arts categories—it is worth saying that we are interested in practice, not in technique. "How-to" courses would not meet our criteria any more than pure theory courses would. What we want is provision for experience informed by reflection, practice experienced within a reflexive theoretical mode.

There are different ways of practicing. Good civic education can make use of *examples* discussed in the classroom as well as those drawn from participants' own direct experience. That is, there is indeed a way to approach practical education, education in *praxis,* that supplements and enriches the always-limited mode of individual direct experience. Examples, of course, are not the same as abstract case studies (in which examples are turned into instances that fit with theory because they are already in the abstract terms of theory). Examples are more like very short stories than they are like case studies: they retain the concreteness and context-embeddedness of good stories (which are more like the realm of experience than that of logic for that very reason). Examples can be explored, interpreted, discussed and, when judgments are made about how to treat them, those judgments can also be explained, explored.

Examples give concrete, particular situations that may be illuminated by principles, generalizations; they also offer a ground against which to test principles for their adequacy. That is, examples can provide the equivalent of shared experience for classes to use in exploring possible judgments. The classroom can itself become an arena for the kind of public talk that is otherwise apparently alien to academia, if stories, examples, discussion from multiple and equally valuable perspectives takes place. Theories can then be brought into discussion not as regnant, not as "the answers," but to see if and how they illuminate (or obscure) the stories, the examples.

In such discussion, what is valued is openness and persuasiveness, not self-interest and correctness. That is, we are thinking here of discussions more like the sort we would like to see among citizens.

Hannah Arendt held that in politics we deal properly with opinion, and hence with persuasion. That is, no one is right, no one is wrong, and all enter as equals—although certainly people can be better and worse informed, more or less self-centered, more or less wise and compassionate. In dealing with each other as equals, we deal with each other in our differences, accepting and working with them.

Academia has tended to deal instead with knowledge and with argument, and has done so in a situation that is hierarchical, not egalitarian. Civic education asks teachers to learn to work with, and be able to judge, a different kind of thinking, speaking, relating to others. Many teachers will need help in developing that kind of pedagogy, that mode of judgment.

We can perhaps say, then, that in civic education we move from teaching knowledge to developing thoughtful opinions; from teaching rational argument (usually deductive) to developing judgment; from rewarding correctness to encouraging persuasiveness, thoughtfulness; from exploring the internal coherence of theories to checking their illuminating usefulness; from valuing the disinterested neutral stance to nurturing the committed; from privileging the ability to read to challenging the ability to hear; from grading writing to encouraging speaking; from teaching respect for those already enshrined as "great" to awakening it toward all. To open the space for the practice of judgment, all those changes, and more, suggest themselves.

Elizabeth K. Minnich writes on political philosophy, women's studies, and the liberal arts curriculum. She is currently teaching philosophy at the Union Graduate School.

"The implicit, inherent message for all Euro-Americans as well as for Americans of other racial and cultural heritages has been and remains that integration/assimilation means negation of one's own cultural values and a melting or blending of the self into the dominant ideal."

The Difficult Dialogue of Curriculum Transformation

by Johnnella E. Butler

During the past 20 years in the United States, we have established Women's Studies, Black Studies, Latino Studies, Asian-American Studies, and Native-American Studies as legitimate scholarly areas of inquiry and as academic majors and minors. The Black Studies movement served as a catalyst for other Ethnic Studies programs and provided a catalyst for Women's Studies to challenge gender bias in the academy. Struggles in Women's Studies to mainstream, balance, and integrate the curriculum have taken place alongside struggles to maintain departments and programs of African-American and the more inclusive Black or Africana Studies, and to develop Puerto Rican Studies, Chicano Studies, Asian-American Studies, and Native-American Studies. The dialogue between Women's Studies and Ethnic Studies is limited, often indirect, and hampered by mutual distrust stemming from racism, sexism, heterosexism, ethnocentrism, and classism. The centrality of each field to women of color, however, can provide a foundation for the two fields to produce complete scholarship and pedagogy, challenging the Eurocentric, male-biased, heterosexist, sexist, racist, and classist orientation of college and university curricula.

The extent of and depth of that challenge is succinctly characterized by an advertisement, "Is the Curriculum Biased? A Statement by the National Association of Scholars" in the November 8, 1989 *Chronicle of Higher Education*. Attention to texts by and about white women and men and women of color is reduced to the argument of standards, supported by the assumption that these texts are inferior and their inclusion decided upon simply on the "principle of proportional representation of authors, classified ethnically, biologically, or geographically. The inclusion of works by white women, and men and women of color is perceived to be for the purpose of simply avoiding" [the discouraging of students for not having encountered] "more works by members of their own race, sex, or ethnic group, [and even if] substantiated, would not justify adding inferior works."[1]

The study of white women, and men and women of color is reduced to simply studying "social problems," and it is argued that "other cultures, minority subcultures, and social problems have long been studied in the liberal arts curriculum in such established disciplines as history, literature, comparative religion, economics, political science, anthropology, and sociology." No attention or validity is given to the reality of most of our curricula either not representing, for example, African or American Indian religions as world religions, or at best insulting them by viewing them from a Eurocentric perspective.

Discussion of the demands for inclusion is reduced to assertions implying the Eurocentric, Anglocentric, colonialist assumptions and perspectives that make it possible to state that "the idea that the traditional curriculum 'excludes' is patently false" and "that the liberal arts oppress minorities and women is yet more ludicrous." Diversity is simplistically reduced to "the idea that people of different sexes, races, or ethnic backgrounds necessarily see things differently." Intellectual honesty is seen to exist only where political realities are ignored or reduced to "polemics," where cultural differences are transcended rather than acknowledged and utilized, and where studies of the West seem curiously separate from the study of the traditions and experiences that make up the United States. Most curiously, in the face of the reality of the near extirpation of American Indians, in the face of the reality of the enslavement of people of African ancestry, in the face of the reality of racism and of the sexist and heterosexist behavior to all women, in the face of these and other like realities and their legacies, the National Association of Scholars publicly advertises its racism, sexism, ethnocentrism, and classism in the patronizing closing of its advertisement:

The National Association of Scholars is in favor of ethnic studies, the study of non-Western cultures, and the study of the special problems of women and minorities in our society, but it opposes subordinating the entire humanities and social science curricula to such studies and it views with alarm their growing politicization. Efforts purportedly made to introduce "other points of view" and "pluralism" often seem in fact designed to restrict attention to a narrow set of issues, tendentiously defined. An examination of many women's studies and minority studies courses and programs discloses little study of other cultures and much excoriation of our society for its alleged oppression of women, blacks, and others. The banner of "cultural diversity" is apparently being raised by some whose paramount interest actually lies in attacking the West and its institutions. . . . We must also reject the allegations of "racism" and "sexism" that are frequently leveled against honest critics of the new proposals, and which only have the effect of stifling much-needed debate.[2]

The "much-needed debate" called upon in the closing statement can hardly take place as long as racism, sexism, heterosexism, ethnocentrism, classism, and colonialism are either ignored or reduced to "a narrow set of issues." Furthermore, until the validity and usefulness of the best of the traditions of both the so-called West and those of its myriad peoples are recognized, studied in their own right, and utilized in scholarship, we will perpetuate a seriously flawed and damaged scholarship and society. As long as the political dimensions of the existing curriculum are obscured and passed off as objective subject content and as long as the past and present realities of white women, women of color, and men of color are deemed a "narrow set of issues," to be studied, at best, from the perspective of their inferiority and deviance, the "much-needed" debate will be a rather lopsided, intellectual game of "defending" the West. Curriculum transformation is not about such games at all.

In my experience, the statement by the National Association of Scholars represents the parameters of the current debate within the academy around Ethnic Studies and Women's Studies. And within this myopic, hostile, ethnocentric context, with its paternalistic overtones, many of us urge a scholarly conversation and sharing between the faculty and content of Ethnic Studies and Women's Studies. I wish to suggest a broader conceptualization of transformative work in the academy, to lend a coherence, a productive perspective, and clear directions for the difficult dialogues that have begun and must continue in order to provide an education worthy of and essential to the well-being of our citizens.

Henry Adams, in his late-nineteenth-century search for unity in thought and action and between the two, oddly enough may be seen as very similar to his contemporary, W. E. B. DuBois, and to more recent scholars and advocates of Black Studies; Asian-American; American-Indian; Latino Studies; and Women's Studies. Adams realized, as they, that his education was useless to cope with rapid social, cultural, and technological change. More distressingly, he realized that his education did not provide him with the attitudes and skills necessary for progress toward a positive end for humanity. Through his efforts to understand human thought and history as energetic forces comparable to the forces of physical, scientific energy, he prophetically predicted that the huge electric dynamos of the Chicago and Paris expos of 1893 and 1900 respectively were symbolic of the coming age in which "the human race may commit suicide by blowing up the world." Furthermore, he explicated the power of the spiritual unity of philosophy, art, and vision. He deplored his own age, of which ours is a direct extension, as having no unity except in "the unsolved mystery of the atom."

The kind of unity that Adams sought was limited and doomed in its inherent ethnocentrism and sexism; nonetheless, it provided a significant step, I think, toward our taking seriously the need for a humaneness in thought and action that might prevent humankind's self-destruction through group, cultural, and societal genocide, and encourage the potential for full human development. Furthermore, as DuBois predicted in 1903, the problem of the twentieth century is the problem of the color line, with all its social, political, economic, and cultural ramifications.[3] The current challenges to academia that white women and women and men of color present to the curriculum are articulations of the problem in academia, just as the Civil Rights and Black Power movements articulated the problem of the color line in the body politic. The greater presence of minorities of color and white women on college and university campuses clearly raises the question of essential change within the academic community structure. Their mere presence, however, does not mandate that the curriculum be changed to reflect the strengths and weaknesses, the beautiful and ugly of our essentially pluralistic collective history. The goal of good, honest scholarship, reflective of the closest approximation of the truth, mandates essential change. Their presence suggests the need to prepare all students to live and work in a rapidly changing and increasingly diverse world. Those of us who have become involved in curriculum transformation efforts are attempting to assist universities, colleges, and their faculty in doing just that.

Most will agree that we are a nation founded essentially on the concept of individualism with a national culture defined by Anglo-American ethnicity with European roots, essentially British and neoclassical Greek and Roman. Serious, unbiased attention to the American historical, social, political, economic, and cultural experiences and present reality of men of color, white women, and women of color in the United States reveals that the democratic ideals of the United States have failed many of its myriad peoples because of the inherent contradiction between the structure and the essence of our projected national culture and the essentially pluralist composition of our people. What Harold Cruse has defined as the "integrationist ethic" conveys not simply "freedom and justice for all," but moreover the myth of the melting pot—the coercion of the American Dream at the expense of one another, a vicious rugged individualism, an ethnocentrism, sexism, classism, and racism maintaining an inherent contradiction between the structure and essence of our national culture and the essentially pluralist composition of our people at a significant, defining, "credo" level.[4] The implicit, inherent message for all Euro-Americans as well as for Americans of other racial and cultural heritages has been and remains that integration/assimilation means negation of one's own cultural values and a melting or blending of the self into the dominant ideal. That dominant ideal, then, defines the greater part of one's cultural and personal identity. In most possibilities for a sharing of cultural values, the values and ways of people of color are appropriated to uses and definitions that result, at best, in distorting compromise. American ethnic, cultural, social, and economic realities are then defined by an individual, bootstrap, competitive, evolving, puritanical ethic. What results, perhaps unwittingly, is the distortion and constantly threatened destruction of a sustaining ethnic potential other than the "American," read "Anglo-American," or subscribers to that norm. Only in short-lived instances where the ethnic group has power and status for a given period of time do we see an apparent flourishing of the democratic ideal in its intended pluralistic concept of "We, the people. . . ."

The ramifications of the integrationist ethic on scholarship are quite visible and incur a figurative as well as concrete violence on the social, cultural, political, and economic realities of most men and women of color in the United States and most white women. It incurs another violence on white men, beginning with an exaggerated sense of self-worth. As a historical tendency stimulated by the Anglo-American ideology (reminder: my use of Anglo-American indicates a cultural, social, political, and economic national heritage), the integrationist ethic subverts and blocks the underlying American propensity toward a democratic pluralism, a pluralism inclusive of the Anglo-American ethic but not defined by that or any one ethic subscribed to by a power structure. It is further supported by racism, which upholds rampant individualism and an Americanism with the implied goal of nullification of all competing subcultures indigenous to what is now the United States. Briefly stated, knowing and acting out of the full, true story of our shared American pasts and presents, and learning that story through a constructive generative process, is the only hope for our becoming a literate nation.

As Paulo Friere has shown, literacy implies more than the ability to read and count. As the history of American slavery reminds us, learning to read and count was closely connected to the slaves perceiving fully their human condition and to the Christian misuse of the *Bible* to justify slavery, and led, if not directly to revolt, to an intense desire for freedom. Literacy is inextricably joined with a freedom that is dependent on our knowing one another, becoming conversant with one another, and building on the best of our traditions in the approximation, if not the achievement, of wholeness.

In the curricular context, the attempt at wholeness includes a comprehensive sense of unity, somewhat reminiscent of Henry Adams and others, but much more transformative. That unity is expressed by:

- The identification of the connections between and interaction among the disciplines (interdisciplinary study would not simply mean bringing several scholars together to investigate a subject. Rather, it would mean an approach to scholarship evolving from the confluence and convergence of disciplinary approaches).

- The study and definition of the experience and the aesthetics of those large groups of people who are neglected, studied not in comparison to the dominant group, not as problems to a dominant group, but in and of themselves and in relation to one another.

- The correction of the distortions of the majority and the minority that have occurred due to the insistence of exclusion.

- The defining and structuring of a curriculum that through its content and process affirms the interconnectedness of human life, experience, and creativity and its constant evolutionary nature.

In such a curriculum, the stories of Euro-American assimilation would find their place in the disciplines and in interdisciplinary study as well as in the transformation of the concept of what and who is American. The Anglo-American experience would take its rightful place as a heritage that has defined much of the national character, to which most Euro-Americans have subscribed, and that has wielded an inordinate amount of power in determining various norms and privileges. The scholarship of Black Studies and other Ethnic Studies, and the scholarship of Women's Studies, as both separate entities and as interdisciplinary fields of study interacting with the traditional disciplines, would then move us to a content and pedagogy that begins to define and characterize a curriculum more reflective of our American cultural reality (and here I use "cultural" in its most comprehensive sense), and more reflective of the need that human beings constantly exhibit to understand who they are in order to act responsibly toward one another in the world.

Given the American social and cultural reality, the greater participation of men and women of color and white women in higher education has far-reaching implications for not only who the students and professors are in our colleges and universities, but also for *what* and *how* we teach. The African-American, the Latino American, the Asian-American, and the American Indian bring with them a cultural and historical reality integral to the understanding of the United States' past and present. Women—Anglo-American and other Euro-American women, and women of color—foreground the diversity implicit in our many misleading collective nouns, such as "women." These realities are vital to laying the groundwork for a productive, vibrant future. Their incorporation into the curriculum began and directs the discussion of curricular change, as well as the more ambitious transformation.

In his 1985 *Report to the Ford Foundation,* the late Nathan Huggins reviews the transition of the American university during the mid-twentieth century from "Cardinal Newman's idealism and from the shaping influence of the German university" to an "unprecedented expansion and transformation." That transformation occurred in regard to curriculum as well as in regard to the composition of the student body. He reminds us that:

> When in the late sixties, black students challenged the curriculum, their main target was the parochial character of the humanities as taught. They saw the humanities as exclusive rather than universal. They saw humanists as arrogant white men in self-congratulatory identification with a grand European culture. To those students, such arrogance justified the charge of "racism."[5]

Consistent with this transformation, humanities scholars, Huggins points out, had become more and more specialized and were even more incompetent, he implies, to meet this challenge than those imbued with Matthew Arnold's conceptualization of the proper liberal arts content that at least went somewhat beyond the confines of Western civilization. Huggins succinctly further reminds us that black students and scholars also began to "challenge the 'objectivity' of mainstream social science," and demanded a "discussion of what they saw to be the inherent racism in these normative assumptions and for a shift in perspective that would destigmatize blacks and reexamine the 'normalcy' of the white middle class."

Catherine Stimpson in her 1986 *Report to the Ford Foundation: Women's Studies in the United States,* argues that it is appropriate to view Women's Studies within the framework of curricular reform beginning in the 1820s, of which the mid-twentieth-century shifts of foci may be seen as a part. She points out that:

> Black studies and the larger black power movement that helped create black studies made several significant contributions to the theory and practice of women's studies, providing an intellectual agenda for women's studies in its initial stages. The black power movement believed that a revolution by the oppressed must be preceded by a transformation of consciousness in order to succeed. The battle for self-esteem proceeded on two fronts—on the popular level through slogans like "black is beautiful" and in institutions of higher learning through the black studies movement. Black studies, like women's studies after it, sought, first, to reclaim the past and, second, to analyze the causes of oppression.[6]

What Huggins and Stimpson refer to is more correctly labeled reform, for early Black Studies and Women's Studies did not demand any fundamental shifts in foci of the entire liberal arts curriculum. The emphasis was on adding the "other" to the curriculum. Indeed, reflecting on the program and departmental status of Women's Studies and Black Studies, we quickly realize that they were most frequently on the periphery of the curriculum, struggling with one another over limited funds. Course approvals, tenure, and reappointments did not come easily. There are many casualties—for example, in Black Studies—of scholars who were denied tenure by white (usually male) professors who have built their careers on studying black people and their lives.[7] The fact that now we have two burgeoning fields of study that by their very nature challenge the accepted subject matter and foci of the liberal arts suggests movement beyond reform to transformation.

In Chapter 8 of *Multicultural Education: Issues and Perspectives*, edited by James and Cherry Banks (Allyn and Bacon, 1990, 1991), "Transforming the Curriculum: Teaching about Women of Color," I define and describe the transformation in the context of scholarship on the United States. Transformation involves taking race, class, gender, and ethnicity seriously as categories of analysis functioning simultaneously separately and together in a matrixlike fashion:

> Essentially, transformation is the process of revealing unity among human beings and the world, as revealing important differences. Transformation implies acknowledging and benefiting from interaction among sameness and diversity, groups and individuals. The maxim on which transformation rests may be stated as an essential affirmation of the West African proverb, "I am because we are. We are because I am." . . . It is in opposition to the European, Western pivotal axiom, on which integration, balancing, and mainstreaming rest. . . . "I think; therefore, I am," as expressed by Descartes.[8]

During the early eighties, many of us in Women's Studies in particular began to understand the difference between reform and transform as we observed that balancing, mainstreaming, and integrating were essentially simply adding women of color to Women's Studies syllabi as an afterthought or as an aberration. The books, *Sturdy Black Bridges* and *But Some of Us Are Brave: Black Women's Studies,* publicly demonstrated the need for transformation, and two early faculty development projects articulated in the academic community, ways of transforming courses: the F.I.P.S.E.-funded Black Studies/Women's Studies, an Overdue Partnership faculty development grant in Massachusetts, and the state-funded Cross Cultural Perspectives in the Curriculum in California.[9]

More recently, focusing on the incorporation of content on women of color into core and introductory courses, Ford has funded eleven Women's

Research Centers to work with the Ethnic Studies components on their campuses. Virginia, through a competitive effort, has funded faculty development projects on incorporating race, class, gender, and ethnicity into the curriculum.[10] Similar efforts are occurring on campuses across the nation, not in insignificant numbers, but not nearly as much as needed. Ethnic Studies and Women's Studies have the content and are developing the methodologies and pedagogies needed to incorporate race, class, gender, and ethnicity into the curriculum. The task calls for approaches to scholarship and teaching beyond those of the traditional disciplines. It also demands dropping courses and texts repetitive of the Euro-American and Western experience from the liberal arts curriculum.

Transformation is in tune with the pluralistic, multidimensional process of scholarship and pedagogy demanded by a pluralistic population. "Reform," "mainstreaming," and "integrating," are more reflective of a monolithic, one-dimensional scholarship and pedagogy.

> Stated succinctly as "I am we," the West African proverb provides the rationale for the interaction and modulation of the categories of race, class, gender, and ethnicity, for the interaction and modulation of their respective "-isms," for the interaction and modulation of the objective and subjective, the rational and the intuitive, the feminine and the masculine, all those things which we, as Westerners, see as either opposite or standing rigidly alone. This is the breakdown of what is called variously critical pedagogy, feminist pedagogy, multifocal teaching, when the end is the comprehension of and involvement with cultural class, racial, and gender diversity toward the end not of tolerance, but rather of an egalitarian world based on communal relationships within humanity.[11]

Transformation of the academy, however, will not occur unless Women's Studies and Ethnic Studies themselves are transformed. *That is, significant curricular change regarding the experiences of women depends on the radical transformation of Women's Studies to reflect all women's experience. Significant curricular change regarding the experience of people of color depends on the radical transformation of Ethnic Studies to reflect the experience of women of color.* Simply put, Women's Studies must divest itself of white-skin privilege, racism, and the feminist insistence on the primacy of gender; Ethnic Studies must divest itself of male-centered scholarship, sexism, and heterosexism, all must lend credibility to gender as a valid, viable, and necessary category of analysis. The emerging dialogue is most productive when viewed as part of the ongoing development of the American university and the restructuring of knowledge as our nation and its needs grow and change. Its rough, jagged edges begin to smooth as we find ways to recognize and incorporate difference, correct omissions and distortions. Clarifying the use of the term "Ethnic Studies" and envisioning a curriculum help to reveal the possible.

The fact that the term Ethnic Studies has come to signify the body of knowledge of people of color in the United States, as well as academic programs and departments organized to study in an interdisciplinary fashion these experiences, is transformative. Ethnic Studies serves as a collective noun for Black Studies, Asian-American Studies, American Indian Studies, and Latino Studies. Programmatically, Ethnic Studies can exist as Black Studies, Asian-American Studies, American Indian Studies, and Latino Studies, independently/in a comparative context. Arguments in the academy over the use of the term generally question its use to the exclusion of Euro-American ethnics. In Werner Sollers's *Beyond Ethnicity*, the discussion of the origin of the term "ethnic" clarifies that it is a time-bound and group-situation-bound term. His work tends to reinforce the historical use of the term that simultaneously affirms assimilation (the melting pot worked) while affirming plural coexistence (cultural pluralism reigns), as if one can have it both ways. Race, gender, and class, while not ignored, do not seem to be taken seriously as categories of definition that also have institutional and cultural manifestations in and of themselves and in the form of their "-isms."[12]

It has become fairly obvious that while most Euro-American ethnic groups maintain an identity around the heritage of their country of origin, most have assimilated in the most significant ways to the Anglo-American norm. Racism has not been a constant factor preventing that assimilation. Scandinavian Studies, for example, may mean studying European Scandinavian countries and populations or it may mean studying assimilated Americans of Scandinavian experience. In the American context, it does not provide us with extensive legal studies, a history that is pervasive throughout and in many ways central to American history, or a distinct cultural experience within the United States that provides distinct and significant paradigms for the study of literature, psychology, sociology, politics, and economics. While the Irish-American, for example, may have more ethnic visibility in some aspects of American life, that experience, because of assimilation, does not provide a centrality, as do the experiences of people of color in the United States.

Furthermore, it is testimony to the peculiar and complex racial and ethnic definitions in the United States that there is confusion as to where the American Jewish experience "fits." Are they Jewish and therefore ethnic? Are they white and therefore assimilated, despite anti-Semitism? Is anti-Semitism the same as racism? Does it have the institutional ramifications of racism? Within a European context, indeed, the study of Semitics and the European Jew may be viewed as Ethnic Studies. In the American context, however, it may be argued that because of white-skin privilege, American Jews have been able to assimilate. Their distinguishing feature is their religion. And yet, anti-Semitism carries many of the outward features of racism.[13]

What has emerged, I think, is a transformation in the American reality and consciousness that sees ethnicity and race as overlapping, making ethnicity applicable as a category to American people of color. Whites, it seems, have for the most part assimilated. Euro-American ethnic differences have evolved for the most part in this century to be variations on a theme that is primarily American (read Anglo-American).[14] People of color have not been allowed, for the most part, to assimilate. Ethnic/racial differences signal "other." The move then within the academy to study the content of Ethnic Studies and Women's Studies may be seen as an effort to examine the beautiful and the ugly of this important aspect of the American experience, in order to reveal and develop the paradigms and methodologies necessary to understand these experiences in and of themselves, in comparison to one another, in the context of the larger American society, and indeed to understand fully American society in its entirety. This describes transformation. It does not stop at simply adding and celebrating diversity, and thereby risking greater polarization. Rather, it demands that we do something with these experiences, this diversity, in order ultimately to understand the whole. It demands that we add, delete, decenter, re-vision and reorganize in order to transform our curricula to reflect a kind of unity, a wholeness that is all-inclusive in its content, methodology, and pedagogy.

A curriculum, methodology, and pedagogy that examines the unity among disciplines, experiences, events, and humans, that explores subject matter comparatively as well as singly, will begin to correct some of the basic ills of the academy:

1. *A lack of a sense of human commonality and communality.*

   Because the curriculum content does not assert or imply a commonality or a communality among humans and human experience, course material seems distant, irrelevant, or perhaps ideal and abstract. And because it is ethnocentric, it is frequently repetitive. Few connections, if any, are apparent between the past, present, and the future; science and math appear formulaic and abstract, distant from humans. The lack of an understood commonality and communality makes it difficult for professors to identify the needs of students who come from backgrounds unlike their own. This lack makes it impossible for professors to draw analogies to experiences with which they are unfamiliar, both when teaching and when deciding on process, or to recognize similar behavior patterns or learning processes. Rarely do students embrace the learning process because they feel connected with the content and the professors in relation to content and process. Rarely do professors feel connected with content and process and with students.

2. *A distorted sense of the value of the aesthetics, ideals, history, and heritage of the Anglo, upper-middle to upper-class white American.*

   Scholars, professors, and students weigh all experience against the stated and implied norm of a white, idealized sense of Western culture. Thus, other aesthetics, ideals, histories and heritages are ignored. They are seen as subordinate to and only within the context of the implied norm, or seen as deviant. In such a way is the literary canon established; historical periods defined; sociological, economic, and political formulae devised; and so on. Failure to achieve the American Dream is ascribed to cultural deprivation and perhaps "lacking the necessaries"—that is, inherent racial/ethnic difference.

3. *A distortion of American history and culture through the distortion of the meaning of race and ethnicity in American social and scholarly contexts.*

The history and heritage of groups of color are presented as additional to, instead of integral to, American history and heritage, that is, if included at all. Thus, there is the accepted version of American history and heritage that is only minimally affected by African-American history and heritage, Asian-American history and heritage, Latino-American history and heritage, American Indian history and heritage, and white women's history and heritage. Similarly, Euro-American history and heritage is modulated by Anglo-American norm imposition and privilege.

4. *A distorted and limited treatment of gender difference and similarities.*

The curriculum is characterized by a valuing of the masculine over the feminine and a simplistic tendency to equate the two to suggest equity and fairness. Failure of women to achieve is often seen as part and parcel of the female reality. Likewise, cultural, academic, social, and political achievements of women are valued less than those of men. This valuing and devaluing is modulated by ethnocentrism, racism, and classism.

5. *A distortion of American class realities.*

In pursuit of the "norm" as coerced by the integrationist ethic, class differences are weighed against the upper-middle to upper-class norm that is part of the Anglo-American ideal. Together with the myth of rugged individualism, the American Dream, the melting pot, racism, sexism, and ethnocentrism, the upper-middle class to upper-class norm allows scholarship and teaching to act as if class differences do not exist or have negligible significance, or to ascribe failure to achieve the American Dream to inherent class characteristics.

6. *A limitation and restriction of education to a static state.*

The entire educational process becomes one that must remain primarily static in order to maintain the imbalance of power sustained by racism, classism, sexism, and ethnocentrism. Only changes defined and limited by the dominant cultural norm are tolerated. Professors generally control and fill "the empty receptacles of students' minds." The "leading out" of the mind inherent in the definition of the verb "to educate" is ignored. Specialization and marketable skills ensure quick returns. Therefore, critical thinking, comprehension of the dynamics of culture and human life, and the relationship of the sciences, humanities, and social sciences to humankind and to one another are devalued and viewed as unnecessary to individual, material well-being. The lack of perceived unity among the different kinds of people, life-styles, classes, cultures, and among disciplines, content, professors, and students, and so on, supports the cultural and personal expression that either imitates or is of the norm. Education maintains that norm instead of catalyzing growth.

7. *A gross limitation of the human potential.*

By the narrow adherence to an idealized norm, we fail to identify and utilize the best of our collective traditions. Hence, a large segment of the American population, both "minority" and "majority," fails to develop as part of the larger culture that which is in them. For example, our national enthusiasm and commitment to foreign language teaching is dampened. Only languages deemed acceptable within the context of the idealized norm are supported. Our tolerance of non-English-speaking peoples is limited. Teaching reading and writing using foreign language or the regional or cultural dialect of English as building blocks is largely disdained, and in some quarters viewed as un-American.

The serious, radical deconstruction and subsequent reconstruction through transformation can ensure the education our students need to strive toward an informed, intelligent, creative, plural, multidimensional, and humane life. Rarely do expediency and moral justice converge. However, if we desire a literate citizenry, then we must encourage an academic atmosphere that corrects distortions and exclusions, and allows for syncretism and an interaction among differences and samenesses so that we see all of our selves as vibrant parts of the past, present, and future of the many dimensions of this nation. Academic institutions, by their very nature and reason for existence, define and perpetuate the national culture. It might be convincingly argued that this purpose has become more and more obscure as the population grows more and more out of touch with the static curriculum. By now, demographic statistics are well known. Numbers of the elite white are dwindling. In addition, the population pool for the majority of colleges and universities is rapidly becoming Latino, Asian-American, African-American, American Indian, and middle- and lower-economic-class white American. The complexion of the elite class reflects flecks of brown and yellow. A curriculum that does not propose and explicate the values of our total population—its past and present, its encounter with technological and social change—will be useless in the working, cultural, and social world of the twenty-first century. Worst of all, it will continue to stifle the human imagination and potential so that fear of one another and protection and isolation from one another will maintain enlarged possibilities for mutual destruction.[15]

Johnnella E. Butler is chair of the American Ethnic Studies Department at the University of Washington in Seattle. Her areas of specialization are African-American literature, comparative American literature, ethnic literature, black studies, and women's studies.

From Transforming the Curriculum: Ethnic Studies and Women's Studies, *edited by Johnnella E. Butler & John C. Walker, copyright © 1991 by the State University of New York Press. Reprinted with permission of the publisher.*

Notes

1. "Is the Curriculum Biased? A Statement by the National Association of Scholars." *Chronicle of Higher Education.* November 8, 1989, p. A23.

2. *Ibid.*

3. W. E. B. Dubois, *The Souls of Black Folk* in John Hope Franklin, ed. *Three Negro Classics* (Signet, 1903) (New York: Avon, 1971).

4. Harold Cruse. "The Creative and Performing Arts and the Struggle for Identity and Credibility" in Harry A. Johnson, ed., *Negotiating the Mainstream: A Survey of the Afro-American Experience* (Chicago: American Library Association, 1972), pp. 47–102.

5. Nathan Huggins, *Afro-American Studies* (New York: Ford Foundation, 1985), p. 13.

6. Catherine Stimpson with Nina Kressner Cobb, *Women's Studies in the United States* (New York: Ford Foundation, 1986), p. 11.

7. This has long been a known, undocumented fact within the Black Studies community. See Michael A. Olivas, "An Elite Priesthood of White Males Dominates the Central Areas of Civil Rights Scholarship," *The Chronicle of Higher Education,* May 24, 1989, pp. B1–B2.

8. Johnnella E. Butler, "Transforming the Curriculum: Teaching about Women of Color," in James and Cherry Banks, eds., *Multicultural Education: Issues and Perspectives* (Boston: Allyn and Bacon, 1990, 1991), p. 152.

9. Roseann P. Bell, Bettye J. Parker, Beverly Guy-Sheftall, eds., *Sturdy Black Bridges: Visions of Black Women in Literature* (New York: Anchor, 1979); Gloria T. Hull, Patricia Bell Scott, Barbara Smith, eds., *But Some of Us Are Brave, Black Women's Studies* (Old Westbury, NY: 1982); Margo Culley and I were the project investigators and codirectors of the F.I.P.S.E. project. See Johnnella E. Butler, "Complicating the Question: Black Studies and Women's Studies in Marilyn Schuster and Susan Van Dyne, eds., *Women's Place in the Academy: Transforming the Liberal Arts Curriculum* (New Jersey: Rowman and Allanheld, 1985). Deborah Rosenfelt and Carol Lee Sanchez codirected the California project at San Francisco State University.

10. The two Virginia projects are at Mary Washington College, Fredericksburg and Virginia Polytechnic Institute and State University, Blacksburg.

11. Butler, pp. 152–153

12. See Chapter 1 in Werner Sollers, *Beyond Ethnicity: Consent and Descent in American Culture* (New York: Oxford, 1986).

13. See Howard Adelman, "Is Jewish Studies Ethnic Studies?" in Johnnella E. Butler and John C. Walter, eds., *Transforming the Curriculum: Ethnic Studies and Women's Studies* (Albany, NY: SUNY Press, 1991). (Forthcoming).

14. For a model transformation of American literature based on American cultural pluralism, see Paul Lauter, ed., *Reconstructing American Literature: Courses, Syllabi, Issues* (Old Westbury, NY: The Feminist Press, 1983).

15. Taking seriously information that is

found in our efforts to correct racist, sexist, classist, and bigoted scholarship in many instances calls for a complete change in the ways we conceptualize our cultural selves. John Pappademos, professor of physics at the University of Illinois at Chicago, as part of a panel presentation at a conference on the core curriculum, sponsored by the Texas Higher Education Coordinating Board (July 21, 1990) presented an unpublished paper on "The Role of Africa in the History of Science." He noted that a survey of introductory physics and physical science texts revealed that of "African and African-American achievements in science there was not a word." While this survey was done in 1980, he said that one or two recent texts "try to remedy the omissions of past and present achievements of women scientists"; but that "Africa and Black people have been stricken from the record as far as science's history is concerned." (p. 1) Demonstrating that ancient Egypt's racial makeup was predominantly Black African, he detailed Black African achievements in science, most of which have been obliterated as such by blatantly racist nineteenth-century scholars (see Martin Bernal, *Black Athena* (New Brunswick, NJ: Rutgers University Press, 1989). From the world's first

scientific method of measuring time, to identifying the retrograde motion of the planet Mars, to quadratic equations, to establishing a thousand years before Galileo (and known to Galileo) that bodies of different mass fall with the same acceleration, he provided sufficient information to prove his point that the Greeks had learned from the Black Egyptians most of what we credit them and other Europeans for. We need to contemplate just what such information means for transforming our curricula; what it means for the reconceptualization of the Origins of Western Civilization and for the excluded and dispossessed cultures of our curricula. Might we not only correct distortions but also learn of different ways of being that might be useful in rescuing ourselves from our oppressive excesses? See Bemal, cited above; John Pappademos, "An Outline of Africa in the History of Physics," *Journal of African Civilization,* Vol. II, No. 1,2 (September 1980, pp. 40–59; Pappademos, "The Newtonian Synthesis in Physical Science, Roots in the Nile Valley," *Journal of African Civilizations,* Vol. VI, no. 2 (November 1984), pp. 84–101. Various works by Ivan Van Sertima and Frank Snowden also address the Black African origins of science and mathematics.

"Schools are influential public cultures which cultivate and produce particular stories of how to live
ethically and politically."

Critical Pedagogy and the New Politics of Cultural Difference

by Henry A. Giroux

At the 1990 California Association for Bilingual Education Conference in San Francisco, ten-year-old Maribel Martinez, one of the winners of the student writing contest, offered in her speech a fundamental insight that is increasingly being taken up as central to reconstructing the meaning and purpose of critical pedagogy as part of a wider movement for democratic educational reform. In her speech, Maribel linked becoming literate to being able to move into different galaxies; in this case, the concept of galaxy served as a metaphor for moving in and out of different languages, ways of life, narratives, and social relationships. While Maribel didn't speak directly in these terms, she was asserting the value of a politics of cultural difference that enlarged her possibilities as a citizen in a democratic society.

For Maribel, being literate meant extending her understanding of justice to different cultural spheres, it meant acting as a border-crosser so that she could explore different linguistic and social worlds; it meant extending the principle of cultural difference as a basis for tolerance, enrichment, and possibility. It also meant living in a world in which she could locate herself not only in her own history but also understand how other students and adults situated themselves in histories with different values, traditions, and voices. For Maribel, to have a voice was to be able to write and speak in the language of cultural diversity in order to broaden the possibilities of one's identity within a global world that is increasingly marked by forms of linguistic, cultural, and social heterogenity and difference.

What does the notion of being a border-crosser suggest for a theory and practice of critical pedagogy? At best, a theory of pedagogy should be grounded in a public philosophy which aims at providing educators with a moral and political vision which extends rather than limits the promise and possibilities of a principled democratic society. Such a vision takes as its primary task reconstructing public schools and universities as places where students are educated as critical citizens capable of thinking critically, taking risks, and exercising some control over the conditions of knowledge production and acquisition. This is a vision of pedagogy linked to the imperatives of a practical hope, one that views the relationship between leadership and schooling as part of the wider struggle to create the lived experience of empowerment for the vast majority.

Today, teaching is most often organized around a claim to authority that is primarily managerial, procedural, and technical. This is a position that defines leadership in terms that are not only profoundly antiutopian, but also incapable of referencing what administrators and teachers actually do in terms of the underlying principles and values that structure their beliefs and actions. At work here is an educational language that ignores its own partiality, that refuses to engage the ideological assumptions that underlie its vision of the future, and reduces teachers to technicians and bad theorists. More specifically, this view of teaching often removes schools from their most vital connections to public life, and more often than not, defines teaching in instrumental rather than enabling terms. In other words, it deskills teachers while purporting to empower them.

In opposition to this view, I want to argue that educators need to do more than provide students with the technical knowledge and skills they will need to fit into an educational system increasingly governed by state mandates, that define schooling through an emphasis on standardization rather than empowerment, achievement rather than equity, testing rather than learning, and choice rather than community. The question is, of course, whose interests and voice shapes this agenda.

This is essentially a question of purpose and meaning, one that underscores the importance of situating the debate about pedagogy within the larger debate of the future of education in this country. I want to stress at the outset the fundamental importance of recognizing that public schools, as well as higher education, do not simply provide students with the knowledge and skills they will need to secure decent employment and the benefits of social mobility; in fact, contrary to the view that schools are merely instructional sites, I want to argue that all forms represent a place that introduces students to particular views of the world and to particular social relations; put simply, schooling is an introduction to somebody's story, it is a place that is deeply political and unarguably normative.

What is important to stress here is that schools are influential public cultures which cultivate and produce particular stories of how to live ethically and politically; schools reproduce selected values, and they harbor in their social relations and teaching practices specific notions regarding what knowledge is of most worth, what it means to know something, and how one might construct representations of themselves, others, and the social environment. Put another way, educating students is really an introduction into how culture is organized, a demonstration of who is authorized to speak about particular forms of culture, and what culture is considered acceptable and what isn't. As an introduction to, preparation for, and legitimation of particular forms of social life, education always presupposes a vision of the future. In this respect, the language of education that students take with them from their school and university experience should embody a vision capable of providing them with a sense of identity, place, and public worth.

It serves us well to remember that schooling is always about the production of stories and narratives, about what it means to locate oneself in the history of a language, culture, and lived experience. With this in mind, I want to reiterate that the current debate specifically in the U.S. about educational reform and, in particular, about cultural literacy rather than literacies represents more than a commentary and conflict over language and culture; it is fundamentally a debate about the relevance of democracy, social criticism, and the status of utopian thought in constituting both one's dreams and the stories that people devise in order to give meaning to their lives. This debate has taken a serious turn in the last decade and now, as before, its terms are being principally set by technocrats and antiutopians. For example, neoconservatives have presented an agenda and purpose for shaping public schooling which under the guise of attempting to revitalize the language of morality have, in reality, launched an attack on some of the most fundamental aspects of democratic public life and the social, moral, and political obligations of responsible, critical citizens.

Within this new public philosophy there is a ruthlessly frank expression of doubt about the viability of democracy. Moreover, its loss of utopian vision is nowhere more evident than in its view of educational reform in which schools are reduced either to low-skill job training or to pedagogical beachheads enlisted in the fight to save what is often labeled as "Western Civilization." In the first instance, schools are fast becoming adjuncts of the corporation, and learning is reduced to mastering the knowledge, skills, and attitudes necessary to develop good work habits. In this position, schooling is about educating students in order to fit them into a job market that offers low-paying and low-level skilled jobs for the many and a limited number of middle-range and high-level jobs at the top for a select few. This is a form of education that imitates the old colonial model of socialization, which educated to pacify in the name of literacy and economic security those subordinate groups whose cultural capital does not bring the right exchange rate in the marketplace of the dominant culture and wider society. Lost from the dominant perspective is the broader concern of providing students with a critical education in the service of creating a public sphere of citizens who are able to exercise power over their lives. Its code word is literacy but its purpose is to get students to adapt to existing configurations of power rather than to teach them how to lead and govern.

More recently, the notion of educational reform has taken a different turn. In this view, it is not only the American economy which is at risk but the very notion of Western Civilization itself. Universities are now defined through the necessity of providing students with the language, knowledge, and values necessary to preserve the "essential" traditions of Western culture. The conservative position on cultural production in the schools has arisen from a recognition by some of its followers that problems faced by the U.S. can no longer be reduced to educating students so they can occupy jobs at entry- and middle-range occupational levels. Instead, the emphasis must be switched to addressing an alleged cultural crisis, which can be traced to the broader ideological tenets of the progressive education movements that dominated the U.S. curriculum after the Second World War, changing the cultural demographics, and the rise of new social movements since the 1960s.

I think it is accurate to say that within the last decade in the U.S. the goal of schooling as a vehicle for social justice and public responsibility has lost ground to the *imperatives* of the marketplace, the *logic* of the test score, and the *undemocratic* emphasis on cultural ethnocentrism. "Making it" in schools is now defined in terms fashioned out of the language of Wall Street — competitive, individualistic, and heartless. Important school problems stemming from inadequate resources, overworked teachers, understaffed schools, visionless administrators, and powerless students are no longer taken seriously as part of the language of educational reform. At the same time, community, democracy, and diversity have become subversive categories as the language of schooling is stripped of its ethical and public functions.

In the most general sense, the educational reform movement of the last decade represents the latest cultural offensive by the new elitists to rewrite the past from the perspective of the privileged and the powerful. This is a perspective that disdains both the democratic implications of democratic citizenship, cultural difference, and forms of pedagogy that engage issues central to developing critical public cultures. In this perspective, questions of language and literacy are situated within a notion of uniformity in which cultural difference, as an articulation of racial, gender, class, and ethnic issues, is consigned to the margins of history and everyday life.

Against this trend, I want to develop a rationale along with some pedagogical principles for developing a politics of cultural difference responsive to the imperatives of a critical democracy. In doing so, I want to emphasize that public schools and institutions of higher learning must be more broadly defined as contradictory agencies and sites of struggle engaged in specific forms of moral and political regulation. That is, they produce different subject positions, knowledges, and forms of ethical address. In doing so, they offer students selected representations, skills, social relations, and disciplinary practices that presuppose particular histories and ways of being in the world.

The moral and political dimension at work here is revealed in the question: Whose history, story, and experience prevails in the school setting? In other words, who speaks for whom, under what conditions, and for what purpose? At the risk of overemphasis, educational institutions and the processes in which they engage are neither apolitical nor objective, as many neoconservatives claim. Simply stated, schools are not neutral institutions designed for either providing students with work skills or with the privileged tools of culture. Instead, they are deeply implicated in forms of inclusion and exclusion that produce particular moral truths and values. In effect, they both produce and legitimate cultural differences as part of their broader project of constructing particular knowledge/power relations and producing specific notions of citizenship. To some, this may sound commonsensical and a bit tiresome. But I think it is imperative to locate all levels of education within a moral and social context in order to assess how a politics and pedagogy of difference might be engaged as part of a discourse fundamental to the reconstruction of a critical democracy.

The problems facing education around the issue of difference in the United States need to be reformulated as a crisis in citizenship and ethics. This suggests that the solution to these problems lies ultimately in the realms of values and politics, not simplistic calls for the creation of a common culture, a monolithic notion of cultural literacy, or a pluralism divorced from the issues of power and struggle. What is at stake is not the semantic differences between pluralism and particularism, or the struggle between Western culture and barbarism, but the creation of a democratic society in which differences are affirmed and interrogated rather than dismissed as essentialist or disruptive. It is not small irony that many conservatives who oppose a politics of difference to the discourse of pluralism are also arguing for measuring citizenship competencies through standardized cultural literacy tests and dismissing the voices of those who have been left out of dominant versions of academic discourse by suggesting that they are incapable of being more than self-referential and doctrinaire. Within this formulation, justice is subordinated to a plea for academic balance while, at the same time, the school curriculum (canon) is defended as being a representative version of Western history that is self-righteously equated with the meaning of civilization itself. There is something ironic in the charge by those in power (white academic males—especially in higher education), that they have been pushed to the margins as a result of their defense of a Eurocentric-based curriculum. In light of the upsurge of racism across the country, this type of logic translates into the self-indulging act by dominant groups of mistaking the call by subordinate groups to defend their views as a form of separatism and aggression. So much for the spirit of critical inquiry. The sentiment echoes what the dominant curriculum suggests and blacks, women, and other subordinate groups generally accept as a given: it is only the voices of white males that count.

At the risk of overstating this issue, the crisis of literacy in this country must be framed as part of a politics of difference that provides students with the opportunity to engage in a deeper understanding of the importance of cultural citizenship and democratic culture while developing classroom relations that prioritize the relationship among diversity, equality, and social justice. The ethical imperative that links difference, schooling, and democracy in institutions of public and higher education should educate students primarily for the responsibilities of learning how to govern. This means organizing curricula in ways that enable students to make judgments about how society is historically and socially constructed, how existing social practices are implicated in relations of equality and justice as well as how they structure inequalities around racism, sexism, and other forms of opposition. It also means offering students the possibilities for being able to make judgments about what society might be, what is possible or desirable outside existing configuration of power.

Students need more than information about what it means to get a job or pass standardized tests that purport to measure cultural literacy; they need to be able to critically assess the relationship between dominant and subordinate traditions in historical, relational, and political terms. What they don't need is to treat history as a closed, singular narrative that simply has to be revered and memorized. Educating for difference, democracy, and ethical responsibility is not about creating passive citizens. It is about providing students with the knowledge, capacities and opportunities to be noisy, irreverent, and vibrant. Central to this concern is the need for students to understand how cultural, ethnic, racial, ideological differences enhance the possibility for dialogue, trust, and solidarity. Within this perspective, difference can be analyzed and constructed within pedagogical contexts that promote compassion and tolerance rather than envy, hatred, and bigotry. The pedagogical and ethical practice which I am emphasizing is one that offers opportunities for students to be border-crossers; as border-crossers, students not only refigure the boundaries of academic subjects in order to engage in new forms of critical inquiry, they also are offered the opportunities to engage the multiple references that construct different cultural codes, experiences, and histories. In this context, a pedagogy of difference provides the basis for students to cross over into diverse cultural zones that offer a critical resource for rethinking how the relations between dominant and subordinate groups are organized, how they are implicated and often structured in dominance, and how such relations might be transformed in order to promote a democratic and just society. Difference in this case does not become a marker for deficit, inferiority, chauvinism, or inequality; on the contrary, it opens the possibilities for constructing pedagogical practices that deepen forms of cultural democracy and enlarge our moral vision.

This means that the debate over the politics of literacy, difference, and culture might be reconstructed to engage the broader issue of how learning that goes on in American education is truly attentive to the problems and histories that construct the actual experiences students face in their everyday lives. A pedagogy of literacy and difference is not based merely on providing students with conflicting paradigms or the dispassionate skills of rhetorical persuasion; on the contrary, it points to pedagogical practices which offer students the knowledge, skills, and values they will need to critically negotiate and transform the world in which they find themselves. The politics of critical literacy and cultural difference engages rather than retreats from those problems that make democracy messy, vibrant, and noisy.

A democratic discourse of literacy and difference provides readers with diverse elements of a critical approach to literacy that ruptures universal versions of reason and linear notions of history; it points to decentering margins as spaces that offer the opportunity for other voices to be spoken and heard. Within this perspective, literacy is not engulfed in a stifling regime of knowledge that refuses to recognize its own partiality, but in a view of uncertainty that makes dialogue and debate possible. It is literacy that both affirms and disrupts in the name of hope committed to the radical responsibility of politics and ethics, and informs the struggle for a better future.

Henry A. Giroux is professor of Education at Miami University in Oxford, Ohio, and the author of Schooling and the Struggle for Public Life: Critical Pedagogy in the Modern Age.

This paper was presented at Ohio Wesleyan's National Colloquium Conference, Fall 1990. Reprinted by permission of the author.

Higher Education and the Practice of Democratic Politics:

A Political Education Reader

"At some point the attenuation of civic spirit and competence will create pathologies with which liberal institutions . . . simply cannot cope. The viability of liberal society depends on its ability to conduct civic education."

"One of the chief failings of the American political system over the past half century has been the inability to encourage average citizens to participate in the search for the public good."

As these quotations suggest, this book is concerned with the state of democracy in the United States today. Editor Bernard Murchland observes that our involvement in civic life is shallow, the public will is enfeebled, and once-honored ideas such as the common good are largely vestigial. In short, we have a weak sense of citizenship.

Critics charge that colleges and universities are failing to ensure that young Americans receive the education that will provide them with the skills—and the disposition—to carry out the tasks that only the citizens of a republic can perform. But the debate about the purposes of *education* is a debate about the nature of *democracy*. Collectively, the authors substantiate the claim that the current academic definition of politics is too narrow—too preoccupied with governments, elections, and interest groups—to comprehend all that is in the public realm. Their perspectives lead them to question the role of the university and the nature of political education—even the very definition of knowledge itself.

This is a book about educating for democratic citizenship—about political education. *Higher Education and the Practice of Democratic Politics* is indispensable reading for anyone concerned with the role of colleges and universities in preparing young Americans for political responsibility, civic competence, and public leadership.